D0940084

CONTENTS

INTRODUCTION

Thank you for purchasing Prima's Official Game Guide to *MMA*. This guide is packed with tips and tactics to help you smash rivals in the cage, whether you're playing online or guiding your warrior along his legendary *MMA* career.

HOW TO USE THIS BOOK

The information in this guide is presented in several chapters—here's what you'll find in each one.

TRAINING

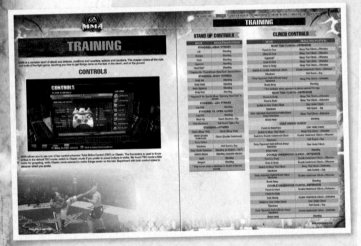

Turn to the next chapter to review the fundamentals of *MMA*'s gameplay. Here we review the fine arts of striking, clinch work, grappling, and positions, and teach you how to conduct business in the cage like a pro.

CREATE A FIGHTER

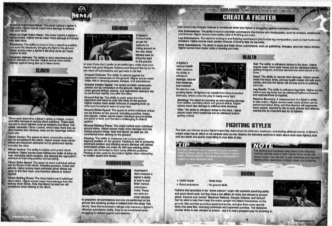

Creating custom fighters is a big part of *MMA*, so we've devoted an entire chapter to the process. Turn here for informative looks at each fighting style and every special move. Handy tables give you the minimum, maximum, and starting stats for each style in every weight class as well.

HOW TO USE THIS BOOK

CAREER MODE

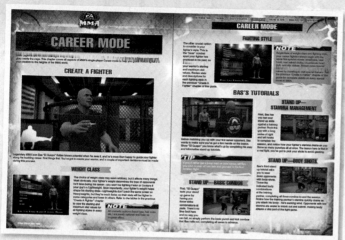

Flip to this chapter for all things Career mode. Here we give tips on completing every training exercise you can perform at the various gyms. A quick-reference table is provided so you can quickly identify which exercises are available at each gym as well.

ONLINE ACTION

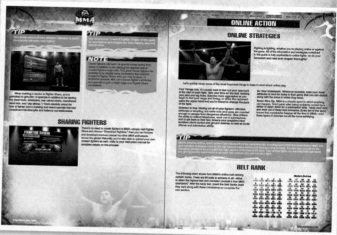

This chapter covers the ins and outs of online play. Turn here to learn about importing Career fighters and your Fighter Share options, along with a recap of vital fighting strategies.

MMA ROSTER

MMA's roster boasts nearly 60 well-known warriors, and we've spared no effort to provide you with a complete look at each one. Flip through the roster sections to view each fighter's stats, moves, and strategies, along with other interesting info such as the fighter's professional record and fight history.

APPENDIX

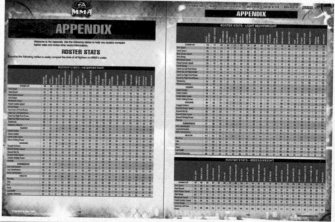

The final pages of the guide provide a variety of quick-reference tables. Flip here for a convenient source of stat comparisons and the like.

TRAINING

MMA is a complex sport of attack and defense, positions and counters, actions and reactions. This chapter covers all the nuts and bolts of the fight game, teaching you how to get things done on the feet, in the clinch, and on the ground.

CONTROLS

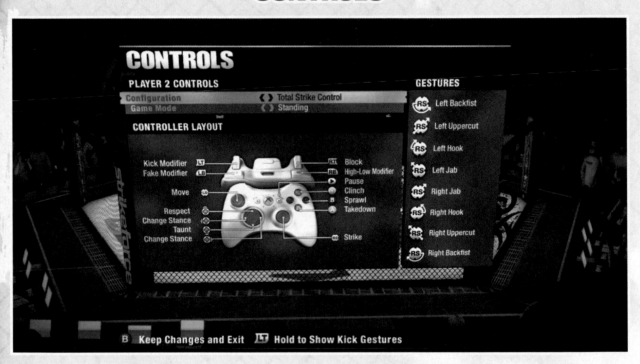

MMA allows you to use one of two control schemes: Total Strike Control (TSC) or Classic. The thumbstick is used to throw strikes in the default TSC mode; switch to Classic mode if you prefer to press buttons to strike. We found TSC mode a little better for grappling, while Classic mode seemed to make things easier on the feet. Experiment with both control styles to discover which you prefer.

TRAINING

STAND UP CONTROLS

MOVE	RESULTING POSTION
STANDING—HEAD STRIKES	
Jab	Standing
Straight	Standing
Hook	Standing
Uppercut	Standing
Head Kick*	Standing
*Requires the "Roundhouse Head Kick" Special Move.	
STANDING—BODY STRIKES	
Body Jab	Standing
Body Hook	Standing
Body Uppercut	Standing
Body Kick	Standing
STANDING—LEG STRIKES	
Leg Kick	Standing
STANDING VS. OPEN GUARD	
Leg Kick	Standing
Stack Up	Guard Stacked—Top
Dive into Guard	Full Guard Tight—Top
STANDING—OTHERS	
Clinch (Muay Thai)	Clinch (Muay Thai)
Clinch (Double Underhook)	Clinch (Double Underhook)
Parry Strikes	
Takedown	Half Guard—Top
Deny Clinch/Takedown	Standing (or Sprawl—Top*)
Switch Stance	Standing (opposite stance)
Taunt	Standing
Respect	Standing
*Only occurs when a takedown is denied at the last second.	

CLINCH CONTROLS

MOVE	RESULTING POSTION
MUAY THAI CLINCH—OFFENSIVE	
Punch to Face	Muay Thai Clinch—Offensive
Elbow to Face	Muay Thai Clinch—Offensive
Uppercut*	Muay Thai Clinch—Offensive
Knee to Face	Muay Thai Clinch—Offensive
Knee to Body	Muay Thai Clinch—Offensive
Switch to Double Underhook Clinch	Double Underhook Clinch—Offensive
Takedown	Half Guard—Top
Deny Opponent Switch/Break Away/Takedown	Muay Thai Clinch—Offensive
Break Away	Standing
*Not available when opponent is pinned against the cage.	
MUAY THAI CLINCH—DEFENSIVE	
Punch to Body	Muay Thai Clinch—Defensive
Knee to Body	Muay Thai Clinch—Defensive
Switch to Over Under Clinch	Over Under Clinch
Takedown	Half Guard—Top
Deny Opponent Submission/Switch/Break Away/Takedown	Muay Thai Clinch—Defensive
Break Away	Standing
OVER UNDER CLINCH	
Punch to Body/Face	Over Under Clinch
Switch to Muay Thai Clinch	Muay Thai Clinch—Offensive
Switch to Double Underhook Clinch	Double Underhook Clinch—Offensive
Takedown	Half Guard—Top
Deny Opponent Switch/Break Away/Takedown	Over Under Clinch
Break Away	Standing
DOUBLE UNDERHOOK CLINCH—OFFENSIVE	
Punch to Body	Double Underhook Clinch—Offensive
Knee to Body	Double Underhook Clinch—Offensive
Switch to Muay Thai Clinch	Muay Thai Clinch—Defensive
Takedown	Side Control—Top
Deny Opponent Switch/Break Away/Takedown	Double Underhook Clinch—Offensive
Break Away	Standing
DOUBLE UNDERHOOK CLINCH—DEFENSIVE	
Punch to Head	Double Underhook Clinch—Defensive
Punch to Body	
Foot Stomp	Double Underhook Clinch—Defensive
Switch to Over Under Clinch	Over Under Clinch
Takedown	Half Guard—Top
Deny Opponent Switch/Break Away/Takedown	Double Underhook Clinch—Defensive
Break Away	Standing

GROUND CONTROLS

MOVE	RESULTING POSTION
GUARD STACKED—TOP	
Punch to Head	Guard Stacked—Top
Punch to Body	Guard Stacked—Top
Move to Full Guard Postured Up—Top	Full Guard Postured Up—Top
Break Away	Standing vs. Open Guard
Deny Opponent Submission/Kick Off/Stand Up	Guard Stacked—Top
GUARD STACKED—BOTTOM	
Upkick to Head	Guard Stacked—Bottom
Kick Opponent Off	Open Guard vs. Standing
Stand Up	Standing
Deny Opponent Submission/Pass/Break Away	Guard Stacked—Bottom
FULL GUARD POSTURED UP—TOP	
Hammerfist to Head	Full Guard Postured Up—Top
Hook to Head	Full Guard Postured Up—Top
Punch to Body	Full Guard Postured Up—Top
Stack Up	Guard Stacked—Top
Pass to Half Guard	Half Guard—Top
Deny Opponent Submission/Stand Up/Pull to Full Guard	Full Guard Postured Up—Top
FULL GUARD POSTURED UP—BOTTOM	
Hammerfist to Head	Full Guard Postured Up—Bottom
Punch to Head	Full Guard Postured Up—Bottom
Pull to Full Guard	Full Guard—Bottom
Stand Up	Standing
Deny Opponent Submission/Pass/Stand Up	Full Guard Postured Up—Bottom
FULL GUARD—TOP	
Punch to Head/Body	Full Guard—Top
Posture Up	Full Guard Postured Up—Top
Pass to Half Guard	Half Guard—Top
Deny Opponent Submission/Sweep/Stand Up	Full Guard—Top
FULL GUARD—BOTTOM	
Punch to Head	Full Guard—Bottom
Heel Strike to Body	Full Guard—Bottom
Stand Up	Standing
Sweep	Half Guard—Top
Deny Opponent Submission/Pass/Stand Up	Full Guard—Bottom

MOVE	RESULTING POSTION
HALF GUARD—TOP	
Punch to Body/Head	Half Guard—Top
Knee to Body	Half Guard—Top
Stand Up	Standing vs. Open Guard
Pass to Side Control	Side Control—Top
Deny Opponent Submission/Stand Up/Recover Full Guard	Half Guard—Top
HALF GUARD—BOTTOM	
Punch to Head	Half Guard—Bottom
Knee to Body	Half Guard—Bottom
Recover Full Guard	Full Guard—Bottom
Stand Up	Standing
Deny Opponent Submission/Pass/Stand Up	Half Guard—Bottom
SIDE CONTROL—TOP	
Punch to Head/Body	Side Control—Top
Pass to Mount	Full Mount Tight—Top
Stand Up	Standing vs. Open Guard
Deny Opponent Submission/Stand Up/Recover Half Guard	Side Control—Top
SIDE CONTROL—BOTTOM	
Punch to Head/Body	Side Control—Bottom
Recover Half Guard	Half Guard—Bottom
Stand Up	Standing
Deny Opponent Submission/Pass/Stand Up	Side Control—Bottom
FULL MOUNT TIGHT—TOP	
Punch to Head	Full Mount Tight—Top
Posture Up	Full Mount—Top
Deny Opponent Submission/Stand Up/Recover Half Guard	Full Mount Tight—Top
FULL MOUNT TIGHT—BOTTOM	
Punch to Body	Full Mount Tight—Bottom
Recover Half Guard	Half Guard—Bottom
Give Up Back	Back Mount—Bottom
Deny Opponent Submission/Pass/Posture Up	Full Mount Tight—Bottom
FULL MOUNT—TOP	
Hammerfist to Head	Full Mount—Top
Hook to Head	Full Mount—Top
Stand Up	Standing vs. Open Guard
Deny Opponent Submission/Recover Half Guard/Give Up Back	Full Mount—Top
FULL MOUNT—BOTTOM	
Hammerfist to Head	Full Mount—Bottom

TRAINING

GROUND CONTROLS, CONT.

MOVE	RESULTING POSTION
Punch to Head	Full Mount—Bottom
Pull to Full Mount Tight	Full Mount Tight—Bottom
Give Up Back	Back Mount—Bottom
Deny Submission	Full Mount—Bottom
BACK MOUNT—TOP	
Punch to Head	Back Mount—Top
Roll to Full Mount	Full Mount—Top
Stand Up	Standing vs. Open Guard
Deny Opponent Submission/Roll/Escape	Full Mount—Top
BACK MOUNT—BOTTOM	
Punch to Head	Back Mount—Bottom
Roll to Full Mount	Full Mount—Bottom
Escape	Standing
Deny Opponent Roll	Back Mount—Bottom
SPRAWL—TOP	
Punch to Head	Sprawl—Top
Pass to Back Mount Side Turtle	Back Mount Side Turtle—Top
Stand Up	Standing
Deny Opponent Submission/Stand Up/Recover Full Guard	Sprawl—Top
SPRAWL—BOTTOM	
Punch to Body	Sprawl—Bottom
Recover Full Guard	Full Guard Tight—Bottom
Stand Up	Standing
Deny Opponent Submission/Pass	Sprawl—Bottom

MOVE	RESULTING POSTION
BACK MOUNT SIDE TURTLE—TOP	
Punch to Head	Back Mount Side Turtle—Top
Pass to Back Mount	Back Mount—Top
Stand Up	Standing vs. Open Guard
Deny Opponent Submission/Stand Up/Recover Half Guard	Back Mount Side Turtle—Top
BACK MOUNT SIDE TURTLE—BOTTOM	
Elbow to Head	Back Mount Side Turtle—Bottom
Recover Half Guard	Half Guard—Bottom
Stand Up	Standing
Deny Opponent Submission/Pass	Back Mount Side Turtle—Bottom
RUBBER GUARD—TOP	
Punch to Body	Rubber Guard—Top
Posture Up	Full Guard Postured Up—Top
Deny Opponent Submission/Sweep	
RUBBER GUARD—BOTTOM	
Punch to Head	Rubber Guard—Bottom
Sweep	Half Guard—Top
Deny Opponent Posture Up	Rubber Guard—Bottom
OPEN GUARD VS. STANDING	
Leg Kick	Open Guard vs. Standing
Stand Up	Standing

STAMINA

Stamina is life in the cage—a measure of a fighter's energy. When a fighter is full of stamina, he's able to unleash furious offense and power his way out of dangerous holds. When a fighter is exhausted, he's barely able to move, let alone defend himself or mount much offense. Conserving stamina and wearing away at your opponent's gas tank is therefore a vital aspect of MMA.

Here are the benefits of having plenty of stamina:

» Your strikes are much faster and more powerful.
» Your movement speed and blocking ability are much higher.
» Your ability to pass guard and apply submission holds is much greater.
» Your ability to deny your opponents' takedowns, passes, sweeps, and submissions is much improved.

CONSERVING STAMINA

The more action
you take in a fight,
the more stamina
you consume.
Winging wild
punches and
grappling
relentlessly will
cause your fighter

to gas out fast, so pick your attacks carefully and conserve
your stamina. Use short bursts of offense to score damage
or bring the fight to a new area, giving your fighter the
chance to recover afterward. Keep plenty of gas in the tank
so you can defend effectively and explode with offense at a
moment's notice.

CATCHING YOUR BREATH

When your fighter
starts sucking
wind, stop
attacking and
play defense to
give him a chance
to recover. If
you're on your
feet, back away

from your rival and start blocking—your stamina slowly refills
while you're not striking or attempting to grapple. As your
stamina returns and your mobility improves, begin dashing
away from aggressive adversaries, looking to set up a shot or
counter.

In the clinch, recover stamina by blocking your rival's
attacks—this also tires him as he struggles to land strikes.
Don't strike back, simply defend as your stamina refills.
Beware of takedowns in the clinch, however—you're more
susceptible to being taken down while you're blocking.

On the
ground, recover
stamina by
blocking your
rival's strikes,
and by denying
his attempts
at improving
position and

applying submissions. This also tires your rival as he
struggles to work. Try to recover your stamina on the ground
before attempting to improve position.

WEARING OUT RIVALS

Attacking your
rival's stamina is
just as important
as protecting
your fighter's
own gas tank.
Body shots
are the best
way to tire your

rivals—these sap their stamina and can even drop opponents
if you land enough flush blows. Throw hard jabs, straights,
and kicks at your opponent's midsection while standing, and
punish his body up close with hard hooks and uppercuts.

In the clinch,
throw punches
and knees to
the body to gas
opponents out,
setting them up
for debilitating
slams. Be careful:
Your stamina
drains quickly

when your clinch strikes are blocked—either transition to
a takedown, break away, or simply pause your assault and
catch your breath.

On the
ground, drill
your opponents'
ribs with
punches and
knees to beat
the stamina out
of them. Tired
opponents are

easier to dominate on the ground because they struggle to
deny passes and submission attempts. Soften opponents up
with body shots, then improve position and lock in a fight-
ending sub.

TRAINING

STRIKING

The fine art of striking is easy to grasp, but challenging to master. Every fight begins on the feet, so it's important to know how to handle yourself in this chaotic position.

PUNCHING

Punches are versatile strikes. String together fast boxing combos of jabs and hooks to back opponents up or get them blocking—this creates opportunities for you to clinch up or shoot in for a takedown. Use punches defensively as well, countering forward-moving opponents. Let's review the various punches you can throw.

Jab

The jab is a long, straight punch thrown by a fighter's lead hand (usually the left). Jabs are the fastest and longest punches you can throw, but they're also the weakest. Jab early and often to find your range and interrupt your opponents' combos as you dash about the ring. Because jabs are thrown so quickly, there's little chance of being countered.

Straight

Jabs thrown with the back hand (usually the fighter's right) are often referred to as "straights." These fast punches pack a bit more power than lead jabs, but they're slightly slower to find their mark. Use straights to counter kicks and hooks, and unleash jab-straight combos to make your fighter wing punches as fast as he's able.

Hook

Hooks are long, versatile punches. They're slightly slower than jabs and straights, but almost as long and much more powerful. Combine hooks with jabs and straights, using the strikes' similar length to back up opponents with fast, dangerous combos. Hooks can really rock opponents if they don't see them coming, so throw plenty of hooks if your fighter has exceptionally fast hands.

Uppercut

Uppercuts are the most powerful punches your fighter can throw aside from special strikes. However, they're also somewhat slow and have a short range. Depending on the opponent and your fighter's hand speed, you may or may not find uppercuts to be effective—fast strikers can easily counter these power shots, so they can get you into trouble. Primarily use uppercuts after you've cornered your opponent near the cage and are hunting for the big KO.

NOTE

This chapter only covers the basics—refer to the next chapter, "Create A Fighter," to learn about every special strike, such as the overhand punch and flying knee.

KICKING

Kicks are powerful strikes with superior range. Certain fighters are not skilled at kicking, however, so consider your warrior's attributes and strengths when deciding how often to include these strikes in your offense. Fighters that can kick effectively have the advantage on the feet, because kicks are great at keeping opponents off balance and at bay.

NOTE

See the next chapter, "Create A Fighter," to learn all about each fighting style, including the meanings behind all of the various fighter attributes. (Foot Speed, Punch Combo Speed, etc.)

Leg Kick

Leg kicks are the only strikes capable of damaging a fighter's legs. If your fighter excels at kicking, use leg kicks like a second jab to help you find your range, interrupt the opponent's attacks, and set up your combos. Batter your rivals' legs to slow them down dramatically, reducing their ability to avoid strikes and taking the power out of their takedowns. Leg kicks can be incredibly effective in any fight, so consider them when devising your game plan.

Body Kick

Body kicks batter a fighter's ribs, damaging his torso and eroding his stamina. Blast your rivals with sharp body kicks to knock the wind from their lungs. Attacking the body is an important strategy in MMA, and the body kick's long range and heavy power make it the ideal strike to use.

Head Kick

Most fighters own the "roundhouse head kick" special move, allowing them to throw feet at their opponents' faces. A shin to the chin can rock anyone if they're caught flush, but head kicks are slow [to] perform and somewhat easy to evade and counter. Only [those] with great kickboxing skill should make liberal use of [advanced] kicks.

BLOCKING

"Protect yourself at all times"—it's the first rule of combat sports. Defense is vital in MMA, and blocking is the most basic technique— simply cover up to conserve stamina and lessen the impact of inbound strikes. Fighters with high Blocking scores can withstand quite a beating while blocking. All fighters block poorly when rocked or gassed, however.

CAUTION

Your fighter is more susceptible to takedowns while blocking, so block less when facing skilled grapplers.

PARRYING

Parrying is more challenging than blocking, but the potential benefits are greater. Block while first gauging your rivals' striking habits, then begin to anticipate their strikes and parry them to the right and left, deflecting their go-to blows. A successful parry means your fighter takes no damage, and he also knocks his rival off balance for an instant, creating a brief window for a counter.

STUFFING TAKEDOWNS

Some fighters have limited striking ability, but are extremely dangerous grapplers. More often than not, these fighters will look to shoot in on the feet for takedowns, using their rudimentary striking as a means of bringing the fight to the mat. When facing a dangerous grappler, be conservative on the feet and remain ready to sprawl as a defense against his takedowns and clinch attempts. Focus on stuffing his shots and keeping the fight upright.

TRAINING

DOWNED OPPONENTS

Occasionally, one standing fighter faces an opponent who's lying on the ground, on his back in open guard. For example, this happens when the top ground fighter decides to stand up and return to his feet. If your fighter is the standing combatant, take advantage of these opportunities by throwing relentless leg kicks at the downed opponent, battering his exposed legs and doing a number on his mobility before letting him up.

When faced with a downed opponent, hit the Takedown button to stack up in guard. Here, you are in position to land some heavy punches, a kneebar, or hit a major pass to side control. Beware of upkicks from the bottom while controlling this precarious position, however—they add up.

If you just want to join your rival on the mat, the safest option is to move forward while pressing the Takedown button— this causes you to dive directly into the downed opponent's full guard, rather than stacking up. Now you can pass to work for arm and neck submissions.

DAMAGE

By default, the only gauge that remains onscreen at all times is the all-important stamina meter. Three other meters are also hidden in the background, though—the head health, torso health, and legs health meters. These deplete as your fighter takes damage to various areas of his body, and they slowly refill when he avoids being hit. When a health meter falls below half, it becomes visible near the stamina gauge to alert you.

NOTE

Suffering regular damage to a body area shortens the length of its health meter over time, making the fighter even more susceptible to further damage to that area.

GETTING ROCKED

When two guys stand and bang, it's not long before someone gets rocked. This usually occurs when one fighter is caught flush with a strike that they didn't see coming. Rock your opponent by interrupting his combos with sharp counter straights and hooks, catching him off guard in exchanges. While rocked, a fighter loses his ability to effectively attack and must focus on defending until his head clears (the head health meter refills).

TIP

Even if your fighter isn't a fantastic grappler, try shooting for a takedown after you've been rocked. Chances are the opponent will be striking wildly and looking for the KO—this makes them easier to surprise. Score a takedown and then let your head clear.

If a fighter's head or body health meter becomes fully depleted, he becomes badly rocked, collapsing to the ground and balling up in self-preservation mode. As the aggressor, wiggle the thumbstick to seize the opportunity and pound out badly rocked foes. If you're the one who's on the floor, mash the indicated button as fast as possible for a chance at recovering your composure and fighting back from the brink of defeat.

WORKING THE CLINCH

The clinch is a strenuous position that quickly takes its toll on both fighters. There's no room to parry or evade while tied up in the clinch, so blocking is your only defensive option against powerful, short range strikes unleashed in the position. The clinch is ideal against elusive strikers because it helps you pin them down—but it should be used with caution when facing powerful grapplers and submission artists, who may use the position to achieve takedowns more easily.

ENTERING THE CLINCH

Your fighter's Clinch Control attribute is the primary determining factor in his ability to tie up foes. First, back up the opponent with a barrage of rapid jabs, straights, and hooks, aiming to corner him near the cage. Clinch once he's trapped and forced to block, mashing him against the fence to gain superior control.

The fighter who initiates a clinch always enters the position with the offensive advantage—the defending fighter must seek to improve his position or break free of the hold. Two clinch options are available, each with its own merits: the Muay Thai clinch and the double underhook clinch.

Muay Thai Clinch

In the Muay Thai clinch, the dominant fighter wraps his hands behind the opponent's neck to keep him close and control his posture. The ample distance between the fighters' torsos allows the aggressor to land devastating knees, punches, and elbows to the defender's head and body. Use the Muay Thai clinch to batter opponents with strikes if you're the brawler sort, breaking free or switching to double underhooks once the adversary begins to block.

TIP

Land knees to the body in the Muay Thai clinch to quickly deplete your rivals' stamina. This sets the stage for a transition to double underhooks and a brutal slam.

Double Underhook Clinch

In the double underhook clinch, the dominant fighter wraps his arms under his opponent's arms and around his back, controlling his adversary's body weight. The closeness of the position makes striking less effective, but also promotes devastating slams. Scoring takedowns from the double underhook clinch lands your fighter in side control—a dominant ground position that's just one pass away from mount. Grapplers and ground fighters should exploit the double underhook clinch to help them secure takedowns.

Over Under Clinch

The over under clinch cannot be directly initiated—it only occurs when the defending clinch fighter manages to improve his position. Neither fighter has the advantage in the over under clinch, unless one of the fighters has the other pinned against the cage, of course. Striking is somewhat limited in this position—blows can be thrown with force, but not in rapid combos. Takedowns are far more likely to occur than knockouts in the over under clinch, making this a favorable position for grapplers and ground fighters.

TIP

If you're an expert grappler and your rival foolishly clinches with you, improve to the over under clinch and then score the takedown.

TRAINING

ADVANCING POSITION

Both fighters are able to improve their position in the clinch. Aggressors can switch directly between the dominant Muay Thai clinch and double underhook positions, while defenders must advance to the over under clinch before they can improve to a dominant posture. Your fighter's Clinch Control attribute is the primary factor in determining his ability to maintain and improve position in the clinch.

> **NOTE**
>
> Your controller vibrates when your rival tries to improve his position or break free of your clinch—immediately deny him to maintain control.

BREAKING AWAY

If your fighter is better at striking than ground fighting, breaking away is usually your best option when the opponent clinches with you. Block strikes and deny takedowns to tire your rival, then use your superior stamina to help you break free. Exhausted fighters are easily controlled in the clinch, so protect your ribs against body shots as you look to break free.

STRIKING FROM THE CLINCH

The confines of the Muay Thai clinch allow the aggressor to inflict plenty of pain. Brutalize opponents with fast knees, punches, and elbows in this dominant striking position, but strike tactfully—you're easier to shrug off and toss to the mat when you open up too much with your strikes.

Clinch fighting is very exhausting, especially when the defending fighter blocks your strikes. Stop attacking to recover stamina and either break away or score a takedown—there's no sense in wasting all of your stamina on a few blocked knees.

CLINCH TAKEDOWNS

Shooting for takedowns on the feet is dangerous—opponents can counter your shots with fast knees or catch you in a dangerous choke. Clinch takedowns are much safer to attempt and easier to accomplish because you've already tied up your foe. They're especially easy to achieve from the over under and double underhook clinch positions.

You land in side control when you complete a takedown from the double underhook clinch.

EXPLOITING THE CAGE

Using the cage to your advantage is the backbone of a strong clinch game. Initiate clinches near the fence, pressing your opponent against the wall  to gain superior control. If you've clinched up in the center of the ring, walk your opponent backward, throwing punches and elbows at his head while maneuvering him into the unyielding steel.

You have the advantage when leaning on your rival against the cage—your clinch strikes are more powerful and your takedowns are more dominant. In fact, the over under clinch takedown lands you in side control instead of half guard when you perform it from this advantageous position.

It's important for defending fighters to break away from cage clinches as soon as possible. Block strikes and deny takedowns to tire the aggressive rival before slipping away. Be especially guarded against takedowns when the opponent has you stuffed against the fence—many land you on your back with the opponent in side control.

THE GROUND GAME

Fights change dramatically once the action hits the mat. Though one fighter may have a modest advantage over his opponent on the feet or in the clinch, the ground game greatly favors one fighter over the other—the man on top.

NOTE

This section focuses on the fundamentals of grappling and various ground positions. Submissions are special moves in *MMA*, so refer to the following "Create A Fighter" chapter to learn about each one.

TIP

Takedowns are also easy to accomplish in the over under clinch, so if your opponent foolishly clinches with you, improve your position and then look for the immediate takedown.

TAKEDOWNS

Before you can work your ground game, you must first bring the fight to the floor. The most straightforward way to do this is by shooting

for takedowns on the feet. Completing a stand up takedown always lands you in your opponent's half guard, ready to apply a kimura submission (assuming you know the submission) or work some ground and pound. The higher your fighter's Takedown score, the more success he'll have shooting in.

Takedowns can also be accomplished from the clinch—these are ideal when the opponent is countering your standing

shots with knees and chokes. Pressure your opponent into giving up the double underhook clinch, which favors takedown slams.

PASSING GUARD

Most takedowns land the aggressor in the opponent's half guard, where little damage can be done outside of light strikes and the possible kimura submission. However, by passing to side control and then to mount, the top fighter places himself in dominant position, ready to rain down devastating fists and elbows. Many more submission opportunities present themselves in the side control and mount positions as well, making a fighter's Passing attribute a major facet of his ground game.

TRAINING

TIP

Throw body strikes to drain your opponents' stamina and get them to block, then pass their guard. Don't strike too frequently, however, or you may lose position.

GROUND AND POUND

The striking advantage is the primary reason why most fighters seek to bring the fight to the floor. The top fighter's punches gain all the force of gravity, while the bottom fighter has little countering power and nowhere to hide. Punish the opponent's body to drain his stamina and force him to block, then pass his guard to improve your position. Keep striking to pass your way to full mount, then posture up to rain down heavy leather.

Ground and pound can also be effectively administered from within an opponent's guard, but this is a far more dangerous position for the top man. This is because the fighter on bottom can land powerful upkicks or slap on inverted kneebars and triangle

chokes when stacked up, while triangles and armbars can be used against postured up foes. Keep out of the opponent's guard when fighting submission experts, working to pass and strike from mount instead.

SUBMISSIONS

Ground and pounders can be brutal, but submission artists are the real sharks of the ground world. Subs can be locked in from almost any position on the ground, so passing guard isn't really a necessary skill for submission practitioners.

CAUTION

Failing a submission battle usually lands you in a compromising position, such as on your back with the opponent on top. Avoid attempting submissions until you've worn down your rival with strikes and are fairly certain you can finish.

Limb Submissions

Manage your stamina carefully when caught in a battle over a leg or arm lock—don't mash the button or you'll quickly gas out. Tap it in short, rapid bursts to apply steady pressure, recovering stamina during the brief pauses between working the hold. The victim automatically escapes if the aggressor runs out of stamina, so be careful not to gas out.

NOTE

The camera zooms in dramatically as submissions are made tighter and pulls back as victims start to break free.

Choke Submissions

Choke holds play
out differently
than limb locks. In
these submission
battles, each
player must
strive to find the
elusive "zone" by
slowly rotating his

thumbstick. The controller vibrates when the zone is found—
stick with it to either tighten the choke or begin to slip free.

NOTE

The "zone" is easier to find when you have lots of stamina.
Release the thumbstick occasionally to recover stamina
and improve your odds of finding the zone.

CAUTION

Don't move your thumbstick too rapidly or you'll never
find the zone during chokes—you'll only gas out your
fighter!

GROUND DEFENSE

Taking someone
down and
pounding on
him is one
thing—defending
yourself on the
ground is a whole
other matter. A
fighter's Blocking,

Grapple Defense, and Ground Get Up attributes are the most
important things to look at when considering his ground
defense.

Blocking

Blocking lessens
the damage from
ground strikes,
taking the sting
out of your rivals'
ground and
pound. Block
your opponents'

strikes to tire them out while minimizing damage and
recovering stamina. Beware, however: your fighter's guard
is easier to pass while blocking, and he's more vulnerable to

submissions as well. Don't block unless you really need to;
focus on improving your position instead.

TIP

If your opponent has you mounted and your head has
taken a pounding, stop blocking and start parrying. This
is riskier than blocking because you could be caught
flush, but in this situation, you'll soon be knocked out
if you continue to block, and parrying a series of blows
gives your head a chance to clear.

Your fighter's
Grapple Defense
attribute is
considered when
he tries to deny
passes, sweeps,
submission
attempts, and
when struggling

to escape from submission holds. His Ground Get Up
attribute determines his ability to kick opponents off him
and pop back up to his feet. Both of these are vital to feeling
comfortable on the ground—the former helps you control the
action, while the latter lets you quickly escape to your feet if
things aren't going your way.

NOTE

Your controller vibrates whenever your rival attempts
to pass, sweep, or submit you. Hit the Deny button
immediately to utilize your fighter's Grapple Defense and
prevent the attempt from succeeding.

The Grapple Defense attribute can be used help you get
back to your feet as well. Recover full guard after a takedown,
then simply focus on denying your opponent's attempts at
improving position. Keep your rival trapped in full guard to
stall the action until the ref is forced to break things up and
return the fight to the feet.

CREATE A FIGHTER

Building your own bad boy is an important facet of MMA, and we've devoted an entire chapter to aiding you in this critical process. Here you'll discover the importance behind every attribute, along with fighting style descriptions, and a complete list of the starting, minimum, and maximum attribute values for each fighting style in every weight class. The chapter concludes with a look at the more than 30 special moves you can bestow upon your warriors, with tips on how to use and combine them. If you're looking for help in creating the ultimate mixed martial artist, look no further.

ATTRIBUTES

The many attributes that determine a fighter's skill and ability in the cage are collectively known as attributes. These numbers form the backbone of every fighter and determine their ability to get things done in the cage. Attribute scores can range from 33 to 100—the higher an attribute, the more dominant the fighter is at that particular aspect of battle.

TIP

Whenever possible, review your opponents' attributes before fights, carefully considering their strengths and looking for holes in their game to exploit.

NOTE

Don't read too much into the attribute averages for a fighter's major attribute categories (Stand Up, Clinch, Ground, etc.)—these can be very deceptive. For example, a fighter may end up with a lackluster Stand Up average if his takedowns are poor—but could still have KO power in his fists. Look over a fighter's complete attributes when gauging his strengths and weaknesses, not just the overall averages.

STAND UP

A fighter's Stand Up attributes are used to measure his skill and ability to strike and evade on the feet. Stand Up attributes are therefore most important to strikers, but even grapplers can benefit from a strong takedown ability, or fast hands that can help them set things up. Here's the meaning behind each Stand Up attribute:

Foot Speed: The speed at which individual kicks are thrown. Higher scores mean swifter individual kicks.

Hand Speed: The speed at which individual punches are thrown. Higher scores mean faster individual punches.

Kick Combo Speed: The speed at which kicks can be thrown in combination. Higher scores mean you can rattle off kick combinations faster.

Kick Range: The length of a fighter's kicks. Higher scores mean a longer reach, which helps you keep opponents at bay and score damage from outside of countering range.

Movement Speed: The speed at which a fighter moves about the cage. Higher scores mean swifter dashes and movements, which help a fighter create angles, slip into and out of striking range, and escape dangerous standing positions.

Punch Combo Speed: The speed at which punches can be thrown in combination. Higher scores mean you can string together blistering punch combos.

Punch Range: The length of a fighter's punches. Higher scores mean a longer reach, which helps you keep opponents at bay and score damage from outside of countering range.

Stand Up Left Foot Power: The power behind a fighter's left kicks. Higher scores mean more damage is inflicted with each blow.

Stand Up Left Hand Power: The power behind a fighter's left punches. Higher scores mean more damage is inflicted with each blow.

Stand Up Right Foot Power: The power behind a fighter's right kicks. Higher scores mean more damage is inflicted with each blow.

Stand Up Right Hand Power: The power behind a fighter's right punches. Higher scores mean more damage is inflicted with each blow.

Takedowns: The ability to shoot in from a standing position and score the takedown, bringing the fight to the ground. Higher scores mean a fighter's standing shots are much tougher to stuff.

Takedown Defense: The ability to deny takedowns on the feet. Higher scores mean better defense against being tied up or taken down.

CLINCH

Clinch attributes determine a fighter's ability to initiate, control, and inflict damage in various clinch positions. These attributes are vital to clinch fighters such as wrestlers and Muay Thai artists, especially Clinch Control, which helps them lock up and maintain their clinches. Here are the meanings behind each attribute:

Clinch Combo: The speed at which consecutive actions can be completed in the clinch. Higher scores mean clinch strikes and takedown attempts can be performed rapidly, one after the other.

Clinch Control: The ability to initiate and control clinch positions. Higher scores mean fighters are better at tying up foes, improving clinch position, and denying the opponent's attempts at improving position and escaping.

Clinch Strike Speed: The speed at which individual strikes can be thrown in the clinch, including punches, knees and elbows. Higher scores mean individual clinch strikes are quick to find their mark, and therefore difficult to defend against.

Clinch Striking Power: The force behind each individual clinch strike. Higher scores mean more damage from the various clinch blows. Note that Stand Up attributes are not considered when striking in the clinch.

GROUND

A fighter's Ground attributes gauge his aptitude for rolling around on the mat. Many fighters seek to bring the fight to the ground, so even if you don't prefer to do battle here, make sure your warrior has good Grapple Defense and Ground Get Up so he can ward off submissions and get back to his feet.

Grapple Defense: The ability to defend against the opponent's maneuvers on the ground. Higher scores mean better skill at denying passes, sweeps, and submissions.

Ground Combo Speed: The speed at which consecutive actions can be completed on the ground. Higher scores mean ground strikes can be performed rapidly, one after the other.

Ground Get Up: The ability to push away from the opponent and return to your feet while on the ground. Higher scores mean better chances of popping back up when you're trying to return to your feet.

Ground Strike Speed: The speed at which individual strikes can be thrown on the ground, including punches, knees, and elbows. Higher scores mean individual ground strikes are quick to land, and therefore challenging to defend against.

Ground Striking Power: The might behind each individual ground strike. Higher scores mean more damage from the various ground blows. Note that Stand Up attributes are not considered when striking on the ground.

Passing: The ability to maneuver into a more advantageous position on the ground. Passing is vital to achieving dominant position and inflicting severe damage with strikes. Submission artists can make do with less passing ability, as subs can be locked in from many different positions. Passing is also used by the bottom fighter when attempting to reclaim guard and sweep.

SUBMISSION

Submission attributes measure a fighter's ability to lock in and finish various submission holds. These are attributes are most valuable to grapplers; all submissions but one are performed on the ground (the climbing armbar is initiated from the Muay Thai clinch). Note that submission ratings only measure a fighter's offensive submission ability; they're not considered when struggling to defend against submissions.

CREATE A FIGHTER

(The Ground attribute Grapple Defense is considered when your fighter is struggling against submission holds.)

Arm Submissions: The ability to lock in and finish submissions that involve arm manipulation, such as armbars, americanas, and kimuras. Higher scores mean better odds of finishing arm subs.

Leg Submissions: The talent for locking in and finishing submissions that involve leg manipulation, such as heel hooks and kneebars. Higher scores mean greater chances of forcing taps via leg locks.

Neck Submissions: The ability to seize and finish choke submissions, such as guillotines, triangles, and rear naked chokes. Higher scores mean better odds of choking out rivals.

HEALTH

A fighter's various Health attributes measure his ability to withstand damage, recover from beatings, and maintain his stamina over grueling fights. All fighters can benefit from these important attributes, which come into play in nearly every fight.

Blocking: The talent for covering up and reducing damage from strikes, including clinch and ground strikes. Higher scores mean less damage is suffered while blocking.

Chin: The ability to withstand strikes to the head. Higher scores mean less chance of being rocked due to head strikes.

Gut: The ability to withstand strikes to the torso. Higher scores mean more body blows can be withstood before getting dropped, and less stamina lost when struck in the torso.

Heart: The ability to recover from damage. Higher scores mean the head, torso, and leg health meters will refill more rapidly, and that the fighter will be less prone to suffering bad cuts.

Leg Health: The ability to withstand leg kicks. Higher scores mean more leg kicks can be withstood before movement and explosiveness is crippled.

Stamina Recovery: A measurement of a fighter's ability to take action. Higher scores mean more actions can be performed before tiring, and that stamina will regenerate more quickly. Stamina is vital to both offense and defense, making this an important attribute for all fighters.

FIGHTING STYLES

The style you choose as your fighter's specialty determines his minimum, maximum, and starting attribute scores. A fighter's weight class has an effect on his attribute attributes as well. Explore the following sections to learn about each base fighting style and see which one seems most fitting to your style of play.

TIP

If certain attributes aren't important to you, consider lowering these ratings down to their minimum values when creating fighters. This gives you extra points to spend on more attractive attributes.

NOTE

The starting and maximum attributes listed in the following sections are the same in both Fighter Share mode and Career mode. Use this info to help determine your favorite fighting style, regardless of which mode you're playing.

BOXING

+ Quick hands   - Weak kicks
+ Good endurance   - No ground skills

Fighters that specialize in the "sweet science" begin with excellent punching ability and good clinch work, but they have a low affinity for kicks and almost no ground game. Improve your boxers' Takedown Defense, Grapple Defense, and Ground Get Up attributes to help them keep the action upright and defend themselves on the ground. Max out their punching speed and power, and give them every special strike that uses fists, including overhands and superman punches. The takedown counter strike is also valuable to boxers—use it to make grapplers pay for shooting in.

BOXING ATTRIBUTES

	HEAVYWEIGHT			LIGHT HEAVYWEIGHT			MIDDLEWEIGHT			WELTERWEIGHT			LIGHTWEIGHT		
	MIN	STARTING	MAX	MIN	STARTING	MAX	MIN	STARTING	MAX	MIN	STARTING	MAX	MIN	STARTING	MAX
STAND UP															
Foot Speed	59	59	81	62	62	84	65	65	86	68	68	89	70	70	89
Hand Speed	68	80	91	71	80	94	73	85	97	75	85	100	75	85	100
Kick Combo Speed	59	59	81	62	62	84	65	65	86	68	68	89	70	70	89
Kick Range	50	50	89	50	50	89	50	50	89	50	50	89	50	50	89
Movement Speed	63	79	84	66	80	88	69	80	92	75	85	100	75	85	100
Punch Combo Speed	68	80	91	71	80	94	73	85	97	75	85	100	75	85	100
Punch Range	75	85	100	75	85	100	75	85	100	75	85	100	75	85	100
Stand Up Left Foot Power	60	60	89	60	60	85	50	50	76	50	50	67	46	46	58
Stand Up Left Hand Power	60	80	95	60	75	90	50	68	81	50	59	71	46	52	62
Stand Up Right Foot Power	60	60	89	60	60	85	50	50	76	50	50	67	46	46	58
Stand Up Right Hand Power	60	80	95	60	75	90	50	68	81	50	59	71	46	52	62
Takedowns	33	33	89	33	33	89	33	33	89	33	33	89	33	33	89
Takedown Defense	33	73	95	33	77	95	33	72	95	33	73	95	33	76	95
CLINCH															
Clinch Combo	68	82	91	71	80	94	73	85	97	75	85	100	75	85	100
Clinch Control	33	80	95	33	80	95	33	80	95	33	78	95	33	80	95
Clinch Strike Speed	68	81	91	71	80	94	73	85	97	75	85	100	75	85	100
Clinch Striking Power	60	80	95	60	79	90	50	70	81	50	59	71	46	52	62
GROUND															
Grapple Defense	33	33	92	33	33	92	33	33	92	33	33	92	33	33	92
Ground Combo Speed	68	81	91	71	80	94	73	83	97	75	85	100	75	85	100
Ground Get Up	33	80	95	33	80	95	33	80	95	33	76	95	33	81	95
Ground Strike Speed	68	81	91	71	80	94	73	85	97	75	85	100	75	85	100
Ground Striking Power	60	80	95	60	80	90	50	70	81	50	59	71	46	51	62
Passing	33	33	89	33	33	89	33	33	89	33	33	89	33	33	89
SUBMISSION															
Arm Submissions	33	33	89	33	33	89	33	33	89	33	33	89	33	33	89
Leg Submissions	33	33	89	33	33	89	33	33	89	33	33	89	33	33	89
Neck Submissions	33	33	89	33	33	89	33	33	89	33	33	89	33	33	89
HEALTH															
Blocking	75	85	100	75	85	100	75	85	100	75	85	100	75	85	100
Chin	33	80	95	33	80	95	33	80	95	33	78	95	33	80	95
Gut	33	80	95	33	80	95	33	80	95	33	78	95	33	80	95
Heart	75	85	100	75	85	100	75	85	100	75	85	100	75	85	100
Leg Health	33	79	95	33	80	95	33	80	95	33	75	95	33	80	95
Stamina Recovery	75	85	100	75	85	100	75	85	100	75	85	100	75	85	100

CREATE A FIGHTER

BRAWLER

+ Powerful puncher   - Bad endurance

+ Can take a beating   - No ground skills

Brawlers are slower than boxers, but their punches can be made even more powerful. Brawlers can also be made more durable and resilient than boxers, though they suffer from a poor maximum stamina rating. Outfit brawlers with many of the same specials you'd give to a boxer, focusing on keeping the fight standing and inflicting punishment with the brawler's heavy hands. Increase your brawlers' Takedowns, Grapple Defense, and Passing attributes to make him an effective ground and pounder, or boost his clinch attributes if you prefer to work from that position instead of the ground.

BRAWLER ATTRIBUTES														
	HEAVYWEIGHT			LIGHT HEAVYWEIGHT			MIDDLEWEIGHT			WELTERWEIGHT			LIGHTWEIGHT		
	MIN	STARTING	MAX	MIN	STARTING	MAX	MIN	STARTING	MAX	MIN	STARTING	MAX	MIN	STARTING	MAX
STAND UP															
Foot Speed	59	59	81	62	62	84	65	65	86	68	68	89	70	70	89
Hand Speed	59	71	86	62	73	89	65	76	92	68	75	95	70	78	95
Kick Combo Speed	59	71	86	62	73	89	65	76	92	68	75	95	70	78	95
Kick Range	50	50	89	50	50	89	50	50	89	50	50	89	50	50	89
Movement Speed	59	59	75	62	62	78	65	65	82	68	68	89	70	70	89
Punch Combo Speed	59	71	86	62	73	89	65	76	92	68	75	95	70	78	95
Punch Range	75	85	100	75	85	100	75	85	100	75	84	100	75	84	100
Stand Up Left Foot Power	60	60	89	60	60	85	50	50	76	50	50	67	46	46	58
Stand Up Left Hand Power	75	85	100	71	81	95	64	72	85	56	64	75	46	55	65
Stand Up Right Foot Power	60	60	89	60	60	85	50	50	76	50	50	67	46	46	58
Stand Up Right Hand Power	75	85	100	71	81	95	64	72	85	56	64	75	46	55	65
Takedowns	33	78	95	33	79	95	33	78	95	33	78	95	33	78	95
Takedown Defense	33	73	95	33	75	95	33	75	95	33	76	95	33	75	95
CLINCH															
Clinch Combo	59	76	86	62	73	89	65	77	92	68	75	95	70	79	95
Clinch Control	75	85	100	75	85	100	75	85	100	75	85	100	75	85	100
Clinch Strike Speed	59	70	86	62	73	89	65	76	92	68	75	95	70	78	95
Clinch Striking Power	75	85	100	71	85	95	64	73	85	56	65	75	49	58	65
GROUND															
Grapple Defense	33	33	92	33	33	92	33	33	92	33	33	92	33	33	92
Ground Combo Speed	59	71	86	62	75	89	65	76	92	68	75	95	70	78	95
Ground Get Up	75	85	100	75	85	100	75	85	100	75	85	100	75	85	100
Ground Strike Speed	59	70	86	62	73	89	65	76	92	68	75	95	70	78	95
Ground Striking Power	75	85	100	71	85	95	64	73	85	56	66	75	49	55	65
Passing	33	33	89	33	33	89	33	33	89	33	33	89	33	33	89
SUBMISSION															
Arm Submissions	33	33	89	33	33	89	33	33	89	33	33	89	33	33	89
Leg Submissions	33	33	89	33	33	89	33	33	89	33	33	89	33	33	89
Neck Submissions	33	80	95	33	78	95	33	78	95	33	75	95	33	78	95

BRAWLER ATTRIBUTES, CONT.

	HEAVYWEIGHT			LIGHT HEAVYWEIGHT			MIDDLEWEIGHT			WELTERWEIGHT			LIGHTWEIGHT		
	MIN	STARTING	MAX	MIN	STARTING	MAX	MIN	STARTING	MAX	MIN	STARTING	MAX	MIN	STARTING	MAX
HEALTH															
Blocking	33	78	95	33	70	95	33	78	95	33	75	95	33	78	95
Chin	75	85	100	75	85	100	75	85	100	75	85	100	75	85	100
Gut	75	85	100	75	85	100	75	85	100	75	85	100	75	85	100
Heart	75	85	100	75	85	100	75	85	100	75	85	100	75	85	100
Leg Health	75	85	100	75	85	100	75	85	100	75	85	100	75	85	100
Stamina Recovery	33	65	89	33	65	89	33	65	89	33	65	89	33	65	89

GENERALIST

+ Variety of skills
+ Good endurance
- Not dominant in any skill
- Lacks power

Generalists are well-rounded fighters with no shining advantage in any area. This makes the generalist style a good fit for counter fighters, or for those who've yet to determine where they prefer to do battle in the cage. Generalists can be made into effective strikers, but their lack of power can get them into trouble against knockout artists. Give generalists a good ground game and strong submissions in at least one category (arm, neck, or leg) to give yourself options on how to finish fights.

GENERALIST ATTRIBUTES

	HEAVYWEIGHT			LIGHT HEAVYWEIGHT			MIDDLEWEIGHT			WELTERWEIGHT			LIGHTWEIGHT		
	MIN	STARTING	MAX	MIN	STARTING	MAX	MIN	STARTING	MAX	MIN	STARTING	MAX	MIN	STARTING	MAX
STAND UP															
Foot Speed	59	67	86	62	67	89	65	68	92	68	68	95	70	70	95
Hand Speed	59	67	86	62	67	89	65	68	92	68	68	95	70	70	95
Kick Combo Speed	59	67	86	62	67	89	65	68	92	68	68	95	70	70	95
Kick Range	50	67	95	50	67	95	50	68	95	50	66	95	50	65	95
Movement Speed	59	66	80	62	69	84	65	68	87	68	68	95	70	70	95
Punch Combo Speed	59	67	86	62	67	89	65	68	92	68	68	95	70	70	95
Punch Range	50	67	95	50	67	95	50	68	95	50	66	95	50	65	95
Stand Up Left Foot Power	60	60	89	60	60	95	50	50	76	50	50	67	46	46	58
Stand Up Left Hand Power	60	60	89	60	60	95	50	50	76	50	50	67	46	46	58
Stand Up Right Foot Power	60	60	89	60	60	95	50	50	76	50	50	67	46	46	58
Stand Up Right Hand Power	60	60	89	60	60	95	50	50	76	50	50	67	46	46	58
Takedowns	33	67	95	33	66	95	33	69	95	33	65	95	33	65	95
Takedown Defense	33	68	95	33	67	95	33	68	95	33	64	95	33	63	95

CREATE A FIGHTER

GENERALIST ATTRIBUTES, CONT.														
	HEAVYWEIGHT			LIGHT HEAVYWEIGHT			MIDDLEWEIGHT			WELTERWEIGHT			LIGHTWEIGHT		
	MIN	STARTING	MAX	MIN	STARTING	MAX	MIN	STARTING	MAX	MIN	STARTING	MAX	MIN	STARTING	MAX
CLINCH															
Clinch Combo	59	65	86	62	67	89	65	68	92	68	68	95	70	71	95
Clinch Control	33	67	95	33	67	95	33	68	95	33	66	95	33	64	95
Clinch Strike Speed	59	67	86	62	67	89	65	68	92	68	68	95	70	70	95
Clinch Striking Power	60	60	89	60	60	85	50	50	76	50	50	67	46	46	58
GROUND															
Grapple Defense	33	67	95	33	67	95	33	68	95	33	66	95	33	65	95
Ground Combo Speed	59	67	86	62	66	89	65	68	92	68	68	95	70	70	95
Ground Get Up	33	67	95	33	66	95	33	68	95	33	63	95	33	65	95
Ground Strike Speed	59	67	86	62	66	89	65	68	92	68	68	95	70	70	95
Ground Striking Power	60	60	89	60	60	85	50	50	76	50	50	67	46	46	58
Passing	33	67	95	33	67	95	33	68	95	33	66	95	33	65	95
SUBMISSION															
Arm Submissions	33	67	95	33	66	95	33	68	95	33	65	95	33	65	95
Leg Submissions	33	67	95	33	66	95	33	68	95	33	65	95	33	65	95
Neck Submissions	33	67	95	33	66	95	33	68	95	33	65	95	33	65	95
HEALTH															
Blocking	33	67	95	33	67	95	33	68	95	33	66	95	33	64	95
Chin	33	67	95	33	66	95	33	68	95	33	65	95	33	65	95
Gut	33	66	95	33	66	95	33	68	95	33	65	95	33	65	95
Heart	33	75	95	33	75	95	33	75	95	33	75	95	33	75	95
Leg Health	33	67	95	33	67	95	33	68	95	33	66	95	33	65	95
Stamina Recovery	75	85	100	75	85	100	75	85	100	75	85	100	75	85	100

JIU JITSU

+ Excellent submissions   - Weak striking

+ Good endurance   - Can't take a hit

Jiu jitsu practitioners excel in the fields of ground offense and defense. They have little talent on the feet, so max out their Movement Speed, Takedowns, and Clinch Control attributes to help them bring the fight to the floor. True jiu jitsu buffs will top off all of their submission attributes and ensure they know how to apply every deadly hold—this makes them extremely dangerous to roll with. Make sure to give your jits fighters the "major pass" and "submission chaining" specials to make them far more deadly on the mat, and boost their pathetic initial Health attributes to help them survive long enough to secure the tap.

JUDO ATTRIBUTES, CONT.

	HEAVYWEIGHT			LIGHT HEAVYWEIGHT			MIDDLEWEIGHT			WELTERWEIGHT			LIGHTWEIGHT		
	MIN	STARTING	MAX	MIN	STARTING	MAX	MIN	STARTING	MAX	MIN	STARTING	MAX	MIN	STARTING	MAX
HEALTH															
Blocking	33	33	89	33	33	89	33	33	89	33	33	89	33	33	89
Chin	33	33	89	33	33	89	33	33	89	33	33	89	33	33	89
Gut	33	70	95	33	71	95	33	75	95	33	70	95	33	70	95
Heart	33	75	95	33	75	95	33	75	95	33	75	95	33	78	95
Leg Health	33	33	89	33	33	89	33	33	89	33	33	89	33	33	89
Stamina Recovery	33	71	95	33	71	95	33	71	95	33	69	95	33	71	95

KICKBOXING

+ Strong striker
+ Good strike defense

- No submission skills
- No ground skills

Kickboxers excel at thrashing adversaries on the feet, but their pathetic grappling ability leaves major holes in their overall game. Plug these up by boosting their Takedown Defense, Clinch Control, Grapple Defense, and Ground Get Up attributes. Kickboxers can end things quickly on the feet—max out their kicking ability, then use leg and body kicks to wear down opponents during fights. Be sure to give your kickboxers plenty of special strikes, such as the "takedown counter strike" and flying knee. The "catch punch" special can also help them turn things around on the ground and get back to their feet.

KICKBOXING ATTRIBUTES

	HEAVYWEIGHT			LIGHT HEAVYWEIGHT			MIDDLEWEIGHT			WELTERWEIGHT			LIGHTWEIGHT		
	MIN	STARTING	MAX	MIN	STARTING	MAX	MIN	STARTING	MAX	MIN	STARTING	MAX	MIN	STARTING	MAX
STAND UP															
Foot Speed	68	77	91	71	80	94	73	82	97	75	85	100	75	85	100
Hand Speed	59	71	86	62	73	89	65	76	92	68	75	95	70	78	95
Kick Combo Speed	68	77	91	71	80	94	73	82	97	75	85	100	75	85	100
Kick Range	75	85	100	75	85	100	75	84	100	75	85	100	75	85	100
Movement Speed	59	66	80	62	69	84	65	72	87	68	75	95	70	78	95
Punch Combo Speed	59	70	86	62	73	89	65	76	92	68	75	95	70	78	95
Punch Range	50	75	95	50	77	95	50	78	95	50	75	95	50	78	95
Stand Up Left Foot Power	75	85	100	71	81	95	64	72	85	56	64	75	49	55	65
Stand Up Left Hand Power	60	78	95	60	74	90	50	66	81	50	59	71	46	51	62
Stand Up Right Foot Power	75	85	100	71	81	95	64	72	85	56	64	75	49	55	65
Stand Up Right Hand Power	60	78	95	60	74	90	50	64	81	50	59	71	46	51	62
Takedowns	33	33	89	33	33	89	33	33	89	33	33	89	33	33	89
Takedown Defense	75	83	100	75	84	100	75	85	100	75	83	100	75	84	100

CREATE A FIGHTER

KICKBOXING ATTRIBUTES, CONT.															
	HEAVYWEIGHT			LIGHT HEAVYWEIGHT			MIDDLEWEIGHT			WELTERWEIGHT			LIGHTWEIGHT		
	MIN	STARTING	MAX	MIN	STARTING	MAX	MIN	STARTING	MAX	MIN	STARTING	MAX	MIN	STARTING	MAX
CLINCH															
Clinch Combo	59	70	86	62	71	89	65	76	92	68	72	95	70	77	95
Clinch Control	33	33	89	33	33	89	33	33	89	33	33	89	33	33	89
Clinch Strike Speed	59	70	86	62	70	89	65	75	92	68	71	95	70	78	95
Clinch Striking Power	60	60	89	60	60	85	50	50	76	50	50	67	46	46	58
GROUND															
Grapple Defense	33	33	92	33	33	92	33	33	92	33	33	92	33	33	92
Ground Combo Speed	59	70	86	62	70	89	65	75	92	68	75	95	70	78	95
Ground Get Up	33	75	95	33	75	95	33	75	95	33	75	95	33	78	95
Ground Strike Speed	59	70	86	62	70	89	65	75	92	68	75	95	70	78	95
Ground Striking Power	60	75	95	60	70	90	50	66	81	50	59	71	46	51	62
Passing	33	33	89	33	33	89	33	33	89	33	33	89	33	33	89
SUBMISSION															
Arm Submissions	33	33	89	33	33	89	33	33	89	33	33	89	33	33	89
Leg Submissions	33	33	89	33	33	89	33	33	89	33	33	89	33	33	89
Neck Submissions	33	33	89	33	33	89	33	33	89	33	33	89	33	33	89
HEALTH															
Blocking	75	85	100	75	85	100	75	85	100	75	85	100	75	85	100
Chin	33	75	95	33	75	95	33	75	95	33	75	95	33	78	95
Gut	33	75	95	33	77	95	33	75	95	33	75	95	33	78	95
Heart	33	75	95	33	78	95	33	75	95	33	75	95	33	78	95
Leg Health	75	85	100	75	85	100	75	85	100	75	85	100	75	85	100
Stamina Recovery	75	85	100	75	85	100	75	84	100	75	85	100	75	85	100

MUAY THAI

+ Great kicks
+ Violent in the clinch

- No submission skills
- No ground skills

Muay Thai artists are powerful kickers and excellent clinch fighters, but their punches lack power and their ground game is laughable. Use their strong kicks to wear down opponents from outside of countering range, clinching up when you really want to pour on the pain. Boost your Muay Thai fighters' Takedown Defense, Clinch Control, Grapple Defense, and Ground Get Up attributes so they can keep the fight upright, defend submissions, and scramble back to their feet after takedowns. Pile on the special strikes as well to add even more depth to their imposing stand up game—the flying knee and "takedown counter strike" are particularly useful.

SAMBO ATTRIBUTES, CONT.

	HEAVYWEIGHT			LIGHT HEAVYWEIGHT			MIDDLEWEIGHT			WELTERWEIGHT			LIGHTWEIGHT		
	MIN	STARTING	MAX	MIN	STARTING	MAX	MIN	STARTING	MAX	MIN	STARTING	MAX	MIN	STARTING	MAX
SUBMISSION															
Arm Submissions	75	85	100	75	85	100	75	85	100	75	85	100	75	85	100
Leg Submissions	75	85	100	75	85	100	75	85	100	75	85	100	75	85	100
Neck Submissions	33	33	89	33	33	89	33	33	89	33	33	89	33	33	89
HEALTH															
Blocking	33	33	89	33	33	89	33	33	89	33	33	89	33	33	89
Chin	33	33	89	33	33	89	33	33	89	33	33	89	33	33	89
Gut	33	78	95	33	75	95	33	75	95	33	70	95	33	75	95
Heart	33	78	95	33	75	95	33	75	95	33	75	95	33	75	95
Leg Health	33	33	89	33	33	89	33	33	89	33	33	89	33	33	89
Stamina Recovery	33	78	95	33	78	95	33	76	95	33	73	95	33	73	95

WRESTLING

+ Clinch control and takedowns
+ Ground and pound

- Weak kicks
- Glass jaw

Wrestlers excel at bringing the fight to the floor and keeping it there, seeking to KO their rivals with vicious ground and pound. Wrestlers are also adept at applying chokes—max out their Neck Submission attribute to make them more versatile and dangerous on the mat. Triangles and head arm chokes are excellent submissions for wrestlers, helping them end the fight from side control or off their back. Top off your wrestlers' Takedowns and Clinch Control attributes as well to help them dictate where the fight is fought, and increase their Grapple Defense and Passing ability so they can work confidently on the ground. The wrestler's major drawbacks are found in his lack of Stand Up ability and poor Health attributes—improving his striking is optional, while boosting the wrestler's Blocking, Chin, and Leg Health attributes is vital.

CREATE A FIGHTER

WRESTLING ATTRIBUTES														
	HEAVYWEIGHT			LIGHT HEAVYWEIGHT			MIDDLEWEIGHT			WELTERWEIGHT			LIGHTWEIGHT		
	MIN	STARTING	MAX	MIN	STARTING	MAX	MIN	STARTING	MAX	MIN	STARTING	MAX	MIN	STARTING	MAX
STAND UP															
Foot Speed	50	50	81	62	62	84	65	65	86	68	68	89	70	70	89
Hand Speed	59	70	86	62	70	89	65	70	92	68	70	95	70	70	95
Kick Combo Speed	59	59	81	62	62	84	65	65	86	68	68	89	70	70	89
Kick Range	50	50	89	50	50	89	50	50	89	50	50	89	50	50	89
Movement Speed	59	66	80	62	69	84	65	70	87	68	75	95	70	72	95
Punch Combo Speed	59	70	86	62	70	89	65	70	92	68	70	95	70	70	95
Punch Range	50	69	95	50	70	95	50	70	95	50	70	95	50	71	95
Stand Up Left Foot Power	60	60	89	60	60	85	50	50	76	50	50	67	46	46	58
Stand Up Left Hand Power	60	70	95	60	70	90	50	65	81	50	59	71	46	51	62
Stand Up Right Foot Power	60	60	89	60	60	85	50	50	76	50	50	67	46	46	58
Stand Up Right Hand Power	60	70	95	60	70	90	50	65	81	50	59	71	46	51	62
Takedowns	75	85	100	75	84	100	75	85	100	75	83	100	75	85	100
Takedown Defense	75	85	100	75	85	100	75	85	100	75	85	100	75	85	100
CLINCH															
Clinch Combo	68	77	91	71	80	94	73	81	97	75	85	100	75	85	100
Clinch Control	75	85	100	75	85	100	75	85	100	75	85	100	75	85	100
Clinch Strike Speed	59	73	86	62	69	89	65	76	92	68	75	95	70	71	95
Clinch Striking Power	75	85	100	71	81	95	64	72	85	56	60	75	49	55	65
GROUND															
Grapple Defense	75	85	100	75	85	100	75	85	100	75	85	100	75	85	100
Ground Combo Speed	68	75	91	71	80	94	73	82	97	75	85	100	75	85	100
Ground Get Up	33	75	95	33	75	95	33	72	95	33	68	95	33	75	95
Ground Strike Speed	68	77	91	71	80	94	73	82	97	75	85	100	75	85	100
Ground Striking Power	75	85	100	71	81	95	64	72	85	56	60	75	49	55	65
Passing	75	85	100	75	85	100	75	85	100	75	85	100	75	85	100
SUBMISSION															
Arm Submissions	33	33	89	33	33	89	33	33	89	33	33	89	33	33	89
Leg Submissions	33	33	89	33	33	89	33	33	89	33	33	89	33	33	89
Neck Submissions	33	75	95	33	75	95	33	70	95	33	70	95	33	75	95
HEALTH															
Blocking	33	33	89	33	33	89	33	33	89	33	33	89	33	33	89
Chin	33	33	89	33	33	89	33	33	89	33	33	89	33	33	89
Gut	33	72	95	33	69	95	33	70	95	33	70	95	33	70	95
Heart	33	75	95	33	75	95	33	75	95	33	75	95	33	75	95
Leg Health	33	33	89	33	33	89	33	33	89	33	33	89	33	33	89
Stamina Recovery	75	85	100	75	83	100	75	85	100	75	81	100	75	82	100

SPECIAL MOVES

Every fighter begins with knowledge of a handful of special moves, but you have the option to bestow many more upon them. The following moves are known to all created fighters from the start:

» Americana   » Heel Hook   » Rear Naked Choke   » Roundhouse Head Kick   » Slip Strikes

When creating a fighter through Fighter Share mode, you're able to give your guys 14 additional special moves. Give these some serious thought and ask yourself a few questions:

What are my fighter's strengths? Select specials that best compliment his fighting style.

What are my fighter's weaknesses? Choose specials that help you keep the fight where you want it by punishing opponents for trying to take you out of your game.

What are my habits as a player? Some special moves are advanced and require expert timing, such as the catch kick and the takedown fake. Shy away from these specials if you're unlikely to make use of them.

NOTE

Created fighters can learn 16 special moves over the course of Career mode, giving Career mode fighters the potential to be a bit more dangerous in the cage. The trade-off is that Fighter Share warriors can be built much faster— their attributes are quickly maxed by spending points, rather than having to guide them through the rigors of Career mode's gyms and training sessions.

SPECIAL MOVES

NAME	TYPE	FROM
Americana	Submission (Arm)	(1) Full Mount Postured Up—Top; (2) Full Mount Tight—Top
Armbar	Submission (Arm)	(1) Full Guard—Bottom; (2) Full Guard Postured Up—Bottom; (3) Side Control—Top; (4) Back Mount Side Turtle—Top
Catch Kick	Parry	Standing
Catch Punch	Parry	(1) Full Guard Postured Up—Bottom; (2) Full Guard Postured Up—Top; (3) Full Mount Postured Up—Top
Climbing Armbar	Submission (Arm)	Muay Thai Clinch—Offensive
Darce Choke	Submission (Neck)	Sprawl—Top
Dashing Takedown	Takedown	Standing
Diving Punch	Strike	Standing vs. Open Guard
Flying Knee	Strike	Standing
Gogoplata	Submission (Neck)	Rubber Guard—Bottom
Guillotine Takedown	Submission (Neck)	Standing
Head Arm Choke	Submission (Neck)	(1) Full Mount Tight—Top; (2) Side Control—Top
Heel Hook	Submission (Leg)	(1) Full Guard Postured Up—Top; (2) Guard Stacked—Top
Inverted Kneebar	Submission (Leg)	Guard Stacked—Bottom
Jump Guard Takedown	Takedown	Muay Thai Clinch—Offensive
Kimura	Submission (Arm)	Half Guard—Top
Kneebar	Submission (Leg)	Full Guard—Top
Major Pass	Strike (?)	Many Ground Positions
Omoplata	Submission (Arm)	Rubber Guard—Bottom
Open Guard Takedown	Strike (?)	Open Guard vs. Standing
Overhand Punch	Strike	Standing
Rear Naked Choke	Submission (Neck)	Back Mount—Top
Roundhouse Head Kick	Strike	Standing
Rubber Guard	Strike (?)	Full Guard—Bottom
Slip Strikes	Parry	Standing
Spinning Backfist	Strike	Standing
Spinning Kick	Strike	Standing
Submission Chaining	Submission (varies)	After a failed Armbar, Omoplata, Rear Naked Choke, or Triangle
Superman Punch	Strike	Standing
Takedown Counter Strike	Strike	Standing
Takedown Fake	Strike (?)	Standing
Teep Kick	Strike	Standing
Triangle Choke	Submission (Neck)	(1) Full Guard—Bottom; (2) Full Guard Postured Up—Bottom; (3) Full Mount Postured Up—Top; (4) Guard Stacked—Bottom

CREATE A FIGHTER

AMERICANA

Type: Submission (Arm)

Available From:

» Full Mount Postured Up—Top
» Full Mount Tight—Top

Failure—Resulting Position:

» Full Guard Postured Up—Bottom

Americanas (also commonly known as "keylocks") are basic arm submissions that can be performed from mount even when the opponent is holding you close and not allowing you to posture up. All created fighters begin with this default special move.

ARMBAR

Type: Submission (Arm)

Available From:

» Full Guard—Bottom
» Full Guard Postured Up—Bottom
» Side Control—Top
» Back Mount Side Turtle—Top

Failure—Resulting Position:

» Full Guard Postured Up—Bottom

Armbars are dangerous arm submissions that can be applied from many different ground positions. Armbars allow fighters to  threaten from top and bottom, and this versatility makes them must-have moves for submission artists. Armbars also combine with the "submission chaining" special—if you own both moves, you can transition from a failed triangle or omoplata directly into an armbar.

CATCH KICK

Type: Parry

Available From:

» Standing

This special allows standing fighters to catch their opponents' kicks and throw them to the ground. Thrown opponents end up in open guard on the ground, vulnerable to leg kicks and grapplers. Catch kicks to frustrate kickboxers, or as another means of bringing the fight to the mat.

CATCH PUNCH

Type: Parry

Available From:

» Full Guard Postured Up—Bottom
» Full Guard Postured Up—Top
» Full Mount Postured Up—Top

This special allows fighters to grab onto their opponent's wrists during ground and pound, thus controlling their ability to attack and defend. Catch your opponent's punches while on top to punch and elbow the bottom man freely—he won't be able to block until he manages to shake off your grip. Catch punches with the opponent trapped in full guard to hamper his ground and pound and make him easier to sweep and submit. The "catch punch" move takes a bit of practice to incorporate, but it can make you a far more worthy adversary on the ground, especially when battling ground and pounders that have poor submission skills.

CLIMBING ARMBAR

Type: Submission (Arm)

Available From:

» Muay Thai Clinch—Offensive

Failure—Resulting Position:

» Full Guard Postured Up—Bottom

The climbing armbar is a unique submission—it's the only one that can be applied from the clinch. This makes the climbing armbar a must-have for submission buffs—wrap up your opponent in the Muay Thai clinch, then use the climbing armbar to drag him to the ground and into an immediate arm lock. This move combines with the "submission chaining" special—if you own both, you can transition from a failed climbing armbar directly into an omoplata.

DARCE CHOKE

Type: Submission (Neck)

Available From:

» Sprawl—Top

Failure—Resulting Position:

» Side Control—Bottom

The Darce choke is a defensive submission that can only be employed after denying a takedown. Stuff your opponents' takedowns at the last second to land in the Sprawl—Top position, then make them pay for their mistake by locking up a Darce. This high-risk move is best used by fighters with good neck submissions—those with lackluster chokes should avoid the Darce because failure moves the opponent into side control.

DASHING TAKEDOWN

Type: Takedown

Available From:

» Standing

The dashing takedown is a fantastic special that adds speed and power to a fighter's shots. Use this special to shoot in for takedowns immediately after dashing, greatly increasing your chances of bringing your rival down. Dashing takedowns are must-have specials for ground fighters and can also be useful to strikers, giving them a means of quickly bringing the fight to the floor after they've been rocked.

DIVING PUNCH

Type: Strike

Available From:

» Standing vs. Open Guard

Fighters that own the diving punch are able to come down upon grounded rivals with force, landing a huge haymaker as they dive into a downed opponent's guard. Combine this move with the catch kick special so you can follow up with haymakers after catching kicks and tossing rivals to the ground. If you don't use the catch kick, set up diving punches by scoring takedowns and then quickly standing up, ready to strike.

FLYING KNEE

Type: Strike

Available From:

» Standing

Flying knees are devastating strikes that target the opponent's head. Skilled strikers can use them to quickly close in from range or to punish opponents they've cornered against the fence. All skilled strikers can benefit from this awesome leaping attack.

CREATE A FIGHTER

GOGOPLATA

Type: Submission (Neck)

Available From:

» Rubber Guard—Bottom

Failure—Resulting Position:

» Side Control—Bottom

Gogoplatas are unique submissions in which the bottom fighter uses his shin to choke out the man on top. You must have the "major pass" special in order to utilize gogoplatas—the major pass is required to enter the rubber guard position, where gogoplatas are available.

GUILLOTINE TAKEDOWN

Type: Submission (Neck)

Available From:

» Standing

Failure—Resulting Position:

» Full Guard—Bottom

The guillotine takedown allows fighters to counter their opponents' takedowns by wrapping them up in a guillotine choke. Submission artists should make good use of guillotines, using them to deny takedowns instead of simply stuffing them. Even if the sub fails, your opponent will be in your full guard, vulnerable to armbars and triangles. Guillotines are the perfect answer to ground and pounders with low grappling defense.

HEAD ARM CHOKE

Type: Submission (Neck)

Available From:

» Full Mount Tight—Top

» Side Control—Top

Failure—Resulting Position:

» Full Guard Postured Up—Bottom

Head arm chokes are dangerous submissions that can be applied from dominant top positions. Fighters with natural neck submission ability, such as wrestlers, should favor head arm chokes over armbars and americanas.

HEEL HOOK

Type: Submission (Leg)

Available From:

» Full Guard Postured Up—Top

» Guard Stacked—Top

Failure—Resulting Position:

» Full Guard Postured Up—Bottom

Heel hooks are basic leg submissions that all created fighters come equipped with. Shoot in for takedowns, stand up, then stack up

your downed opponent and slap on a heel hook. Or use the catch kick special to toss opponents to the ground, stacking them up and applying a heel hook afterward. If your fighter is good at leg submissions, look for heel hooks whenever you end up in the opponents' guard.

INVERTED KNEEBAR

Type: Submission (Leg)

Available From:

» Guard Stacked— Bottom

Failure— Resulting Position:

» Open Guard vs. Standing

The inverted kneebar is an advanced defensive submission that can only be applied when stacked up on the ground. Use inverted kneebars to turn the tables on aggressive ground and pounders, snaring them in unexpected leg locks. The inverted kneebar is the only limb lock that can be applied in this precarious position, making it very useful to submission masters.

JUMP GUARD TAKEDOWN

Type: Takedown

Available From:

» Muay Thai Clinch— Offensive

The jump guard takedown is a risky maneuver that gives grapplers an effective means of bringing the fight to the ground from the Muay Thai clinch position. If the move is successful, the victim ends up on the ground, tied up in his opponents' full guard. If the move is denied, the instigator ends up on his back, faced with a standing adversary. This move is most useful to submission fighters who excel at neck submissions, as it lands them in position to lock up an immediate triangle from their back. Armbars can also be secured from full guard, but if you're good at armbars, you should really be using the "climbing armbar" special from the Muay Thai clinch instead.

KIMURA

Type: Submission (Arm)

Available From:

» Half Guard— Top

Failure— Resulting Position:

» Open Guard vs. Standing

Kimuras are nasty joint locks that attack a fighter's shoulder. These arm submissions can only be applied from the top half

guard position, but this is the default position that fighters land in after scoring most takedowns. All arm submission enthusiasts should know their way around kimuras—you don't even need to pass guard before applying these dangerous subs!

KNEEBAR

Type: Submission (Leg)

Available From:

» Full Guard— Top

Failure— Resulting Position:

» Side Control— Bottom

Kneebars are similar to armbars, except that they're used to attack the knee joint instead of the elbow. This move goes well with the diving punch—land a haymaker on your way into your opponents' guard, then slap on a kneebar and end the show. Kneebars are high-risk leg locks that can land you in hot water if you fail them, so only leg submission experts need apply.

MAJOR PASS

Type: Strike

Available From:

» Many Ground Positions

The major pass is a vital special for all ground fighters. This move can be used instead of regular passes to greatly improve position on the ground, moving a fighter from half guard to mount, for example. The major pass is also required to enter the rubber guard position and utilize omoplatas and gogoplatas.

Major passes can give fighters a huge advantage, but beware: these high-risk, high-reward moves can be countered. Simply denying a major pass counters it, causing the instigator to lose valuable position. The following tables detail exactly how the major pass operates, showing where you'll end up after using it from each available ground position.

CREATE A FIGHTER

MAJOR PASS		
FROM	RESULTING POSITION	COUNTER RESULTING POSITION
MAJOR PASS—TOP POSITIONS		
Guard Stacked—Top	Side Control—Top	Half Guard—Bottom
Full Guard Postured Up—Top	Side Control—Top	Half Guard—Bottom
Full Guard—Top	Side Control—Top	Side Control—Bottom
Half Guard—Top	Full Mount Tight—Top	Side Control—Bottom
MAJOR PASS—BOTTOM POSITIONS		
Full Guard Postured Up—Bottom	Half Guard—Top	Half Guard—Bottom
Full Guard—Bottom	Rubber Guard—Bottom	Full Guard Postured Up—Bottom
Side Control—Bottom	Full Guard—Bottom	Full Mount - Bottom
Full Mount Tight—Bottom	Full Guard—Top	Full Mount—Bottom

OMOPLATA

Type: Submission (Arm)

Available From:

» Rubber Guard—Bottom

Failure—Resulting Position:

» Side Control—Bottom

Omoplatas are advanced high-risk arm submissions that can only be performed if you know the "major pass" special, which is required to reach rubber guard. Omoplatas work with the "submission chaining" special, allowing fighters to transition from a failed omoplata directly into an armbar—provided they know how to perform armbar submissions.

OPEN GUARD TAKEDOWN

Type: Strike

Available From:

» Open Guard vs. Standing

This unique special allows a downed fighter to trip up his standing adversary, bringing him to the mat and moving swiftly into his guard. Grapplers can benefit greatly from the open guard takedown, as it gives them another means of bringing the fight to the floor. Look for kneebars and heel hooks directly following these sneaky leg trips.

OVERHAND PUNCH

Type: Strike

Available From:

» Standing

The overhand punch is a favorite among power punchers. These long, looping blows pack tremendous power, inflicting significant damage even when blocked. Dash forward and throw overhands to help you close in from range. You can also throw overhands after dashing right or left, battering opponents from odd angles. Combine overhands with takedown fakes to keep the opponent guessing and potentially catch him off guard.

REAR NAKED CHOKE

Type: Submission (Neck)

Available From:

» Back Mount—Top

Failure—Resulting Position:

» Full Guard—Bottom

All created fighters have the ability to perform rear naked chokes. These fundamental submissions are only available from the back mount position and are usually locked in after a dominated fighter gives up his back by rolling over to avoid strikes when mounted. If your fighter has talent for neck subs, use rear naked chokes to end fights after smashing your adversaries from the mount. Rear naked chokes also combine with the "submission chaining" special, allowing you to transition from a failed choke directly into an armbar—provided you know how to perform that move.

ROUNDHOUSE HEAD KICK

Type: Strike

Available From:

» Standing

Every created fighter knows how to perform a roundhouse head kick. This special is required to perform head kicks in *MMA*, so roster fighters who do not know this move (such as Randy Couture) cannot kick their opponents' heads.

RUBBER GUARD

Type: Strike

Available From:

» Full Guard—Bottom

The "major pass" special move is required to advance from full guard to rubber guard—a high-level ground position used by the bottom fighter to control the top opponent. In the rubber guard, the bottom fighter wraps his leg up and behind the top fighter's head, trapping the top man close and limiting his ability to attack. The advanced omoplata and gogoplata submissions are available from rubber guard.

SLIP STRIKES

Type: Parry

Available From:

» Standing

All created fighters know how to slip strikes, bobbing and weaving to avoid being hit as they trade blows with rivals. Slip strikes when you wish to plant your feet and remain "in the pocket" against other strikers, dodging their attacks and quickly countering with blows of your own. Slipping and countering effectively makes you a dangerous striker capable of turning out anyone's lights, but you're easier to take down while slipping punches and exchanging.

SPINNING BACKFIST

Type: Strike

Available From:

» Standing

The spinning backfist is a beloved unorthodox strike capable of rocking opponents who don't see it coming. Sneak spinning backfists into your standing assaults, hoping to catch rivals off guard with speed and damage of the blow. Spinning backfists have a lackluster range, so don't rely on them to help you close in from afar—use flying knees, overhands, and superman punches to accomplish that goal instead.

SPINNING KICK

Type: Strike

Available From:

» Standing

Spinning kicks are excellent strikes that add versatility to a fighter's stand up game. They're thrown at the opponent's head by default, but by using the High-Low Modifier trigger, you can also unleash spinning kicks to the body—these have great range and a tremendous impact, and knock a significant amount of stamina from your foe.

SUBMISSION CHAINING

Type: Submission (Varies)

Available From:

» After a failed Armbar, Omoplata, Rear Naked Choke, or Triangle

Failure—Resulting Position:

» Varies

The awesome "submission chaining" special grants tap-out experts the ability to transition from one failed submission directly into another, provided they know how to perform each of the subs. Failed triangles and rear naked chokes can be rolled into armbars; failed armbars can be rolled into omoplatas; and failed omoplatas can be rolled back into armbars. By learning the armbar, major pass, omoplata, and "submission chaining" specials, a fighter can transition endlessly between failed armbars and omoplatas!

When one of the aforementioned submissions fails, you'll have a brief opportunity to use the "submission chaining" special to lock in another. Quickly press the indicated button, which appears near your stamina meter—if the opponent beats you to it, he'll break free of your submission chain and gain the advantage.

CREATE A FIGHTER

SUPERMAN PUNCH

Type: Strike

Available From:
» Standing

The superman punch is a powerful straight thrown with a fighter's whole body behind it. Use these spectacular blows to close in from range with a quick and powerful punch. Follow takedown fakes with superman punches to catch your opponent off guard.

TAKEDOWN COUNTER STRIKE

Type: Strike

Available From:
» Standing

This fantastic special causes fighters to automatically counter takedowns with knees to the aggressor's face. Simply deny takedowns quickly to deliver a knee to the opponent's head that staggers him for a brief time, allowing you to follow up with quick strikes or a takedown of your own. All fighters can benefit from this special move, especially when facing mat grapplers. If you keep eating counter knees when shooting in, try for clinch takedowns instead.

TAKEDOWN FAKE

Type: Strike

Available From:
» Standing

The takedown fake is a seemingly unspectacular special, but creative fighters can use it to great effect. Perform takedown fakes to keep the opponent off guard, helping you set up your offense. Takedown fakes count as dashes, so you can combo other specials off of them, such as overhands and superman punches. Fake the takedown and then land a power shot to rock your rivals and keep them guessing.

TEEP KICK

Type: Strike

Available From:
» Standing

The teep is a frontal push kick aimed at the mid section. It's purpose is primarily defensive; it is used to keep the opponent at bay. Teeps can be used as offensive setups as well, driving the wind from opponents' lungs, draining their stamina, and momentarily stunning them. If your fighter excels at kicking, be sure to implement teeps into your stand up game.

TRIANGLE CHOKE

Type: Submission (Neck)

Available From:
» Full Guard—Bottom
» Full Guard Postured Up—Bottom
» Full Mount Postured Up—Top
» Guard Stacked—Bottom

Failure—Resulting Position:
» Side Control—Bottom

Triangles are nasty, high-risk choke submissions in which the bottom fighter uses his legs to choke out the top man. Triangles are

generally applied from the bottom but can also be slapped on from mount when you tire of beating on your victim. Triangles combine with the "submission chaining" special, allowing you to transition from a failed triangle directly into an armbar—provided you know how to perform that move. If your fighter's better at chokes than joint locks, use triangles to tap out enemies instead of armbars and americanas.

CAREER MODE

MMA Legends are not born overnight. Only through years of dedication and hard work can one hope to achieve success and glory inside the cage. This chapter covers all aspects of *MMA*'s single-player Career mode to help you guide novice fighters of your creation to the heights of the MMA world.

CREATE A FIGHTER

Legendary MMA icon Bas "El Guapo" Rutten knows potential when he sees it, and he's more than happy to guide your fighter along his budding career. First things first: You've got to create your warrior, and a couple of important decisions must be made during this process.

WEIGHT CLASS

The choice of weight class may seem arbitrary, but it affects many things. Most obviously, your fighter's weight determines the type of opponents he'll face during his career—you won't be fighting Fedor or Couture if your guy's a Lightweight. More importantly, your fighter's weight helps shape his starting attributes—Lightweights don't pack the same power as Heavyweights, but they're much faster, so their attributes will be higher in some categories and lower in others. Refer to the tables in the previous "Create A Fighter" chapter to view the starting and maximum attribute values for all fighting styles in every weight class.

NOTE

All cosmetic options (head type, hair color, etc.) are purely optional and have no in-game effect.

CAREER MODE

FIGHTING STYLE

The other crucial option to consider is your fighter's style. This is the "base" combat sport your fighter has practiced in his past, so it determines many of your warrior's starting and maximum attribute values. Review attributes and descriptions for each fighting style in the previous "Create A Fighter" chapter of this guide.

NOTE

Regardless of weight class and fighting style, your career fighters always begin with the same five special moves: americana, heel hook, rear naked choke, roundhouse head kick, and slip strikes. Sixteen more special moves can be learned over the course of your career by traveling to visit special trainers. See the previous "Create A Fighter" chapter of this guide for complete details on every special move in *MMA*.

BAS'S TUTORIALS

Before matching you up with your first career opponent, Bas wants to make sure you've got a firm handle on the basics. Show "El Guapo" you know what's up by completing his easy and informative stand up tutorials.

TIP

If you'd rather get a jump start on your career, tell Bas you wish to skip all tutorials and proceed to the final amateur fight.

STAND UP—BASIC COMBOS

First, "El Guapo" tests your stand up game by having you throw strike combinations at pads. There's no time limit here and no way you

can fail, so simply perform the basic punch and kick combos that Bas calls out, completing all seven to advance.

STAND UP— STAMINA MANAGEMENT

Next, Bas has you test your stand up skills against a training partner. Rock the guy with a long series of right and left hooks to complete the

session, and notice how your fighter's stamina drains as you throw so many punches all at once. The lesson here is that in a real fight, you've got to pick your shots to avoid gassing.

STAND UP—BODY SHOTS

Bas's third stand up tutorial asks you to wear down opponents with body shots. Throw the indicated body combinations at the training

partner, completing all three combos to end the session. Notice how the training partner's stamina quickly drains as you attack his body—he's sucking wind. Opponents with low stamina are easier to knock out and submit, making body attacks a vital part of the fight game.

STAND UP—MOVEMENT

The fourth stand up tutorial underscores the fine art of footwork. Imitate the onscreen prompts to make your fighter dash in every direction, swiftly striking and evading. Dashing is a vital maneuver; it makes you difficult to hit while you quickly move into or out of striking distance. Use dashes to help you set up your offense, slip punches, and quickly escape from countering range.

STAND UP—DEFENSE

Rutten's final stand up tutorial tests your ability to block and parry. First, simply block and defend against the training partner's barrage of strikes. Block four blows, then parry four more to complete the session. Blocking is easy, but it only reduces damage—parrying causes you to avoid strikes and sets up counters, but this requires timing and practice.

AMATEUR FIGHT 1

Satisfied with your knowledge of the fundamentals, Bas lines you up with your first amateur fight. Feel free to spar before the fight if you feel like getting in a bit of practice beforehand. The amateur fight is very easy—the opponent offers little resistance. Pressure him with fast, simple combos to show off your striking and score the quick KO.

CLINCH—COMBOS

You've proven your stand up game is sharp—now Bas wants to gauge your clinch ability. Initiate a clinch against the sparring partner, then perform the basic clinch strike combos that Bas outlines for you. Break away after completing the first combo, then tie up again and perform a second combo to complete the exercise.

CLINCH—CAGE CONTROL

Next, show Bas that you know how to use the cage to your advantage in the clinch. Tie up with the opponent and shove him against the cage, then switch to a double underhook clinch and score a takedown. Opponents are easier to control when pressed up against the cage, and takedowns are much easier to accomplish here, so make good use of this dominant clinch position.

AMATEUR FIGHT 2

Bas has already lined up another amateur fight for you, and he wants to see you work the clinch in this one. Again, feel free to spar for as long as you like before accepting the fight. This is another easy contest—back the opponent up with strikes, then use the clinch to control him against the cage, working him over with knees and elbows until he drops to the floor.

TIP

Be methodical with strikes in the clinch to maintain control.

CAREER MODE

GROUND—BASIC COMBOS

Bas is impressed—all that remains to be seen is your ground game. In the first tutorial, shoot in for a takedown to bring the opponent to the mat. Once there, simply perform the basic ground strike combos to work the opponent over from half guard, thereby completing the exercise. Ground strikes are an important way of scoring points with the judges and opening up passing opportunities.

GROUND—MOVING TO MOUNT

Bring the action to the mat in the second ground tutorial, then use strikes to set up your passes. Pass to full mount and posture up to rain down fists on your training partner. Complete the ground strike combos from full mount to complete the test.

GROUND—CONTROL

In the third ground tutorial, lock up into the double underhook clinch position, then slam your training partner to the mat with a huge takedown. Pass to mount and then simply deny your partner's attempt at improving position to complete the exercise. The more tactful you are with your ground and pound, the better you'll be at maintaining control.

GROUND—SUBMISSION DEFENSE

You're mounted by your training partner at the start of this short test and must deny one submission attempt by him to advance. Hit the button the moment your controller begins to vibrate to deny the sub attempt and complete the challenge.

GROUND—LIMB SUBMISSIONS

Now for the fun stuff. Bas wants to see you finish a limb submission— press the Submission button to lock in an americana and then finish the sub by methodically tapping the Submission button to tighten the hold. Don't button mash while applying limb locks—this will burn out your stamina before the submission can be fully applied. Tap the button in short bursts to manage your stamina as you work at securing the sub.

NOTE

The camera zooms in as submissions become tighter and zooms out as the defender slips free.

GROUND—CHOKE SUBMISSIONS

Next, Bas wants you to lock in a choke hold. Can do! Press the Submission button to initiate a rear naked choke, then rotate the left stick to "find the zone" when the submission circle appears. Your controller vibrates whenever you find the invisible, moving "zone," and the zone briefly appears—try to follow it by continuing to rotate the thumbstick, squeezing tighter and tighter each time you find the zone until you force the tap.

FINAL AMATEUR FIGHT

Bas is impressed with your grappling skill and has booked your third and final amateur fight. Put everything you've learned to practice in this bout, picking your opponent apart with standing strikes, smashing him against the cage in the clinch, and pounding him out or submitting him on the mat. Fight your fight and finish him however you like to convince Bas that you've got what it takes to become a champion.

LEAGUE CONTRACTS

Now that you've shown Bas that you're no stranger to the cage, "El Guapo" is finally ready to take you under his wing. Bas's sole desire is to steer your career toward fame and glory, and he'll regularly contact you in person, over the phone, and via email to keep in touch as the two of you manage your fighter's career.

After choosing your fighting league, Brandy sends you your first fight contract. Bas is a hands-on manager and always picks your opponents for you, so simply review the contract to see who you're up against.

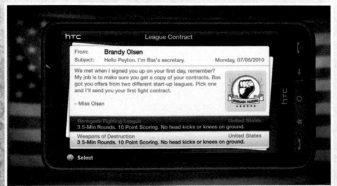

Bas's secretary, Brandy Olsen, soon sends you your first league contract. Choose to fight in either "Weapons of Destruction" or the "Renegade Fighting League." Both organizations feature the exact same rules and regulations, so the choice is completely arbitrary—pick whichever name or logo you like best.

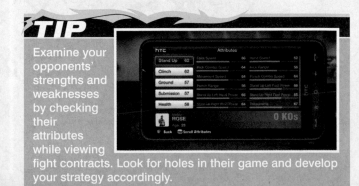

CAREER MODE

HITTING THE GYM

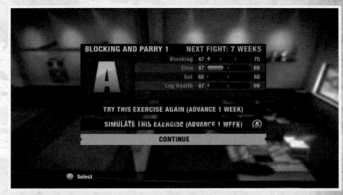

Bas knows that spending time in the gym is crucial to improving your skills, and he insists that you go through eight weeks of intense training after you accept each fight. This is your time to grow and improve—the harder you work at building your fighter's skills in the gym, the better things will go on fight night!

Keep in mind that the green coloring is just an estimate—it's possible to achieve even greater improvement if you manage to ace the workout. You're given a letter grade following every exercise: "D" means you did poorly, while "A" means you excelled. Achieve "A" ratings to receive the most gain from each exercise and boost your fighters skills as quickly as possible. Earning "A" ratings can also lead to advanced exercises.

WORK SMART—FIGHT HARD

When scrolling through all of those exercises, examine their improvement charts carefully—they can be a little deceptive. The listed attributes are the ones you'll improve by training in the exercise—the green coloring next to them shows your estimated improvement after a good workout session. Attribute points are gained each time you fill a meter beyond one of its white lines, and some meters have more lines than others, meaning you'll gain several attribute points by the time you completely fill the meter.

SIMULATING WORKOUTS

Simulating exercises allows you to boost your fighter's attributes without having to undergo the same workout over and over. Once you've earned an "A" grade, feel free to simulate the exercise as many times as you like to instantly gain top benefits. Your highest letter grade in each workout is always displayed next to their names as you scroll through them.

SPECIAL TRAINERS

Rutten's gym is stocked with everything you need to improve your fighter's fundamental attributes, but to truly become a legend, you'll

need to travel and train with other specialists. Fortunately, "El Guapo" has amazing connections and will soon have you visiting gyms around the world after you breeze through your first two professional bouts. Keep racking up wins to unlock more special trainers, and make sure to visit these valuable masters as often as your fight earnings allow.

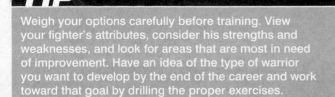

TIP

Weigh your options carefully before training. View your fighter's attributes, consider his strengths and weaknesses, and look for areas that are most in need of improvement. Have an idea of the type of warrior you want to develop by the end of the career and work toward that goal by drilling the proper exercises.

SPECIAL MOVES

Special trainers can also teach your fighter new special moves, which make your warrior far more dangerous. Each trainer offers a variety of special moves, as listed below. See the previous "Create A Fighter" chapter for complete details on all special moves.

Special Trainers—First Group

International Jiu Jitsu: Armbar, catch punch, submission chaining, triangle choke

Miletich Fighting Systems: Dashing takedown, diving punch, spinning kick, takedown fake

Xtreme Couture: Darce choke, head arm choke, major pass

Special Trainers—Second Group

Ballistic Boxing: Catch kick, guillotine takedown, overhand punch, takedown counter strike

Bushido Club: Climbing armbar, inverted kneebar, kimura

Eight Venoms: Flying knee, spinning backfist, superman punch, teep kick

Inferno International Gym: Gogoplata, jump guard takedown, omoplata, open guard takedown

> **NOTE**
>
> Your fighter can only learn 16 special moves over the course of his career, so choose wisely. Refer to the previous "Create A Fighter" chapter for complete details on special moves, including tips for choosing moves that best compliment your fighting style. Don't worry about failing special move challenges, either—you can retry them as many times as it takes to learn the move.

TRAINING EXERCISES

Most training exercises are simple and straightforward, but some are quite challenging. Here we provide tips to help you ace every workout. See the previous "Special Trainers" table to learn where each exercise can be attempted.

> **NOTE**
>
> The higher your fighter's attributes, the easier it'll be for him to achieve "A" ratings. If you're having trouble beating a certain exercise, just keep working at it. Your fighter's attributes will steadily increase, even when low ratings are achieved, and you'll eventually make the grade.

STAND UP EXERCISES

Blocking and Parry 1

Major Benefit: Chin

Minor Benefits: Blocking, Gut, Leg Health

Simply maintain a defensive blocking posture throughout this exercise, allowing your training partner to whale away at you with strikes. The exercise completes with an "A" after you block 10 blows.

Blocking and Parry 2

Major Benefits: Gut, Blocking

Minor Benefits: Chin, Leg Health

Parry 10 strikes in 30 seconds to ace this drill. Your sparring partner will throw rights and lefts, often throwing two strikes per side—just keep parrying right and left until you've slapped away 10 punches and kicks.

Blocking and Parry 3

Major Benefits: Leg Health, Blocking

Minor Benefits: Chin, Gut

You cannot dash or attack during this 30-second exercise, yet you must not allow the aggressive sparring partner knock you out. Hold the block button as you circle away from your sparring partner's back (power) hand. Keep your distance, and if your partner ever corners you, slip and parry his strikes as you look for an escape.

CAREER MODE

Blocking and Parry 4

Major Benefit: Blocking

Minor Benefits: Chin, Gut, Leg Health

Without fighting back, survive for a full minute against an aggressive sparring partner to complete this exercise. Block constantly as you move and dash away from your opponent, circling around his lead (weak) hand. Parry and slip strikes whenever your partner corners you, bobbing and weaving to avoid damage as you search for a way to create distance again.

Boxing Combo 1

Major Benefit: Punch Combo Speed

Minor Benefits: Punch Range, Stand Up Left Hand Power, Stand Up Right Hand Power, Hand Speed

Perform a simple series of punch combinations against a heavy bag to complete this exercise. The combos are of the basic jab-hook variety and there's plenty of time, so the challenge here is minimal. Complete all six of the following combos to earn an "A" grade:

Combo 1: Left jab.

Combo 2: Left jab, left jab.

Combo 3: Left jab, right straight.

Combo 4: Left jab, right straight, left jab, right straight.

Combo 5: Left jab, right straight, left hook.

Combo 6: Left jab, right straight, left hook, right hook.

Boxing Combo 2

Major Benefit: Hand Speed

Minor Benefits: Stand Up Left Hand Power, Stand Up Right Hand Power, Punch Combo Speed, Punch Range

Body shots are the focus of this boxing exercise—throw hands at the heavy bag, completing all of the following combos in under 30 seconds:

Combo 1: Left body hook.

Combo 2: Left body hook, right body hook.

Combo 3: Right body straight, left body hook, right body hook.

Combo 4: Left body jab, right body hook, left body uppercut, right body hook.

Combo 5: Left body jab, left body jab, right body uppercut, left body hook, right body straight.

Combo 6: Left body jab, right body straight, left body hook, right body hook, left body uppercut.

Boxing Combo 3

Major Benefits: Stand Up Left Hand Power

Minor Benefits: Hand Speed, Punch Combo Speed, Stand Up Right Hand Power, Punch Range

Complete a series of seven punch combinations within 20 seconds to complete this challenge. The combos are short, but so is your time, so you can't afford to make mistakes. Here are the combos you must throw:

Combo 1: Left jab, right straight.

Combo 2: Left jab, left jab, right hook.

Combo 3: Left jab, right straight, left hook.

Combo 4: Right straight, left hook, right uppercut.

Combo 5: Left jab, left jab, right straight.

Combo 6: Right body straight, left body hook, right body hook.

Combo 7: Right body straight, left body hook, right body hook, left body hook.

Boxing Combo 4

Major Benefits: Stand Up Right Hand Power

Minor Benefits: Stand Up Left Hand Power, Hand Speed, Punch Combo Speed, Punch Range

Land four three-strike combos in 30 seconds to complete this relatively simple boxing exercise. Any strikes will do, but you've got to land them in quick succession or you'll be forced to start over. Speed is key—throw a flurry of jabs and straights at your partner's jaw, stringing together combos of quick punches to complete the lesson before the bell.

Movement and Range 1

Major Benefit: None

Minor Benefits: Movement Speed, Stamina Recovery, Punch Range, Kick Range

Simply dash in each indicated direction before time expires to complete this easy exercise. (Flick the thumbstick in a direction to dash.)

Movement and Range 2

Major Benefits: Movement Speed, Kick Range

Minor Benefits: Punch Range, Stamina Recovery

Land any three unblocked strikes and then dash away from the opponent—do this four times to complete this simple exercise.

Wade in with fast jabs and straights, dashing backward the moment you've landed three unblocked blows.

Movement and Range 3

Major Benefits: Movement Speed, Punch Range

Minor Benefits: Kick Range, Stamina Recovery

Avoid being knocked out by an aggressive sparring partner in this exercise, but beware: You can't attack or block. Defend yourself by dashing away from your partner—first dash backward, then dash either right or left, whichever leads you away from your partner's back hand. Continue to dash backward and around your opponent. Survive for 45 seconds to ace the training.

Movement and Range 4

Major Benefit: Movement Speed

Minor Benefits: Punch Range, Kick Range, Stamina Recovery

You have 50 seconds to knock down an intermediate sparring partner in this final Movement and Range lesson, and the faster you do so, the better your grade will be. You can't block or parry, and your sparring partner is very aggressive—dash to sidestep his strikes, using footwork to create angles as you wing shots at his chin.

Kick Boxing Combo 1

Major Benefit: Kick Combo Speed

Minor Benefits: Kick Range, Stand Up Left Foot Power, Stand Up Right Foot Power, Foot Speed

Sling combos of fists and feet at your trainer's Muay Thai pads in this exercise. The combos are a little tricky until you gain a grasp of the game's kicking dynamic. Here are the combos you must perform:

Combo 1: Left jab, right head kick.

Combo 2: Right hook, left head kick.

Combo 3: Left jab, right jab, left leg kick.

Combo 4: Right straight, left hook, right head kick

Combo 5: Left head kick, right straight, left jab.

Combo 6: Right leg kick, left jab, right hook, left head kick.

Kick Boxing Combo 2

Major Benefit: Foot Speed

Minor Benefits: Stand Up Left Foot Power, Stand Up Right Foot Power, Kick Combo Speed, Kick Range

Complete a series of five punch and kick combos against a sparring partner in this exercise. The partner will occasionally move, making things a little more challenging. You have 30 seconds to land all of the following combos:

CAREER MODE

Combo 1: Right straight, left hook, right body kick.

Combo 2: Left jab, left jab, right leg kick.

Combo 3: Left jab, right hook, left hook, right body kick.

Combo 4: Left jab, right straight, left hook, right body kick.

Combo 5: Left leg kick, left leg kick, right hook, left body kick.

Kick Boxing Combo 3

Major Benefits: Stand Up Left Foot Power

Minor Benefits: Foot Speed, Kick Combo Speed, Stand Up Right Foot Power, Kick Range.

Unleash a number of advanced kickboxing combos against your trainer's pads in this lesson. You have 45 seconds to bang out the following tricky combos:

Combo 1: Left jab, right straight, left body kick.

Combo 2: Right straight, left hook, right head kick.

Combo 3: Left body jab, right body kick, left jab, right hook.

Combo 4: Right straight, left hook, right hook, left body kick.

Combo 5: Right leg kick, left jab, right straight, left body kick.

Combo 6: Left jab, left jab, right straight, left hook, right head kick.

Kick Boxing Combo 4

Major Benefits: Stand Up Right Foot Power

Minor Benefits: Stand Up Left Foot Power, Foot Speed, Kick Range, Kick Combo Speed

Land five challenging combos against a mobile sparring partner to clear this final Kick Boxing Combo challenge. Your partner will move and strike you back, making things quite difficult. Back him into a corner with a flurry of rapid punches, then focus on completing all of the following combos within 70 seconds:

Combo 1: Right leg kick, right leg kick, left jab, right straight.

Combo 2: Left jab, left jab, right hook, left body kick.

Combo 3: Left jab, right straight, left hook, right body kick.

Combo 4: Right leg kick, left hook, right body hook, left body kick.

Combo 5: Left jab, right body straight, left hook, right head kick.

Takedown Defense 1

Major Benefit: Ground Get Up

Minor Benefits: Takedown Defense, Stamina Recovery, Takedowns

Remain ready to sprawl at all times during this easy exercise, and simply focus on denying your training partner's takedown attempts. If he ever manages to drag you down, immediately shove him away and return to your feet so you may continue to stuff more takedowns. Stuff five shots to complete the exercise with an "A" grade.

Takedown Defense 2

Major Benefits: Ground Get Up, Takedown Defense

Minor Benefits: Takedowns, Stamina Recovery

Your partner takes you down at the start of this lesson, landing in your half guard. Shrug him off and get back to your feet immediately to complete the challenge. The faster you return to your feet, the better your grade—try reclaiming full guard and even sweeping your partner if you can't seem to stand up from half guard.

Takedown Defense 3

Major Benefit: Takedown Defense

Minor Benefits: Ground Get Up, Stamina Recovery, Takedowns

You must remain on your feet for a full minute to beat this challenge. Your sparring partner doesn't strike at you, so simply stand before him, ready to sprawl against his takedowns and deny his clinch attempts. Strive to stuff his takedowns immediately; if you're a little slow, you may stuff the shot but end up in the sprawl position with your partner trapped beneath you—although this is a dominant position, you are no longer standing on your feet and have therefore failed the exercise!

Takedown Defense 4

Major Benefit: Takedown Defense

Minor Benefits: Ground Get Up, Stamina Recovery, Takedowns

Your training partner scoops and slams you to the ground at the start of this exercise—you end up trapping him in half guard. Deny his passes as you work to recover full guard, then shove him away and rise back up to your feet. You have plenty of time to work, but the faster you reach your feet, the better your grade.

CLINCH EXERCISES

Clinch Combo 1

Major Benefits: Clinch Combo, Clinch Striking Power

Minor Benefits: Clinch Striking Power, Clinch Strike Speed, Stamina Recovery

Tie up with your training partner and complete the clinch strike combos before breaking away again. Just keep clinching and striking until you complete all five combos.

Combo 1: Clinch, right punch, right punch, break.

Combo 2: Clinch, left elbow, left elbow, break.

Combo 3: Clinch, right punch, right punch, left elbow, break.

Combo 4: Clinch, right elbow, right elbow, left elbow, break.

Combo 5: Left jab, right straight, clinch, left punch, left elbow, break.

Clinch Combo 2

Major Benefits: Clinch Strike Speed, Clinch Striking Power

Minor Benefits: Stamina Recovery, Clinch Combo

Rattle off a series of five kickboxing and clinch strike combos against an active sparring partner in this exercise. You have a full minute to complete the following advanced combos, so take your time and don't stress over a few mistakes:

Combo 1: Left jab, left jab, clinch, right punch, right punch, break.

Combo 2: Right leg kick, left body hook, clinch, right punch, right punch, right elbow, break.

Combo 3: Right body kick, left jab, clinch, left elbow, left jab, right elbow, break.

Combo 4: Left jab, right straight, right hook, clinch, left elbow, left elbow, right punch, break.

Combo 5: Left jab, right body straight, left body hook, clinch, right punch, right elbow, right punch, break.

Clinch Combo 3

Major Benefits: Clinch Striking Power, Clinch Strike Speed, Clinch Combo

Minor Benefits: Stamina Recovery

Clinch and smash your training partner with various strike combos to clear this lesson. You have 45 seconds to work, but avoid making too many errors. The combos you must complete are as follows:

Combo 1: Clinch, right punch, right punch, break.

Combo 2: Clinch, right elbow, right elbow, left elbow, break.

Combo 3: Left jab, left jab, clinch, right punch, right punch, break.

Combo 4: Right body kick, left jab, clinch, left elbow, left punch, right elbow, break.

Combo 5: Left jab, right body straight, left body hook, clinch, right punch, right elbow, right punch, break.

Clinch Combo 4

Major Benefit: Clinch Striking Power

Minor Benefits: Clinch Strike Speed, Clinch Combo, Stamina Recovery

Execute five clinch strike combos against an intermediate sparring partner to complete this exercise. You have 70 seconds to land five three-hit combos, and any clinch strikes will do the trick. Throw strikes to set up your clinches, landing three fast strikes after tying up. Break away after landing three strikes to complete the combo, then tie up again and land some more. Shove away from your training partner if he initiates a clinch—you must be the instigator for your strikes to tally.

CAREER MODE

Clinch Control 1

Major Benefit: Clinch Control

Minor Benefits: Clinch Control, Stamina Recovery

Practice your mastery over clinch control in this easy exercise. First enter the Muay Thai clinch against the training partner, then break away, then enter the double underhook clinch. Repeat this sequence to complete the lesson.

Clinch Control 2

Major Benefit: Clinch Control

Minor Benefits: Stamina Recovery

You must deny five of your training partner's clinch attempts to clear this exercise, and you fail instantly if he manages to tie you up even once. Your partner will throw strikes at you as well—but he can't knock you out or rock you, so simply let him tee off and don't bother blocking. Remain ready to stuff his clinch attempts when they eventually come.

Clinch Control 3

Major Benefit: Clinch Control

Minor Benefits: Stamina Recovery

Hurl a flurry of fast strikes at your sparring partner, backing him up toward the cage before tying up in the Muay Thai clinch. Muscle him against the cage and deny his escapes as you switch to the double underhook clinch. Slam your partner to the mat with a huge double underhook takedown to at last complete the lesson. The most challenging part of all of this is getting into the clinch and maintaining position—you need excellent clinch control to succeed, so keep practicing to strengthen your ability. Make sure you're the one to initiate the clinch as well—your rival cannot be the one to instigate it.

GROUND EXERCISES

Grappling 1

Major Benefit: Grapple Defense

Minor Benefits: Passing, Stamina Recovery

This exercise starts you off in your training partner's guard and asks you to pass to full mount. Your partner offers little resistance, so just keep passing until you reach the full mount position.

Grappling 2

Major Benefits: Grapple Defense, Passing

Minor Benefit: Stamina Recovery

You begin this exercise in full mount and must simply deny your sparing partner's attempts at improving position. Don't strike or block; simply remain ready to stuff your partner's moves the moment your controller begins to shake.

Grappling 3

Major Benefit: Passing

Minor Benefits: Grapple Defense, Stamina Recovery

Sweep your training partner the moment this exercise begins, then start working your way to full mount. Throw a few strikes to set up your passes, battering your partner's ribs to erode his stamina and make passing easier. Reach full mount within 90 seconds to complete the lesson—the faster you get there, the better your grade.

Grappling 4

Major Benefits: Passing

Minor Benefits: Grapple Defense, Stamina Recovery

Beat this lesson by surviving for one full minute without allowing your training partner to mount you. You begin in your partner's guard—strive to keep top position by denying his sweep attempts. Keep your partner planted on his back for the whole minute to earn an "A."

Ground Combos 1

Major Benefit: Ground Combo Speed

Minor Benefits: Ground Striking Power, Ground Strike Speed, Stamina Recovery

From your training partner's guard, use strikes to help you pass to mount. Your partner offers little resistance, so just keep passing until you reach the full mount position. If you're having trouble passing, pause to recover stamina and then throw a series of strikes to distract the opponent before making another attempt.

Ground Combos 2

Major Benefits: Ground Striking Speed, Ground Striking Power

Minor Benefits: Ground Combo Speed, Stamina Recovery

This exercise is similar to Ground Combos 1, except that this sparring partner is far more resistant to your passes. Use plenty of strikes to distract him before attempting each pass, targeting his body to drain his stamina and make passing easier. Beware his attempts to reclaim guard and be swift at denying him—this will wear him out as well.

Ground Combos 3

Major Benefits: Ground Striking Power, Ground Strike Speed

Minor Benefits: Ground Combo Speed, Stamina Recovery

You begin this lesson in the sprawl position and must pass around your partner, taking his side and then his back. The faster you manage to sink in your hooks, the better your grade will be. Deny your partner's escape attempts as you pass around, taking his back quickly to secure the "A" grade.

Ground Combos 4

Major Benefit: Ground Striking Power

Minor Benefits: Ground Strike Speed, Ground Combo Speed, Stamina Recovery

Your partner has you mounted at the start of this exercise, and you must turn the tables by recovering guard, sweeping, and then mounting him. You have two full minutes to work, but the faster you manage to reach mount, the better your score will be. Your opponent isn't too difficult to sweep, but the better your fighter's passing ability, the easier time he'll have at clearing this final Ground Combos lesson.

Takedowns 1

Major Benefit: None

Minor Benefits: Takedowns, Stamina Recovery, Takedown Defense

Shoot in on your easy training partner and plant him on the mat nine times to ace this exercise. Time is against you, so stand up after each successful takedown and get ready to set up your next shot.

CAREER MODE

Takedowns 2

Major Benefit: Takedowns

Minor Benefits: Stamina Recovery, Takedown Defense

Score nine takedowns on an intermediate sparring partner without being taken down yourself to beat this lesson. Be the aggressor and drive your partner to the mat, then immediately stand up so you can do it again. Shoot in the moment your partner rises to plant him on his back again and again, keeping a rhythm going and giving your partner very little chance at stopping you or taking you down.

Takedowns 3

Major Benefit: Takedowns

Minor Benefits: Stamina Recovery, Takedown Defense

This challenge is similar to Takedowns 2, except that the sparring partner is far more aggressive with his shots. Stuff his initial takedown and then shoot in to score your own. Quickly stand back up and then hit another takedown the moment your partner begins to rise. Keep this pattern going until you land nine takedowns.

Takedowns 4

Major Benefit: Takedowns

Minor Benefits: Stamina Recovery, Takedown Defense

This difficult challenge is similar to its predecessors, except that your expert sparring partner is very skilled at sprawling against your shots and taking you down. Shoot in for a takedown the moment he strikes, then stand back up and immediately dash away—your partner has the "open guard takedown" special and can trip you up with his feet from his back, bringing you to the mat and causing you to fail! Make sure to dash away after standing up from each takedown.

SUBMISSION EXERCISES

NOTE

Submission exercises can be very challenging to beat when you have little skill. Keep drilling them to build your submission ability, making these challenges easier.

Arm Submissions 1

Major Benefit: None

Minor Benefits: Arm Submissions, Grapple Defense, Stamina Recovery

Lock in an americana the moment this easy exercise begins and apply bursts of pressure to force your novice training partner to tap.

Arm Submissions 2

Major Benefit: Arm Submissions

Minor Benefits: Grapple Defense, Stamina Recovery

This lesson is similar to Arm Submissions 1, except that the opponent is far more difficult to submit. Use an americana and be sure to maximize your stamina by pressing the Submission button in short, regular bursts. The greater your fighter's arm submission skill, the easier it will be to finish the hold.

Arm Submissions 3

Major Benefit: Arm Submissions

Minor Benefits: Grapple Defense, Stamina Recovery

This final Arm Submission lesson is by far the most challenging—only those with great skill at arm subs will walk away with an "A." Lock in that americana and use short bursts of pressure to tighten the hold, looking to secure the tap. Expect a great struggle by your training partner—if you can tap this guy out, you can tap out anyone.

Choke Submissions 1

Major Benefit: None

Minor Benefits: Neck Submissions, Grapple Defense, Stamina Recovery

Finish your novice training partner with a rear naked choke (or any other choke) in this exercise. After initiating the choke, slowly rotate the left thumbstick to find the invisible "zone"—your controller rattles when you hit it. Stick with the zone once you find it to squeeze tighter and tighter until the choke is fully applied.

Choke Submissions 2

Major Benefit: Neck Submissions

Minor Benefits: Grapple Defense, Stamina Recovery

Tap an intermediate training partner with a rear naked choke to clear this lesson. Strive to find the elusive "zone" and stick with it when your controller begins to vibrate. Remember not to rotate the thumbstick too quickly and to release it to recoup stamina. The better your fighter is at applying neck submissions, the easier this challenge will be.

Choke Submissions 3

Major Benefit: Neck Submissions

Minor Benefits: Grapple Defense, Stamina Recovery

The final Choke Submission challenge is most difficult—expect to struggle greatly against your seasoned training partner.

Only those with a high neck submission score will be able to secure the choke against this worthy foe. Slip into a rear naked choke at the start of the challenge and strive to find that elusive "zone." Keep practicing to improve your skill until you're finally able to secure the tap.

Leg Submissions 1

Major Benefit: Leg Submissions

Minor Benefits: Grapple Defense, Stamina Recovery

Finish a heel hook (or any other leg submission) on your novice training partner to ace this easy exercise. Simply initiate the heel hook from your starting position and apply pressure in bursts of button presses until you force the tap.

Leg Submissions 2

Major Benefit: Leg Submissions

Minor Benefits: Grapple Defense, Stamina Recovery

Tap an intermediate training partner with a heel hook to clear this lesson. Apply the submission at the start of the exercise and use short bursts of pressure to conserve stamina while securing the hold. The higher your fighter's talent for leg submissions, the easier this challenge will be.

Leg Submissions 3

Major Benefit: Leg Submissions

Minor Benefits: Grapple Defense, Stamina Recovery

Grab hold of your expert partner's leg and battle to tap him out with a heel hook in this final Leg Submission challenge. You must have exceptional leg sub skill to force the tap against your seasoned partner—practice to build your ability. If you can finish this guy with a leg lock, you can finish anyone.

CAREER MODE

Submission Defense 1

Major Benefit: None

Minor Benefits: Stamina Recovery, Arm Submissions, Leg Submissions, Neck Submissions

Your sparring partner has you mounted—survive against his onslaught of submission attempts until time expires. You fail if you're ever caught up in a submission battle, so don't bother blocking those strikes—focus solely on denying each submission attempt until you hear the bell.

Submission Defense 2

Major Benefit: Grapple Defense

Minor Benefits: Stamina Recovery, Arm Submissions, Leg Submissions, Neck Submissions

Defend against an even more skilled submission artist's holds in this exercise. Focus on denying his submission attempts, but also try to recover guard and sweep to nullify his submission options.

Submission Defense 3

Major Benefit: Grapple Defense

Minor Benefits: Stamina Recovery, Arm Submissions, Leg Submissions, Neck Submissions

This exercise is similar to the last—simply deny your partner's onslaught of submission attempts to achieve an "A" grade. Again, try to improve your position when the opportunity allows to potentially negate your partner's subs.

Submission Defense 4

Major Benefit: Grapple Defense

Minor Benefits: Stamina Recovery, Arm Submissions, Leg Submissions, Neck Submissions

Your training partner is an elite grappler in this final lesson, but your tactics remain the same: Simply strive to deny all submission attempts and complete the exercise with an "A" grade.

FIGHT NIGHT

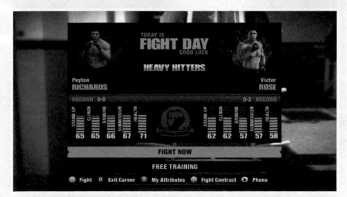

The time has finally come. You've put in the hard work—now you get to show the world what you're capable of. Keep the following tips in mind to increase your odds of getting your hand raised on fight night.

FIGHT YOUR FIGHT

Your knowledge of your opponent's strengths and weaknesses is the best thing you've got going for you in each fight. Study your rival's attributes while viewing the fight contract, looking for his highest and lowest scores. Perhaps he's got weak legs, or a glass jaw? Or maybe he lacks grappling defense, which makes him susceptible to submissions. Think of the best places to bring the fight against your opponents—and be aware of dangerous areas you should avoid.

CONSERVE YOUR STAMINA

Play it cool once the cage doors seal—you've got all night to finish the bum in front of you. Running out of stamina makes everything more difficult, both offense and defense, so it's something you must avoid. Use footwork and feints to pressure your opponent without expending much stamina. Get him to open up with strikes, then capitalize with counter shots or a fast takedown—whichever your fighter would prefer.

Don't overcommit when striking, and remain tactical and methodical when battling in the clinch and on the ground. Try to keep your opponent working in each position, but keep an eye on your own stamina and look for short breaks in the action where your fighter can catch a few breaths.

CONTROL AND CONQUER

Fighting is intense, but do your best to consider your surroundings as you mix things up on the feet. Use the cage to your advantage by keeping near the center, then applying slow but steady pressure to carefully back your opponent up and pinning him against the cage to limit his mobility and gain the advantage in the clinch.

Keep your surroundings in mind when retreating as well. Avoid backing directly away from your opponent—circle away instead, moving backward and then away from your opponent's back (power) hand.

NEVER QUIT

Anything can happen in a fight—your very first punch might be sharply countered, rocking you and putting you in deep water right from the get-go. Never give up and always struggle to survive in these situations—it doesn't take long for your fighter to recover, and you might end up rocking your opponent just as easily.

Clinch or shoot for a takedown when you get rocked, closing the distance and controlling position for a moment until your head clears. Relax and focus when caught in submissions, working methodically to defend and slip free of holds. As long as you have enough stamina, it's often possible to escape from desperate situations and gain a chance to fight back and turn the tables on your opponent.

FIGHT RESULTS

Statistical feedback is displayed following each fight, along with the judge's scorecards (regardless of whether they were needed to determine the outcome). Use this data to help you fine-tune your game. For example, if your fighter seems to tire rapidly and you always seem to throw a high number of strikes during fights, you're probably being a little too busy. Try slowing down and picking your shots with more care, using footwork instead of simply winging combos.

ONLINE ACTION

To truly count yourself among *MMA*'s elite, you've got to challenge your skills against other players. Fortunately, *MMA* features a dedicated online community full of fight fans, all ready to mix things up with their favorite created warriors.

Before you dive into the frenzy of online *MMA*, you'll either need to create a fighter, import one of your Career mode fighters, or download a fighter that another player has created and uploaded via Fighter Share.

CREATING ONLINE FIGHTERS

Eager to test your skills online, but not interested in working to max out a Career fighter's attributes? No sweat—just go to Fighter Share and choose the "Create A Fighter" option. Here you can build your ideal online warrior simply by choosing his fighting style and weight, then distributing points to his various attributes. Give some thought to the type of fighter you want to build and modify his attributes accordingly.

NOTE

A fighter's starting, minimum, and maximum attribute values are determined by his fighting style (boxing, wrestling, etc.) and his weight class (Heavyweight, Middleweight, etc.). Set these options before fiddling with a fighter's attribute scores, and see the previous "Create A Fighter" chapter of this guide for complete attribute tables for all fighting styles in every weight class.

When building a warrior in Fighter Share, you're permitted to give him 14 specials in addition to his starting five (heel hook, americana, rear naked choke, roundhouse head kick, and "slip strikes.") Think carefully about the type of fighter you're building and select specials that best compliment his strengths and balance out weaknesses.

SHARING FIGHTERS

There's no need to create fighters in *MMA*—simply visit Fighter Share and choose "Download Fighters," then you can browse and download warriors created by other *MMA* enthusiasts across the globe! Naturally, you're also able to upload your own created fighters as well—refer to your instruction manual for complete details on this process.

ONLINE ACTION

ONLINE STRATEGIES

Fighting is fighting, whether you're playing online or against the game. All of the information and strategies contained in this guide is fully applicable to online fights, so do your homework and read each chapter thoroughly!

Let's quickly recap some of the most important things to keep in mind about online play.

Feel Things Out. It's usually best to feel out your opponent at the start of each fight. Take your time on the feet, working your jabs and leg kicks. Become more aggressive as you begin to find your range and timing, or when the opponent gains the upper hand and you're forced to change the pace of the fight.

Defense Is Key. Maxing out all of your fighters' offensive attributes is tempting, but make sure your guys are rounded enough to escape from dangerous situations. Give strikers the ability to defend takedowns, work out of submissions, and to get back to their feet. Ensure your grapplers have excellent clinch control and ground defense as well as brutal offense and submission ability.

Do Your Homework. Whenever possible, scan your rivals' attributes to look for holes in their game that you can exploit, along with the areas in which they excel.

Never Give Up. MMA is a chaotic sport in which anything can happen. Don't panic after being suddenly rocked by a striker or taken down by a submission whiz—keep your cool and work out of these bad scenarios. Every fan of the sport knows that comebacks happen all the time in MMA—and these types of victories are all the more satisfying.

TIP

Before jumping online, watch some Fight Replays from the Leaderboards. Scouting users from the leaderboard helps you gain valuable strategies used by the top fighters online without first having to lose to them. You can stay current on the prevailing strategies by just watching fight replays of the best of the best. *Your* ranked fights are automatically uploaded, too, giving you the opportunity to go back and analyze why you lost each fight.

BELT RANK

The following chart shows how *MMA's* online belt ranking system works. There are 90 belts to achieve in all—strive to attain the highest belt and consider yourself a true *MMA* champion!"

Masters Division

1	2	3	4	5
6	7	8	9	10
11	12	13	14	15
16	17	18	19	20
21	22	23	24	25
26	27	28	29	30
31	32	33	34	35
36	37	38	39	40
41	42	43	44	45

46	47	48	49	50
51	52	53	54	55
56	57	58	59	60
71	62	63	64	65
76	67	68	69	70
71	72	73	74	75
76	77	78	79	80
81	82	83	84	85
86	87	88	89	90

MMA ROSTER

ALISTAIR OVEREEM
"DEMOLITION MAN"

ALISTAIR OVEREEM
Born: Hounslow, England

Specialty: Muay Thai

Weight Classes: Heavyweight, Light Heavyweight

▶ FIGHT RECORD ◀

33—11—0 (WIN—LOSS—DRAW) (1 NC)

WINS: 13 (T)KOS (39.39%)
19 Submissions (57.58%)
1 Decision (3.03%)

LOSSES: 6 (T)KOS (54.55%)
2 Submissions (18.18%)
3 Decisions (27.27%)

OPPONENT	RESULT	METHOD	DATE	ROUND	TIME
Brett Rogers	Win	TKO (Punches)	5/15/10	1	3:40
Kazuyuki Fujita	Win	KO (Knee)	12/31/09	1	1:15
James Thompson	Win	Submission (Guillotine Choke)	10/25/09	1	0:33
Tony Sylvester	Win	Submission (Guillotine Choke)	10/17/09	1	1:23
Gary Goodridge	Win	Submission (Kimura)	11/9/08	1	1:47
Mirko Filipovic	NC	No Contest (Knee to the Groin)	9/23/08	1	N/A
Mark Hunt	Win	Submission (Keylock)	7/21/08	1	1:11
Tae Hyun Lee	Win	KO (Punches)	6/15/08	1	0:36
Paul Buentello	Win	Submission (Knees to the Body)	11/16/07	2	3:42
Sergei Kharitonov	Loss	KO (Punch)	9/17/07	1	4:21
Michael Knaap	Win	Submission (Guillotine Choke)	6/23/07	1	3:29
Mauricio Rua	Loss	KO (Punches)	2/24/07	1	3:37
Ricardo Arona	Loss	Submission (Punches)	9/10/06	1	4:28
Antonio Rogerio Nogueira	Loss	TKO (Corner Stoppage)	7/1/06	2	2:13
Vitor Belfort	Win	Decision (Unanimous)	6/9/06	3	5:00
Fabricio Werdum	Loss	Submission (Kimura)	5/5/06	2	3:43
Nikolajus Cilkinas	Win	Submission (Armbar)	3/18/06	1	1:42
Sergei Kharitonov	Win	TKO (Knees)	2/26/06	1	5:13
Mauricio Rua	Loss	TKO (Punches)	8/28/05	1	6:42
Igor Vovchanchyn	Win	Submission (Guillotine Choke)	6/26/05	1	1:20
Vitor Belfort	Win	Submission (Guillotine Choke)	4/23/05	1	9:36
Antonio Rogerio Nogueira	Loss	Decision (Unanimous)	2/20/05	3	5:00
Hiromitsu Kanehara	Win	TKO (Doctor Stoppage)	10/31/04	2	3:52
Rodney Glunder	Win	Submission (Guillotine Choke)	10/10/04	1	N/A
Tomohiko Hashimoto	Win	TKO (Knees)	12/31/03	1	0:36
Chuck Liddell	Loss	KO (Punches)	8/10/03	1	3:09
Mike Bencic	Win	Submission (Strikes)	6/8/03	1	3:44
Aaron Brink	Win	Submission (Guillotine Choke)	3/16/03	1	0:53
Bazigit Atajev	Win	TKO (Knee to the Body)	12/23/02	2	4:59
Dave Vader	Win	TKO (Doctor)	10/13/02	2	N/A
Moise Rimbon	Win	Submission (Choke)	10/13/02	1	1:03
Yusuke Imamura	Win	TKO (Knee and Punches)	7/20/02	1	0:44
Vesa Vuori	Win	TKO (Punches)	5/26/02	1	2:15
Sergey Kaznovsky	Win	Submission (Armbar)	4/26/02	1	3:37
Roman Zentsov	Win	Submission (Keylock)	3/17/02	1	N/A
Stanislav Nuschik	Win	TKO (Knees)	3/18/01	1	0:53
Vladimer Tchanturia	Win	Submission (Rear Naked Choke)	2/24/01	1	1:06
Peter Verschuren	Win	Submission (Keylock)	12/12/00	1	1:06
Bobby Hoffman	Loss	KO (Punch)	6/15/00	1	9:39
Yuriy Kochkine	Loss	Decision	5/20/00	2	5:00
Yasuhito Namekawa	Win	Submission (Armbar)	4/20/00	1	0:45
Can Sahinbas	Win	KO (Knee)	3/5/00	1	2:21
Chris Watts	Win	KO (Knee to the Body)	2/6/00	1	3:58
Yuriy Kochkine	Loss	Decision (Majority)	10/28/99	2	5:00
Ricardo Fyeet	Win	Submission (Guillotine Choke)	10/24/99	1	1:39

ALISTAIR OVEREEM

ATTRIBUTES

ATTRIBUTE	HEAVYWEIGHT	LIGHT HEAVYWEIGHT
Stand Up	**88**	**87**
Foot Speed	86	90
Hand Speed	86	90
Kick Combo Speed	86	90
Kick Range	96	75
Movement Speed	83	83
Punch Combo Speed	88	90
Punch Range	75	90
Stand Up Left Foot Power	97	92
Stand Up Left Hand Power	97	92
Stand Up Right Foot Power	97	92
Stand Up Right Hand Power	97	92
Takedowns	80	80
Takedown Defense	80	80
Clinch	**88**	**88**
Clinch Combo	88	90
Clinch Control	80	80
Clinch Strike Speed	88	90
Clinch Striking Power	97	92
Ground	**88**	**88**
Grapple Defense	90	90
Ground Combo Speed	88	90
Ground Get Up	80	80
Ground Strike Speed	88	90
Ground Striking Power	96	92
Passing	90	90
Submission	**82**	**82**
Arm Submissions	90	90
Leg Submissions	60	60
Neck Submissions	98	98
Health	**78**	**78**
Blocking	70	70
Chin	60	60
Gut	90	90
Heart	70	70
Leg Health	99	99
Stamina Recovery	80	80

SPECIAL MOVES

NAME	TYPE	FROM
Americana	Submission (Arm)	(1) Full Mount Postured Up—Top; (2) Full Mount Tight—Top
Armbar	Submission (Arm)	(1) Full Guard—Bottom; (2) Full Guard Postured Up—Bottom; (3) Side Control—Top; (4) Back Mount Side Turtle—Top
Catch Kick	Parry	Standing
Catch Punch	Parry	(1) Full Guard Postured Up—Bottom; (2) Full Guard Postured Up—Top; (3) Full Mount Postured Up—Top
Diving Punch	Strike	Standing vs. Open Guard
Flying Knee	Strike	Standing
Guillotine Takedown	Submission (Neck)	Standing
Head Arm Choke	Submission (Neck)	(1) Full Mount Tight—Top; (2) Side Control—Top
Kimura	Submission (Arm)	Half Guard—Top
Major Pass	Strike	Every Ground Position
Overhand Punch	Strike	Standing
Rear Naked Choke	Submission (Neck)	Back Mount—Top
Roundhouse Head Kick	Strike	Standing
Takedown Counter Strike	Strike	Standing
Teep Kick	Strike	Standing

STAND UP STRATEGIES

A powerful heavyweight, Alistair is nothing short of dominant on the feet. All of his strikes are devastating, though his kick range suffers dramatically when fighting at Light Heavyweight. Alistair's one stand up drawback lies in his lackluster movement speed; close in fast with flying knees and follow up with brutal combos.

Fighting against: Alistair Overeem—When fighting Alistair, don't linger in front of him for long. Exploit his average movement speed to create angles and get out of bad situations. Lead with leg kicks to slow Overeem down and set up combos. Though offensively powerful, Alistair has poor blocking and a weak chin, and can therefore be picked apart by savvy strikers.

CLINCH STRATEGIES

Alistair's a bully in the clinch, quickly piling on devastating strikes that can buckle foes in short order. Lock up into the Muay Thai clinch and batter your adversary with elbows and knees. Clinching up is a good idea when Alistair's chin starts to fail him on the feet. Use the clinch to score takedowns as well, setting up Alistair to end the fight with kimuras or head arm chokes.

Fighting against: Alistair Overeem—Overeem's clinch strikes are fast and powerful, but he comes up short in the control department. When Alistair clinches up with you, block to reduce damage and tire him, then look to reverse the clinch, break away, or turn the tables with a sudden takedown.

GROUND STRATEGIES

A well-rounded fighter, Overeem can take care of business on the ground. Though his takedowns and takedown defense leave something to be desired, Alistair has solid passing and grapple defense attributes, which help him control the action once it hits the mat. Alistair's ground strikes are as devastating as those he throws on his feet or in the clinch, and he's capable of ending the fight very quickly with a fast arm or neck submission. Overeem has plenty of these submissions in his repertoire, so he can tap opponents out from several different angles on the ground.

Fighting against: Alistair Overeem—Alistair is a tough nut to crack on the ground, so expect a grueling battle on the mat. Pass his guard to avoid falling into armbars, working methodically to score damage and control the action without sacrificing position. Pound Overeem's body and deny his attempts to get off his back to drain his stamina as you move toward a dominant ground position. Overeem is tough to tap, so wear him down before locking in a sub.

ANDREAS KRANIOTAKES

"BIG DADDY"

ANDREAS KRANIOTAKES
Born: Koblenz, Germany

Specialty: Judo

Weight Class: Heavyweight

> FIGHT RECORD <

7—2—0 (WIN—LOSS—DRAW)

WINS	LOSSES
6 (T)KOs (85.71%)	1 (T)KO (50%)
1 Submission (14.29%)	1 Decision (50%)

OPPONENT	RESULT	METHOD	DATE	ROUND	TIME
Gerald Turek	Loss	KO (Punches)	3/27/10	1	0:10
Nandor Guelmino	Win	TKO (Punches)	12/20/09	1	3:37
Waldemar Giesbrecht	Win	TKO (Punches)	10/2/09	1	1:45
Jerry Otto	Loss	Decision (Unanimous)	10/19/08	2	5:00
Lars Klug	Win	TKO (Punches)	9/27/08	1	2:22
Alexander Stefanovic	Win	Submission (Strikes)	6/14/08	1	1:17
Kevin Pohie	Win	TKO (Punches)	3/29/08	1	1:41
Andreas Paulus	Win	TKO (Corner Stoppage)	7/16/05	2	1:32
Attila Attila	Win	TKO (Punches)	7/16/05	2	1:55

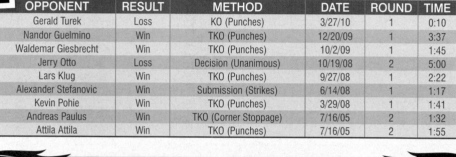

SPECIAL MOVES		
NAME	TYPE	FROM
Americana	Submission (Arm)	(1) Full Mount Postured Up—Top; (2) Full Mount Tight—Top
Catch Kick	Parry	Standing
Catch Punch	Parry	(1) Full Guard Postured Up—Bottom; (2) Full Guard Postured Up—Top; (3) Full Mount Postured Up—Top
Dashing Takedown	Takedown	Standing
Diving Punch	Strike	Standing vs. Open Guard
Flying Knee	Strike	Standing
Guillotine Takedown	Submission (Neck)	Standing
Major Pass	Strike	Every Ground Position
Overhand Punch	Strike	Standing
Rear Naked Choke	Submission (Neck)	Back Mount—Top
Takedown Fake	Strike	Standing

ANDREAS KRANIOTAKES

ATTRIBUTES	
ATTRIBUTE	HEAVYWEIGHT
Stand Up	**74**
Foot Speed	70
Hand Speed	70
Kick Combo Speed	70
Kick Range	71
Movement Speed	70
Punch Combo Speed	70
Punch Range	75
Stand Up Left Foot Power	70
Stand Up Left Hand Power	05
Stand Up Right Foot Power	70
Stand Up Right Hand Power	85
Takedowns	80
Takedown Defense	80
Clinch	**76**
Clinch Combo	70
Clinch Control	80
Clinch Strike Speed	70
Clinch Striking Power	85
Ground	**76**
Grapple Defense	80
Ground Combo Speed	70
Ground Get Up	80
Ground Strike Speed	70
Ground Striking Power	90
Passing	70
Submission	**50**
Arm Submissions	50
Leg Submissions	50
Neck Submissions	50
Health	**83**
Blocking	80
Chin	80
Gut	90
Heart	90
Leg Health	90
Stamina Recovery	70

STAND UP STRATEGIES

One of the weaker fighters in the Heavyweight division, Andreas Kraniotakes boasts respectable punching power on the feet, but suffers from a lack of speed and range. Keep pressure on opponents when fighting as Kraniotakes, strategically backing them into a corner to reduce their ability to move. Shoot a takedown when the time is right to unload some of Andreas's lethal ground and pound.

Fighting against: Andreas Kraniotakes—When fighting Andreas on the feet, expect him to wade in with hooks, quickly changing levels to bring the fight to the mat. Always be ready to stuff a takedown, and use good footwork to exploit Kraniotakes's lack of movement speed, picking him apart with calculated attacks. Target his suspect chin and batter his body to wear away at his unimpressive stamina.

CLINCH STRATEGIES

Kraniotakes's clinch strikes are slow but heavy. He has solid control in the clinch, so use this position to soften up rivals with strikes, setting them up for a heavy double underhook takedown that puts Kraniotakes close to mount.

Fighting against: Andreas Kraniotakes—When facing Kraniotakes in the clinch, exploit his sluggish strikes to land more of your own—but be wary of his takedowns and be ready to stuff them. Focus on battering Kraniotakes's body to drain his stamina.

GROUND STRATEGIES

Kraniotakes's best position in a fight is on the ground, raining heavy leather down on his foes. His submission skills are not good, so focus on passing him to mount, where he can pour on the ground and pound. Kraniotakes's "major pass" special can help move you into dominant position very quickly.

Fighting against: Andreas Kraniotakes—The last place you want to be is underneath Andreas in a fight—his ground and pound is his strongest suit. Get to your feet as soon as possible to pick him apart with blistering strikes. Or, if ground fighting's your game, look to sweep Andreas from the bottom and tap him out. Andreas has solid grappling defense, but tapping him is certainly possible with an accomplished submission wiz.

ANDREI ARLOVSKI
Born: Minsk, Belarus

ANDREI ARLOVSKI
"PITBULL"

› FIGHT RECORD ‹
15—8—0 (WIN—LOSS—DRAW)

WINS	LOSSES
11 (T)KOs (73.33%)	6 (T)KOs (75%)
3 Submissions (20%)	2 Decisions (25%)
1 Decision (6.67%)	

Specialty: Muay Thai
Weight Class: Heavyweight

OPPONENT	RESULT	METHOD	DATE	ROUND	TIME
Antonio Silva	Loss	Decision (Unanimous)	5/15/10	3	5:00
Brett Rogers	Loss	TKO (Punches)	6/6/09	1	0:22
Fedor Emelianenko	Loss	KO (Punch)	1/24/09	1	3:14
Roy Nelson	Win	KO (Punch)	10/4/08	2	3:14
Ben Rothwell	Win	KO (Punches)	7/19/08	3	1:13
Jake O'Brien	Win	TKO (Punches)	3/1/08	2	4:17
Fabricio Werdum	Win	Decision (Unanimous)	4/21/07	3	5:00
Marcio Cruz	Win	KO (Punches)	12/30/06	1	3:15
Tim Sylvia	Loss	Decision (Unanimous)	7/8/06	5	5:00
Tim Sylvia	Loss	TKO (Punches)	4/15/06	1	2:43
Paul Buentello	Win	KO (Punch)	10/7/05	1	0:15
Justin Eilers	Win	TKO (Punches)	6/4/05	1	4:10
Tim Sylvia	Win	Submission (Achilles Lock)	2/5/05	1	0:47
Wesley Correira	Win	TKO (Punches)	4/2/04	2	1:15
Vladimir Matyushenko	Win	KO (Punch)	9/26/03	1	1:59
Ian Freeman	Win	TKO (Punches)	11/22/02	1	1:25
Pedro Rizzo	Loss	KO (Punches)	3/22/02	3	1:45
Ricco Rodriguez	Loss	TKO (Punches)	6/29/01	3	1:23
Aaron Brink	Win	Submission (Armbar)	11/17/00	1	0:55
John Dixson	Win	KO (Punches)	5/13/00	1	N/A
Roman Zentsov	Win	TKO (Punches)	4/9/00	1	1:18
Michael Tielrooy	Win	Submission (Guillotine Choke)	4/9/00	1	1:25
Viacheslav Datsik	Loss	KO (Punch)	4/9/99	1	6:05

SPECIAL MOVES		
NAME	**TYPE**	**FROM**
Armbar	Submission (Arm)	(1) Full Guard—Bottom; (2) Full Guard Postured Up—Bottom; (3) Side Control—Top; (4) Back Mount Side Turtle—Top
Dashing Takedown	Takedown	Standing
Diving Punch	Strike	Standing vs. Open Guard
Flying Knee	Strike	Standing
Guillotine Takedown	Submission (Neck)	Standing
Heel Hook	Submission (Leg)	(1) Full Guard Postured Up—Top; (2) Guard Stacked—Top
Inverted Kneebar	Submission (Leg)	Guard Stacked—Bottom
Kneebar	Submission (Leg)	Full Guard—Top
Major Pass	Strike	Every Ground Position
Overhand Punch	Strike	Standing
Rear Naked Choke	Submission (Neck)	Back Mount—Top
Roundhouse Head Kick	Strike	Standing
Teep Kick	Strike	Standing

ANDREI ARLOVSKI

ATTRIBUTES	
ATTRIBUTE	**HEAVYWEIGHT**
Stand Up	**80**
Foot Speed	71
Hand Speed	87
Kick Combo Speed	77
Kick Range	80
Movement Speed	83
Punch Combo Speed	87
Punch Range	95
Stand Up Left Foot Power	70
Stand Up Left Hand Power	83
Stand Up Right Foot Power	70
Stand Up Right Hand Power	83
Takedowns	80
Takedown Defense	80
Clinch	**81**
Clinch Combo	87
Clinch Control	70
Clinch Strike Speed	87
Clinch Striking Power	80
Ground	**77**
Grapple Defense	70
Ground Combo Speed	87
Ground Get Up	80
Ground Strike Speed	87
Ground Striking Power	80
Passing	60
Submission	**53**
Arm Submissions	65
Leg Submissions	35
Neck Submissions	60
Health	**76**
Blocking	70
Chin	55
Gut	85
Heart	70
Leg Health	80
Stamina Recovery	99

STAND UP STRATEGIES

Arlovski is fast and fluid on the feet, but his strikes don't pack the same punch as the division's heaviest hitters. Use Arlovski's speed to land a few strikes on your way into a Muay Thai clinch, where Andrei is free to inflict damage without fear of leaving his vulnerable chin exposed to counters.

Fighting against: Andrei Arlovski—Though quick on his toes, Arlovski's chin is among worst in the Heavyweight division. When fighting Andrei, frustrate him on the feet with crisp counter jabs and hooks. Arlovski always comes in shape and boasts great stamina recovery, so look for the knockout instead of softening up the body. Wear Andrei out with leg kicks if he's outmaneuvering you.

CLINCH STRATEGIES

With a glass jaw to protect, Arlovski is wise to close the distance. Use Andrei's fast hands to get your opponent thinking "boxing," then quickly clinch up and deliver some rapid Muay Thai combos. Don't become overzealous with clinch strikes, however; focus on keeping the position, wearing down your opponent from the safety of the clinch, and thereby protecting Andrei's chin.

Fighting against: Andrei Arlovski—Arlovski throws fast combos in the clinch, but as with his standing strikes, they don't have the impact that you'd expect from a Heavyweight Muay Thai fighter. Arlovski's clinch control is also lacking; exploit this to break away from the clinch when he opens up with strikes, or turn the tables with a sudden takedown.

GROUND STRATEGIES

Arlovski's not entirely out of his element on the ground, but it's not his ideal place. He's not good at passing guard, and his grappling defense is low enough for those with skill to tap him out. Unless you're battling against a really poor grappler, quickly get Arlovski back up to his feet whenever the action hits the mat.

Fighting against: Andrei Arlovski—Though he's trained in a variety of submissions, Arlovski's tap out attributes leave much to be desired. Don't fear his subs when fighting against Andrei on the ground; instead, look to bring the fight to the mat to exploit his lack of grappling defense. Or simply avoid the ground entirely if you're an explosive striker—Arlovski's chin is the primary target in any fight.

BILLY EVANGELISTA

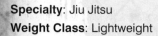
BILLY EVANGELISTA
Born: Parlier, California

Specialty: Jiu Jitsu
Weight Class: Lightweight

> FIGHT RECORD <

10—0—0 (WIN—LOSS—DRAW) (1 NC)

WINS
4 (T)KOs (40%)
6 Decisions (60%)

OPPONENT	RESULT	METHOD	DATE	ROUND	TIME
Jorge Gurgel	Win	Decision (Unanimous)	11/6/09	3	5:00
Mike Aina	NC	No Decision (Overturned by CSAC)	5/15/09	2	3:42
Harris Sarmiento	Win	Decision (Unanimous)	1/22/09	3	3:00
Luke Caudillo	Win	Decision (Unanimous)	10/3/08	3	5:00
Nam Phan	Win	Decision (Split)	6/27/08	3	5:00
Marlon Sims	Win	KO (Punch)	3/29/08	3	0:39
Clint Coronel	Win	Decision (Split)	9/29/07	3	5:00
Ryan Bixler	Win	Decision (Unanimous)	7/24/07	5	5:00
Alexander Crispim	Win	TKO	3/31/07	3	3:48
Isaiah Hill	Win	TKO (Punches)	2/10/07	1	1:39
Ryan Healy	Win	TKO (Punches and Elbows)	1/13/06	2	2:06

	ROCKSTAR ENERGY DRINK	
BILLY EVANGELISTA	LIGHTWEIGHT BOUT	JOACHIM HANSEN
	BORN	
10-0	RECORD	19-10
5' 8"	HEIGHT	5' 10"
155 lbs	WEIGHT	155 lbs

SPECIAL MOVES		
NAME	TYPE	FROM
Americana	Submission (Arm)	(1) Full Mount Postured Up—Top; (2) Full Mount Tight—Top
Armbar	Submission (Arm)	(1) Full Guard—Bottom; (2) Full Guard Postured Up—Bottom; (3) Side Control—Top; (4) Back Mount Side Turtle—Top
Catch Kick	Parry	Standing
Catch Punch	Parry	(1) Full Guard Postured Up—Bottom; (2) Full Guard Postured Up—Top; (3) Full Mount Postured Up—Top
Dashing Takedown	Takedown	Standing
Diving Punch	Strike	Standing vs. Open Guard
Guillotine Takedown	Submission (Neck)	Standing
Kimura	Submission (Arm)	Half Guard—Top
Major Pass	Strike	Every Ground Position
Rear Naked Choke	Submission (Neck)	Back Mount—Top
Roundhouse Head Kick	Strike	Standing
Superman Punch	Strike	Standing
Takedown Fake	Strike	Standing

BILLY EVANGELISTA

ATTRIBUTES	
ATTRIBUTE	LIGHTWEIGHT
Stand Up	**75**
Foot Speed	94
Hand Speed	94
Kick Combo Speed	96
Kick Range	70
Movement Speed	94
Punch Combo Speed	96
Punch Range	70
Stand Up Left Foot Power	54
Stand Up Left Hand Power	58
Stand Up Right Foot Power	56
Stand Up Right Hand Power	56
Takedowns	66
Takedown Defense	77
Clinch	**84**
Clinch Combo	96
Clinch Control	90
Clinch Strike Speed	92
Clinch Striking Power	58
Ground	**83**
Grapple Defense	90
Ground Combo Speed	96
Ground Get Up	88
Ground Strike Speed	96
Ground Striking Power	62
Passing	71
Submission	**33**
Arm Submissions	33
Leg Submissions	33
Neck Submissions	33
Health	**83**
Blocking	71
Chin	77
Gut	90
Heart	97
Leg Health	83
Stamina Recovery	82

STAND UP STRATEGIES

Like most Lightweight fighters, Evangelista has fast hands that lack the power of heavier strikers. Use Billy's furious combos to pick opponents apart while constantly forcing them backward, toward the cage. Clinch up when the time is right, then press them into the cage wall and start doing some real damage with knees and elbows.

Fighting against: Billy Evangelista—Billy's lackluster blocking and chin can get him into trouble on the feet. When striking against Billy, slow him down with leg kicks and go for fast headshot counters, but always be ready to shrug off a clinch or takedown attempt.

CLINCH STRATEGIES

Evangelista is most imposing in the clinch and he's one of the better clinch fighters in the Lightweight division. Lock up and deliver punishing shots, forcing Evangelista's foe against the cage to add even more weight to each blow. Work methodically to ensure your rival isn't able to break away and just keep wearing him down with calculated strikes.

Fighting against: Billy Evangelista—Evangelista's a handful in the clinch, so when fighting against him, it's best not to let him take the fight there. Always be ready to counter his clinch attempts and avoid getting cornered near the cage. If you do end up in the clinch, block Billy's blows to tire him out and escape or improve position the moment his stamina begins to dwindle.

GROUND STRATEGIES

Billy can handle himself on the ground, boasting impressive attributes across the board. However, with amateur-level submission skills, Billy is at his best when posturing up and raining down with his fists. Billy has a hard time passing the guard of seasoned grapplers, so bringing the fight to the mat is purely optional and should be primarily used against those with poor ground skills.

Fighting against: Billy Evangelista—Though a handful from the top position, Evangelista has trouble passing guard to get into dominant ground and pound submissions. Exploit this weakness by sweeping Billy when rolling with him, putting him on his back and working to keep him there. Billy isn't easy to submit, so focus on wearing him down from the top position, scoring points with the judges until a chance to end the fight presents itself. The longer you can keep Evangelista on his back, the better.

BOB SAPP
Born: Seattle, Washington

BOB SAPP
"THE BEAST"

> FIGHT RECORD <
11—6—1 (WIN—LOSS—DRAW)

WINS	LOSSES
7 (T)KOs (63.64%)	2 (T)KOs (33.33%)
3 Submissions (27.27%)	4 Submissions (66.67%)
1 Other (9.09%)	

Specialty: Brawler

Weight Class: Heavyweight

OPPONENT	RESULT	METHOD	DATE	ROUND	TIME
Sascha Weinpolter	Win	Submission (Forearm Choke)	3/27/10	1	2:03
Rameau Thierry Sokoudjou	Loss	TKO (Punches)	10/6/09	1	1:31
Bobby Lashley	Loss	Submission (Punches)	6/27/09	1	3:17
Ikuhisa Minowa	Loss	Submission (Achilles Lock)	5/26/09	1	1:15
Akihito Tanaka	Win	TKO (Punches)	12/31/08	1	5:22
Jan Nortje	Loss	TKO (Punches)	2/23/08	1	0:55
Bobby Ologun	Win	TKO (Punches)	12/31/07	1	4:10
Jong Wang Kim	Win	TKO (Punches)	11/5/05	1	0:08
Alan Karaev	Win	KO (Punch)	7/6/05	1	3:44
Min Soo Kim	Win	KO (Punch)	3/26/05	1	1:12
Jerome LeBanner	Draw	Draw	12/31/04	4	3:00
Kazuyuki Fujita	Loss	Submission (Soccer Kicks)	5/22/04	1	2:15
Sumiyabazar Dolgorsuren	Win	Towel (Foot Injury)	3/14/04	1	5:00
Stefan Gamlin	Win	Submission (Guillotine Choke)	9/21/03	1	0:52
Yoshihiro Takayama	Win	Submission (Armbar)	12/31/02	1	2:16
Antonio Rodrigo Nogueira	Loss	Submission (Armbar)	8/28/02	2	4:03
Kiyoshi Tamura	Win	TKO (Punches)	6/23/02	1	0:11
Yoshihisa Yamamoto	Win	TKO (Punches)	4/28/02	1	2:44

SPECIAL MOVES		
NAME	**TYPE**	**FROM**
Americana	Submission (Arm)	(1) Full Mount Postured Up—Top; (2) Full Mount Tight—Top
Catch Punch	Parry	(1) Full Guard Postured Up—Bottom; (2) Full Guard Postured Up—Top; (3) Full Mount Postured Up—Top
Dashing Takedown	Takedown	Standing
Diving Punch	Strike	Standing vs. Open Guard
Guillotine Takedown	Submission (Neck)	Standing
Kimura	Submission (Arm)	Half Guard—Top
Major Pass	Strike	Every Ground Position
Overhand Punch	Strike	Standing
Rear Naked Choke	Submission (Neck)	Back Mount—Top
Takedown Fake	Strike	Standing

BOB SAPP

ATTRIBUTES	
ATTRIBUTE	HEAVYWEIGHT
Stand Up	**72**
Foot Speed	70
Hand Speed	75
Kick Combo Speed	70
Kick Range	65
Movement Speed	70
Punch Combo Speed	78
Punch Range	88
Stand Up Left Foot Power	70
Stand Up Left Hand Power	06
Stand Up Right Foot Power	70
Stand Up Right Hand Power	98
Takedowns	53
Takedown Defense	33
Clinch	**72**
Clinch Combo	70
Clinch Control	60
Clinch Strike Speed	70
Clinch Striking Power	88
Ground	**64**
Grapple Defense	40
Ground Combo Speed	70
Ground Get Up	70
Ground Strike Speed	70
Ground Striking Power	88
Passing	51
Submission	**33**
Arm Submissions	33
Leg Submissions	33
Neck Submissions	33
Health	**59**
Blocking	60
Chin	51
Gut	87
Heart	33
Leg Health	71
Stamina Recovery	52

"The Beast" has the worst ground game in the Heavyweight division, so avoid hitting the mat at all costs. If you are taken down, focus solely on denying passes and submissions from the bottom, and get back up to your feet. Sapp can do some damage from the top position, but his poor grappling attributes make it difficult to maintain any sort of dominant stature for long.

Fighting against: Bob Sapp—Sapp can KO anyone while on his feet, but his ground game is garbage. If you have even modest grappling skills, fight smart and take "The Beast" to the mat as soon as chance permits. Use feints and footwork to set up takedowns without exposing yourself to Sapp's heavy hands, and once you bring the fight to the floor, work to pass Sapp's guard and make the big man squeal with a sub.

STAND UP STRATEGIES

Bob Sapp has some of the heaviest hands in the Heavyweight division and boasts good range on his punches—but that's about all he brings with him into the cage. "The Beast" suffers from a terrible chin, not to mention poor striking and movement speed. Sapp definitely wants to keep the fight on the feet, but you can't be overaggressive with him. Always be ready to stuff a takedown or clinch attempt, and forget about throwing anything beyond a two-punch combo—you can't risk leaving Bob's chin exposed. Frustrate your opponent with counter punches instead, looking for that one big punch that rocks your rival and hands you the victory.

Fighting against: Bob Sapp—"The Beast" isn't to be trifled with on the feet as he's capable of KO'ing anyone if just one of his meat hooks finds its mark. If you have even modest ground skills, take the fight to the mat against Sapp as soon as you're able and submit this unskilled grappler to avoid any chance of begin caught by one of his heavy blows. If your ground game is no better than Bob's, exploit his lack of speed by dashing into and out of attack range, slipping his punches while scoring with strikes of your own. Work Sapp's vulnerable legs to slow him down to a crawl and hammer his glass jaw for the KO.

CLINCH STRATEGIES

Sapp's strikes don't lose much oomph in the clinch, so tie up with opponents whenever possible to protect his flimsy chin. Batter your rival with heavy shots from the clinch, but work carefully to prevent Sapp from losing position due to his unimpressive clinch control.

Fighting against: Bob Sapp—When fighting against Bob in the clinch, his heavy blows remain worthy of concern. Block to reduce damage and wear him out, looking to escape or score a takedown after the big man has tired. You don't need to fear takedowns from the clinch from Sapp, who has a dismal ground game, so simply look to reduce damage and improve your position when tied up with him.

GROUND STRATEGIES

75

GESIAS CAVALCANTE
Born: Rio de Janeiro, Brazil

Specialty: Jiu Jitsu
Weight Class: Lightweight

GESIAS CAVALCANTE
"JZ"

> FIGHT RECORD <
15—3—1 (WIN—LOSS—DRAW) (1 NC)

WINS	LOSSES
5 (T)KOs (33.33%)	3 Decisions (100%)
7 Submissions (46.67%)	
3 Decisions (20%)	

OPPONENT	RESULT	METHOD	DATE	ROUND	TIME
Katsunori Kikuno	Win	Decision (Split)	7/10/10	2	5:00
Tatsuya Kawajiri	Loss	Decision (Unanimous)	5/26/09	2	5:00
Shinya Aoki	Loss	Decision (Unanimous)	4/29/08	2	5:00
Shinya Aoki	NC	NC (Aoki Injured by Illegal Elbows)	3/15/08	1	3:46
Andre Amado	Win	Submission (Armbar)	9/17/07	1	4:48
Vitor Ribeiro	Win	TKO (Punches)	9/17/07	1	0:35
Nam Phan	Win	TKO (Punches)	6/2/07	1	0:26
Caol Uno	Win	Decision (Majority)	10/9/06	2	5:00
Rani Yahya	Win	Submission (Guillotine Choke)	10/9/06	1	0:39
Hiroyuki Takaya	Win	KO (Flying Knee)	8/5/06	1	0:30
Hidetaka Monma	Win	TKO (Punches)	5/3/06	1	2:08
Michihiro Omigawa	Win	KO (Punches)	12/3/05	1	0:49
Ryan Schultz	Draw	Draw	7/9/05	3	5:00
Henry Matamoros	Win	Decision (Unanimous)	4/2/05	3	5:00
Cengiz Dana	Win	Submission (Guillotine Choke)	12/18/04	3	4:55
Bart Palaszewski	Win	Submission (Guillotine Choke)	11/20/04	1	1:03
Sebastian Korschilgen	Win	Submission (Kimura)	9/4/04	1	1:32
Joachim Hansen	Loss	Decision (Majority)	7/16/04	3	5:00
Brad Mohler	Win	Submission (Achilles Lock)	3/27/04	1	1:32
Justin Wisniewski	Win	Submission (Guillotine Choke)	2/27/04	1	1:53

SPECIAL MOVES		
NAME	**TYPE**	**FROM**
Americana	Submission (Arm)	(1) Full Mount Postured Up—Top; (2) Full Mount Tight—Top
Armbar	Submission (Arm)	(1) Full Guard—Bottom; (2) Full Guard Postured Up—Bottom; (3) Side Control—Top; (4) Back Mount Side Turtle—Top
Catch Punch	Parry	(1) Full Guard Postured Up—Bottom; (2) Full Guard Postured Up—Top; (3) Full Mount Postured Up—Top
Darce Choke	Submission (Neck)	Sprawl—Top
Dashing Takedown	Takedown	Standing
Diving Punch	Strike	Standing vs. Open Guard
Flying Knee	Strike	Standing
Guillotine Takedown	Submission (Neck)	Standing
Head Arm Choke	Submission (Neck)	(1) Full Mount Tight—Top; (2) Side Control—Top
Heel Hook	Submission (Leg)	(1) Full Guard Postured Up—Top; (2) Guard Stacked—Top
Inverted Kneebar	Submission (Leg)	Guard Stacked—Bottom
Kimura	Submission (Arm)	Half Guard—Top
Kneebar	Submission (Leg)	Full Guard—Top
Major Pass	Strike	Every Ground Position
Overhand Punch	Strike	Standing
Rear Naked Choke	Submission (Neck)	Back Mount—Top
Roundhouse Head Kick	Strike	Standing
Takedown Fake	Strike	Standing
Teep Kick	Strike	Standing
Triangle Choke	Submission (Neck)	(1) Full Guard—Bottom; (2) Full Guard Postured Up—Bottom; (3) Full Mount Postured Up—Top; (4) Guard Stacked—Bottom

GESIAS CAVALCANTE

ATTRIBUTES	
ATTRIBUTE	LIGHTWEIGHT
Stand Up	**79**
Foot Speed	89
Hand Speed	98
Kick Combo Speed	97
Kick Range	70
Movement Speed	97
Punch Combo Speed	98
Punch Range	70
Stand Up Left Foot Power	63
Stand Up Left Hand Power	65
Stand Up Right Foot Power	63
Stand Up Right Hand Power	65
Takedowns	80
Takedown Defense	80
Clinch	**84**
Clinch Combo	97
Clinch Control	81
Clinch Strike Speed	97
Clinch Striking Power	63
Ground	**89**
Grapple Defense	94
Ground Combo Speed	98
Ground Get Up	91
Ground Strike Speed	98
Ground Striking Power	65
Passing	90
Submission	**73**
Arm Submissions	65
Leg Submissions	66
Neck Submissions	90
Health	**95**
Blocking	90
Chin	92
Gut	96
Heart	99
Leg Health	99
Stamina Recovery	99

STAND UP STRATEGIES

Gesias is a jiu jitsu practitioner by trade, but he also owns some of the best kickboxing in the Lightweight division. Cavalcante's hands and feet are fast and powerful; use them to break down adversaries as you set up takedowns to unleash some lethal ground and pound. Don't fear being dragged to the mat; "JZ" can perform nasty triangles off his back. Counter takedown attempts with guillotines and Darce chokes if you can to instantly employ some of Cavalcante's jiu jitsu.

Fighting against: Gesias Cavalcante—Cavalcante is dangerous on his feet, but fighting against him on the ground is even worse. Avoid shooting for takedowns against him and focus on beating him in the stand up game instead. Cavalcante has few drawbacks on the feet, but it's the least dangerous place to fight him.

CLINCH STRATEGIES

Use Cavalcante's clinch to assail opponents with lightning-fast strike combos. Gesias has solid clinch control, but it's best to use the position to bring the fight to the ground rather than linger in the hold—Cavalcante is far more gifted on the ground.

Fighting against: Gesias Cavalcante—Gesias's clinch offense is strong, but his control isn't spectacular. Beware the takedown when battling Cavalcante in the clinch, and break away as soon as you're able, returning to calculated striking exchanges to get the job done.

GROUND STRATEGIES

Though Gesias is well rounded, his best game is on the ground. Use Cavalcante's furious strikes to set up clinch or takedown opportunities, moving the fight to the mat to do some real damage. Gesias has fantastic ground offense as well as defense, and he can finish a fight very quickly with a sudden head arm choke, triangle, or rear naked choke. Favor Cavalcante's choke submissions—they're far better than his joint locks.

Fighting against: Gesias Cavalcante—Gesias is a monster on the ground, so strive to keep the fight on the feet. If he scores a takedown, work to stand up as quickly as possible before he can do much damage with his rapid ground and pound. Avoid lingering in positions where Gesias can apply chokes and try luring him into going for limb submissions—these are easier to reverse, landing you in top position where you can escape back up to your feet more easily.

JAY HIERON
Born: Long Island, New York

Specialty: Wrestling

Weight Class: Welterweight

EA SPORTS
MMA

JAY HIERON
"THE THOROUGHBRED"

> FIGHT RECORD <
19—4—0 (WIN—LOSS—DRAW)

WINS	LOSSES
6 (T)KOs (31.58%)	3 (T)KOs (75%)
5 Submissions (26.32%)	1 Decision (25%)
8 Decisions (42.11%)	

OPPONENT	RESULT	METHOD	DATE	ROUND	TIME
Joe Riggs	Win	Decision (Unanimous)	1/30/10	3	5:00
Jesse Taylor	Win	Decision (Unanimous)	8/15/09	3	5:00
Jason High	Win	KO (Punch)	1/24/09	1	1:04
Chris Kennedy	Win	Decision (Unanimous)	10/11/08	3	5:00
Mark Miller	Win	TKO (Punches)	4/4/08	1	2:10
Delson Heleno	Win	TKO (Leg Injury)	12/29/07	1	4:00
Donnie Liles	Win	Decision (Unanimous)	11/3/07	3	4:00
Brad Blackburn	Loss	TKO (Punches)	6/1/07	1	0:40
Donnie Liles	Win	Submission (Guillotine Choke)	3/17/07	1	2:49
Victor Moreno	Win	Submission (Rear Naked Choke)	2/2/07	1	1:55
Chris Wilson	Loss	Decision (Unanimous)	11/2/06	3	4:00
Amos Sotelo	Win	Submission (Guillotine Choke)	9/9/06	1	0:26
Jake Ellenberger	Win	Decision (Unanimous)	6/3/06	3	4:00
Steve Schneider	Win	TKO (Punches)	3/11/06	1	0:55
Jonathan Goulet	Loss	TKO (Cut)	10/3/05	3	1:05
Pat Healy	Win	Decision (Unanimous)	7/30/05	3	5:00
Adam Lynn	Win	Decision (Unanimous)	5/19/05	3	5:00
Ronald Jhun	Win	TKO (Cut)	3/19/05	1	4:34
Georges St. Pierre	Loss	TKO (Punches)	6/19/04	1	1:42
Fabio Holanda	Win	Decision (Unanimous)	4/30/04	3	5:00
Fernando Munoz	Win	Submission (Punches)	4/24/04	1	0:33
Jermaine Johnson	Win	Submission (Rear Naked Choke)	12/14/03	1	1:02
Keith Plate	Win	TKO (Punches)	7/19/03	1	1:28

SPECIAL MOVES		
NAME	TYPE	FROM
Americana	Submission (Arm)	(1) Full Mount Postured Up—Top; (2) Full Mount Tight—Top
Catch Kick	Parry	Standing
Catch Punch	Parry	(1) Full Guard Postured Up—Bottom; (2) Full Guard Postured Up—Top; (3) Full Mount Postured Up—Top
Darce Choke	Submission (Neck)	Sprawl—Top
Dashing Takedown	Takedown	Standing
Diving Punch	Strike	Standing vs. Open Guard
Flying Knee	Strike	Standing
Guillotine Takedown	Submission (Neck)	Standing
Head Arm Choke	Submission (Neck)	(1) Full Mount Tight—Top; (2) Side Control—Top
Major Pass	Strike	Every Ground Position
Overhand Punch	Strike	Standing
Rear Naked Choke	Submission (Neck)	Back Mount—Top
Roundhouse Head Kick	Strike	Standing
Superman Punch	Strike	Standing
Takedown Fake	Strike	Standing

JAY HIERON

ATTRIBUTES	
ATTRIBUTE	WELTERWEIGHT
Stand Up	**78**
Foot Speed	83
Hand Speed	86
Kick Combo Speed	88
Kick Range	74
Movement Speed	89
Punch Combo Speed	91
Punch Range	76
Stand Up Left Foot Power	65
Stand Up Left Hand Power	70
Stand Up Right Foot Power	64
Stand Up Right Hand Power	70
Takedowns	90
Takedown Defense	80
Clinch	**86**
Clinch Combo	95
Clinch Control	86
Clinch Strike Speed	95
Clinch Striking Power	71
Ground	**88**
Grapple Defense	99
Ground Combo Speed	96
Ground Get Up	81
Ground Strike Speed	96
Ground Striking Power	71
Passing	86
Submission	**55**
Arm Submissions	44
Leg Submissions	33
Neck Submissions	90
Health	**82**
Blocking	80
Chin	81
Gut	88
Heart	77
Leg Health	78
Stamina Recovery	90

STAND UP STRATEGIES

Jay Hieron's striking game is average, and is best used to set up clinch attempts and takedowns. "The Thoroughbred" has a suspect chin, so find a way to close the distance and begin grappling with his opponents. Use Jay's flying knees and superman punch to close in from the outside as well.

Fighting against: Jay Hieron—When fighting against Hieron, keep the battle on the feet. Always be ready to stuff his powerful takedowns as you pick away at Jay with leg kicks and straights, wearing him down by eroding his lackluster defense.

CLINCH STRATEGIES

Hieron is a worthy grappler and can work the clinch to great effect. Use Jay's clinch to tie up with opponents, controlling the position as you wear them down with strikes. Look for double underhook takedowns that land Jay in side control, ready to end the fight with a suffocating head arm choke.

Fighting against: Jay Hieron—The more distance you can keep between yourself and Jay Hieron in a fight, the better. Use jabs and leg kicks to score points while keeping "The Thoroughbred" at range. Hieron has good clinch control, so expect a struggle to break free after he latches on.

GROUND STRATEGIES

With outstanding grappling defense and good passing ability, Jay Hieron can battle on the mat with little fear. Set up Jay's powerful takedowns on the feet, or slam opponents to the mat from the clinch, positioning him to end the night with a head arm choke from side control. Unleash Jay's devastating ground and pound to open up opportunities to pass guard and lock in subs.

Fighting against: Jay Hieron—Jay's grappling defense is basically impenetrable, so avoid the ground game when fighting against him. Keep the wrestler at range and try to catch him on the chin when he dives in to grapple. Deny Hieron's attempts at passing guard and struggle to return to your feet after each takedown to "The Thoroughbred" lands.

JEFF MONSON
"THE SNOWMAN"

❯ FIGHT RECORD ❮

36—11—0 (WIN—LOSS—DRAW)

WINS	LOSSES
2 (T)KOs (5.56%)	2 (T)KOs (18.18%)
22 Submissions (61.11%)	2 Submissions (18.18%)
12 Decisions (33.33%)	7 Decisions (63.64%)

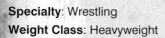

Specialty: Wrestling

Weight Class: Heavyweight

OPPONENT	RESULT	METHOD	DATE	ROUND	TIME
Jason Guida	Win	Submission (Rear Naked Choke)	8/21/10	2	3:04
Ubiratan Marinho Lima	Win	Decision (Unanimous)	7/10/10	3	5:00
Shamil Abdurahimov	Loss	Decision (Majority)	5/14/10	3	5:00
Travis Wiuff	Loss	Decision (Split)	4/24/10	3	5:00
Francisco Nonato	Win	Submission (Guillotine Choke)	3/13/10	1	2:27
John Brown	Win	Decision (Split)	1/16/10	3	5:00
Pedro Rizzo	Loss	Decision (Unanimous)	9/12/09	3	5:00
Jimmy Ambriz	Win	Submission (Rear Naked Choke)	7/11/09	1	1:09
Sergei Kharitonov	Win	Submission (North-South Choke)	4/5/09	1	1:42
Sergei Maslobojev	Win	Submission (North-South Choke)	3/29/09	2	2:30
Roy Nelson	Win	Decision (Unanimous)	3/21/09	3	5:00
Ricco Rodriguez	Win	Decision (Unanimous)	12/13/08	3	5:00
Jimmy Ambriz	Win	Submission (North-South Choke)	10/11/08	1	1:50
Mark Kerr	Win	Submission (Rear Naked Choke)	9/27/08	1	3:17
Josh Barnett	Loss	Decision (Unanimous)	5/18/08	3	5:00
Hakim Goram	Win	Decision (Unanimous)	12/9/07	3	5:00
Pedro Rizzo	Loss	TKO (Punches)	9/1/07	3	2:40
Kazuyuki Fujita	Win	Submission (Rear Naked Choke)	4/8/07	1	6:37
Tim Sylvia	Loss	Decision (Unanimous)	11/18/06	5	5:00
Anthony Perosh	Win	TKO (Punches)	7/8/06	1	2:22
Marcio Cruz	Win	Decision (Split)	4/15/06	3	5:00
Branden Lee Hinkle	Win	Technical Submission (North-South Choke)	2/4/06	1	4:35
Marc Emmanuel	Win	Submission (Rear Naked Choke)	11/26/05	1	0:58
Devin Cole	Win	Decision	10/15/05	3	5:00
Jay White	Win	Submission (Rear Naked Choke)	9/16/05	1	1:23
Rich Wilson	Win	Submission (Armbar)	7/2/05	1	1:56
Tengiz Tedoradze	Win	Submission (Rear Naked Choke)	4/30/05	1	1:59
Jay White	Win	Submission (Injury)	2/26/05	1	4:07
Brian Stromberg	Win	Submission (Rear Naked Choke)	1/8/05	1	N/A
Tengiz Tedoradze	Win	Submission (Rear Naked Choke)	12/18/04	1	3:51
Pat Stano	Win	TKO (Knee to the Body)	10/15/04	2	3:11
Carlos Clayton	Win	Decision	8/28/04	3	5:00
Don Richards	Win	Submission (North-South Choke)	6/5/04	2	2:25
Joe Nye	Win	Submission (Rear Naked Choke)	8/16/03	1	3:02
Mike Delaney	Win	Submission (Choke)	7/19/03	1	4:27
Forrest Griffin	Loss	Decision	6/29/02	4	4:00
Ricco Rodriguez	Loss	TKO (Punches)	1/11/02	3	3:00
Roman Roytberg	Win	Submission (North-South Choke)	7/21/01	1	N/A
Chuck Liddell	Loss	Decision (Unanimous)	12/16/00	3	5:00
Tim Lajcik	Win	Decision	9/22/00	2	5:00
Bob Gilstrap	Win	Decision (Unanimous)	7/29/00	3	5:00
David Dodd	Loss	Submission (Armbar)	4/2/99	1	0:46
Roger Neff	Win	Decision	3/1/99	3	5:00
Tom Sauer	Loss	Submission (Rear Naked Choke)	8/22/98	1	3:47
John Renfroe	Win	Submission (Strikes)	8/2/98	1	2:45
Cy Cross	Win	Submission (Choke)	3/14/98	1	3:47
Luther Norberg	Win	Decision (Unanimous)	11/21/97	1	N/A

JEFF MONSON

ATTRIBUTES	
ATTRIBUTE	HEAVYWEIGHT
Stand Up	**76**
Foot Speed	80
Hand Speed	80
Kick Combo Speed	76
Kick Range	75
Movement Speed	80
Punch Combo Speed	80
Punch Range	75
Stand Up Left Foot Power	65
Stand Up Left Hand Power	78
Stand Up Right Foot Power	65
Stand Up Right Hand Power	75
Takedowns	80
Takedown Defense	85
Clinch	**82**
Clinch Combo	80
Clinch Control	90
Clinch Strike Speed	80
Clinch Striking Power	80
Ground	**87**
Grapple Defense	99
Ground Combo Speed	86
Ground Get Up	75
Ground Strike Speed	80
Ground Striking Power	90
Passing	93
Submission	**86**
Arm Submissions	95
Leg Submissions	66
Neck Submissions	99
Health	**86**
Blocking	80
Chin	80
Gut	99
Heart	90
Leg Health	80
Stamina Recovery	90

SPECIAL MOVES		
NAME	TYPE	FROM
Americana	Submission (Arm)	(1) Full Mount Postured Up—Top; (2) Full Mount Tight—Top
Armbar	Submission (Arm)	(1) Full Guard—Bottom; (2) Full Guard Postured Up—Bottom; (3) Side Control—Top; (4) Back Mount Side Turtle—Top
Catch Kick	Parry	Standing
Catch Punch	Parry	(1) Full Guard Postured Up—Bottom; (2) Full Guard Postured Up—Top; (3) Full Mount Postured Up—Top
Darce Choke	Submission (Neck)	Sprawl—Top
Dashing Takedown	Takedown	Standing
Diving Punch	Strike	Standing vs. Open Guard
Guillotine Takedown	Submission (Neck)	Standing
Head Arm Choke	Submission (Neck)	(1) Full Mount Tight—Top; (2) Side Control—Top
Heel Hook	Submission (Leg)	(1) Full Guard Postured Up—Top; (2) Guard Stacked—Top
Kimura	Submission (Arm)	Half Guard—Top
Kneebar	Submission (Leg)	Full Guard—Top
Major Pass	Strike	Every Ground Position
Overhand Punch	Strike	Standing
Rear Naked Choke	Submission (Neck)	Back Mount—Top
Spinning Backfist	Strike	Standing
Takedown Counter Strike	Strike	Standing
Takedown Fake	Strike	Standing

STAND UP STRATEGIES

Monson is a fantastic grappler, but his stand up game leaves much to be desired. His strikes are slower and weaker than most Heavyweights, and his lack of range forces him to close into countering range when exchanging. Focus on bringing the fight to the clinch or ground, where Monson can quickly secure a submission victory.

Fighting against: Jeff Monson—"The Snowman" is a fearsome ground fighter, so attack his shortcomings by keeping the fight on the feet. Stuff Monson's clinch attempts and takedowns, keeping your distance to exploit Jeff's lack of reach. Monson's body is tough to damage, so punish his vulnerable legs with kicks and target his suspect chin for the KO.

CLINCH STRATEGIES

Jeff is strong in the clinch, boasting excellent control over the position. His strikes gain a bit of power in the clinch as well. Use Monson's clinch to wear opponents down as you work for a takedown. Get the fight to the floor without delay and start looking for submissions.

Fighting against: Jeff Monson—Don't clinch up when fighting Monson—this only puts him in range to land heavier shots and score takedowns. Outstrike the stocky grappler by staying at range and always being ready to deny his clinch attempts. Monson works slowly in the clinch; deny his takedowns and strive to break free as soon as possible.

GROUND STRATEGIES

"The Snowman" is a brilliant wrestler with fantastic ground and pound, submissions, and chokes. When using Monson, strive to bring the fight to the mat before he suffers too much damage on the feet. Use his dashing takedown to quickly close in, or work for takedowns from the clinch. Use Jeff's heavy ground and pound to set up submissions, favoring armbars, kimuras, and chokes over his leg locks.

Fighting against: Jeff Monson—The ground is not where you want to be when fighting against Monson. His grappling defense is too high to make him prone to submissions, and his ability to finish a fight in seconds following a takedown must be respected. Take "The Snowman" out of his element by keeping the fight on the feet with sprawls. Nullify Jeff's submissions if he takes you down and stand up the moment you're able.

JOACHIM HANSEN
Born: Oslo, Norway

JOACHIM HANSEN
"HELLBOY"

> FIGHT RECORD <
19—10—1 (WIN—LOSS—DRAW)

WINS	LOSSES
7 (T)KOs (36.84%)	1 (T)KO (10%)
5 Submissions (26.32%)	4 Submissions (40%)
7 Decisions (36.84%)	4 Decisions (40%)
	1 Other (10%)

Specialty: Kickboxing

Weight Classes: Welterweight, Lightweight

OPPONENT	RESULT	METHOD	DATE	ROUND	TIME
Hiroyuki Takaya	Loss	KO (Punches)	5/29/10	1	4:27
Bibiano Fernandes	Loss	Decision (Split)	3/22/10	2	5:00
Shinya Aoki	Loss	Submission (Armbar)	10/6/09	2	4:56
Shinya Aoki	Win	TKO (Punches)	7/21/08	1	4:19
Kultar Gill	Win	Submission (Armbar)	7/21/08	1	2:33
Eddie Alvarez	Loss	Decision (Unanimous)	5/11/08	2	5:00
Kotetsu Boku	Win	Decision (Unanimous)	3/15/08	2	5:00
Kazuyuki Miyata	Win	Submission (Rear Naked Choke)	12/31/07	2	1:33
Eiji Mitsuoka	Loss	Decision (Majority)	11/8/07	3	5:00
Jason Ireland	Win	Submission (Armbar)	2/24/07	3	2:33
Shinya Aoki	Loss	Submission (Gogoplata)	12/31/06	1	2:24
Luiz Azeredo	Win	KO (Knee)	4/2/06	1	7:09
Tatsuya Kawajiri	Loss	DQ (Kick to Groin)	2/17/06	1	0:08
Hayato Sakurai	Loss	Decision (Unaminous)	9/25/05	2	5:00
Yves Edwards	Win	Decision (Split)	9/25/05	2	5:00
Kenichiro Togashi	Win	Decision (Unanimous)	8/20/05	3	5:00
Masakazu Imanari	Win	KO (Knee)	7/17/05	1	2:34
Caol Uno	Win	KO (Knee)	3/26/05	3	4:48
Sergey Golyaev	Win	Submission (Rear Naked Choke)	10/15/04	1	3:24
Gesias Cavalcante	Win	Decision (Majority)	7/16/04	3	5:00
Metin Yakut	Win	TKO (Punches)	4/5/04	2	3:50
Vitor Ribeiro	Loss	Submission (Arm Triangle Choke)	12/14/03	2	2:37
Takanori Gomi	Win	Decision (Majority)	8/10/03	3	5:00
Rumina Sato	Win	TKO (Punches)	3/18/03	1	2:09
Takumi Nakayama	Win	Decision (Majority)	12/14/02	3	5:00
Sami Hyyppa	Win	Submission	10/19/02	1	4:00
Rafles la Rose	Draw	Draw	8/31/02	2	5:00
Olof Inger	Win	Decision	11/24/01	N/A	N/A
Jani Lax	Loss	Submission (Rear Naked Choke)	12/2/00	1	9:25
Marcus Peltonen	Win	TKO	11/6/99	1	1:38

Joachim
HANSEN
Specialty Kickboxing
Record 19-10

JOACHIM HANSEN

ATTRIBUTES

ATTRIBUTE	WELTERWEIGHT	LIGHTWEIGHT
Stand Up	**79**	**79**
Foot Speed	99	99
Hand Speed	99	99
Kick Combo Speed	99	99
Kick Range	70	70
Movement Speed	99	99
Punch Combo Speed	99	99
Punch Range	70	70
Stand Up Left Foot Power	60	60
Stand Up Left Hand Power	60	60
Stand Up Right Foot Power	60	60
Stand Up Right Hand Power	60	60
Takedowns	80	80
Takedown Defense	80	80
Clinch	**84**	**83**
Clinch Combo	99	99
Clinch Control	80	80
Clinch Strike Speed	99	99
Clinch Striking Power	60	55
Ground	**86**	**85**
Grapple Defense	75	75
Ground Combo Speed	99	99
Ground Get Up	90	90
Ground Strike Speed	99	99
Ground Striking Power	65	60
Passing	90	90
Submission	**55**	**55**
Arm Submissions	66	66
Leg Submissions	33	33
Neck Submissions	66	66
Health	**92**	**92**
Blocking	90	90
Chin	70	70
Gut	99	99
Heart	99	99
Leg Health	99	99
Stamina Recovery	99	99

SPECIAL MOVES

NAME	TYPE	FROM
Armbar	Submission (Arm)	(1) Full Guard—Bottom; (2) Full Guard Postured Up—Bottom; (3) Side Control—Top; (4) Back Mount Side Turtle—Top
Catch Kick	Parry	Standing
Catch Punch	Parry	(1) Full Guard Postured Up—Bottom; (2) Full Guard Postured Up—Top; (3) Full Mount Postured Up—Top
Diving Punch	Strike	Standing vs. Open Guard
Flying Knee	Strike	Standing
Gogoplata	Submission (Neck)	Rubber Guard—Bottom
Major Pass	Strike	Every Ground Position
Omoplata	Submission (Arm)	Rubber Guard—Bottom
Overhand Punch	Strike	Standing
Rear Naked Choke	Submission (Neck)	Back Mount—Top
Roundhouse Head Kick	Strike	Standing
Rubber Guard	Strike	Full Guard—Bottom
Takedown Counter Strike	Strike	Standing
Teep Kick	Strike	Standing
Triangle Choke	Submission (Neck)	(1) Full Guard—Bottom; (2) Full Guard Postured Up—Bottom; (3) Full Mount Postured Up—Top; (4) Guard Stacked—Bottom

STAND UP STRATEGIES

One of the fastest fighters on his feet, Hansen is known for exceptional footwork and lightning-quick strikes. Use his great movement speed to create angles and dictate the pace of the stand up game.

Joachim's power leaves something to be desired, particularly when fighting at Welterweight, so use his speed to slip in with strikes and counter aggressive foes. Unleash Joachim's flying knee special to rock opponents from range.

Fighting against: Joachim Hansen—Hansen's chin is somewhat fragile; exploit this when fighting against him, looking to score the KO blow. Joachim also has holes in his grappling defense, so when Hansen starts slinging combos, skilled ground fighters should look for the takedown, aiming to work their submissions on the mat.

CLINCH STRATEGIES

Though fast as ever in the clinch, Hansen is unable to utilize his outstanding footwork in this position. Avoid the clinch when using Joachim, seeking instead to pick apart foes with crisp kickboxing combos. If the opponent manages to clinch up, deny his takedowns and unleash some fast strikes to make him think twice about tying up again.

Fighting against: Joachim Hansen—Joachim's speed makes him dangerous in the clinch, but his lack of control creates opportunities for damage and takedowns in this position. Use the clinch against Hansen when he's too hard to tag on the feet. Attack his fragile jaw and look for the takedown to set up a fight-ending submission.

GROUND STRATEGIES

Hansen is an effective offensive wrestler, but his poor grappling defense leaves him exposed to submission experts. Hansen should avoid the ground game if the opponent is a skilled tap-out artist. However, if the opponent isn't a practiced grappler, shoot for takedowns to keep the opponent guessing and unleash some of Joachim's blistering ground and pound. "Hellboy" has poor submission skill, so don't get caught up with the grappling game if he's been planted on his back; get up quickly, returning to fight on the feet.

Fighting against: Joachim Hansen—When Hansen becomes overconfident with his striking combos, take him down and exploit his lack of ground defense by tapping him out. Beware Joachim's ability to sweep and pop back up to his feet; strive to maintain dominant position against him as you work to secure the tap.

www.primagames.com

MMA
EA SPORTS

MARIUS ZAROMSKIS
"THE WHITEMARE"

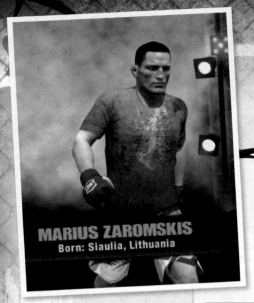

MARIUS ZAROMSKIS
Born: Siaulia, Lithuania

Specialty: Kickboxing

Weight Class: Welterweight

> FIGHT RECORD <

13—5—0 (WIN—LOSS—DRAW)

WINS	LOSSES
10 (T)KOs (76.92%)	4 (T)KOs (80%)
1 Submission (7.69%)	1 Other (20%)
1 Decision (7.69%)	
1 Other (7.69%)	

OPPONENT	RESULT	METHOD	DATE	ROUND	TIME
Evangelista Santos	Loss	TKO (Punches)	6/16/10	1	2:38
Nick Diaz	Loss	TKO (Punches)	1/30/10	1	4:38
Myung Ho Bae	Win	KO (Head Kick)	10/25/09	1	0:19
Jason High	Win	KO (Head Kick)	7/20/09	1	2:22
Hayato Sakurai	Win	TKO (Head Kick and Punches)	7/20/09	1	4:03
Seichi Ikemoto	Win	Decision (Unanimous)	4/5/09	2	5:00
Jedrzej Kubski	Win	TKO (Punches)	11/8/08	1	0:50
Che Mills	Loss	TKO (Doctor Stoppage)	5/10/08	1	5:00
Ross Pointon	Win	TKO (Doctor Stoppage)	12/1/07	2	3:39
Ross Mason	Win	KO (Flying Knee)	7/14/07	3	2:03
Damien Riccio	Win	TKO (Cut)	2/10/07	3	4:30
Darius Swierkosz	Win	Submission (Triangle Choke)	11/12/06	2	N/A
Che Mills	Loss	KO (Knee)	8/20/06	1	4:49
Afnan Saeed	Win	TKO (Punches)	5/28/06	1	1:21
Kazys Grigaliunas	Win	KO	2/19/06	1	1:57
Jack Mason	Win	TKO	11/27/05	1	3:18
Ricardas Jancevicius	Loss	N/A	2/4/00	N/A	N/A
Viktoras Kontrimas	Win	N/A	2/4/00	N/A	N/A

SPECIAL MOVES		
NAME	**TYPE**	**FROM**
Diving Punch	Strike	Standing vs. Open Guard
Flying Knee	Strike	Standing
Guillotine Takedown	Submission (Neck)	Standing
Head Arm Choke	Submission (Neck)	(1) Full Mount Tight—Top; (2) Side Control—Top
Major Pass	Strike	Every Ground Position
Rear Naked Choke	Submission (Neck)	Back Mount—Top
Roundhouse Head Kick	Strike	Standing
Spinning Backfist	Strike	Standing
Spinning Kick	Strike	Standing
Takedown Counter Strike	Strike	Standing
Teep Kick	Strike	Standing
Triangle Choke	Submission (Neck)	(1) Full Guard—Bottom; (2) Full Guard Postured Up—Bottom; (3) Full Mount Postured Up—Top; (4) Guard Stacked—Bottom

MARIUS ZAROMSKIS

ATTRIBUTES	
ATTRIBUTE	WELTERWEIGHT
Stand Up	**81**
Foot Speed	97
Hand Speed	97
Kick Combo Speed	97
Kick Range	75
Movement Speed	92
Punch Combo Speed	97
Punch Range	70
Stand Up Left Foot Power	75
Stand Up Left Hand Power	70
Stand Up Right Foot Power	75
Stand Up Right Hand Power	70
Takedowns	75
Takedown Defense	75
Clinch	**86**
Clinch Combo	97
Clinch Control	80
Clinch Strike Speed	97
Clinch Striking Power	70
Ground	**86**
Grapple Defense	90
Ground Combo Speed	97
Ground Get Up	90
Ground Strike Speed	97
Ground Striking Power	70
Passing	75
Submission	**33**
Arm Submissions	33
Leg Submissions	33
Neck Submissions	33
Health	**91**
Blocking	90
Chin	80
Gut	90
Heart	90
Leg Health	99
Stamina Recovery	99

STAND UP STRATEGIES

Zaromskis is a gifted kickboxer with exceptional speed and able to obliterate opponents with furious striking barrages. His takedown defense isn't spectacular, however, so Marius must strike with care when facing a grappling artist. Use his great footwork to set up his array of special stand up moves, battering enemies with spinning kicks and backfists, and flying knees.

Fighting against: Marius Zaromskis—Though an offensive force on the feet, Zaromskis's poor takedown defense and susceptible chin can be exploited. Bait Marius into unleashing wild strikes, then look for heavy headshot counters or stuff him on his back with a quick takedown. Even if you aren't much of a ground fighter, sprinkle in takedowns when you fight Zaromskis to give him something to worry about on the feet—there's no need to fear his offense off his back.

CLINCH STRATEGIES

Marius retains his striking speed in the clinch, but his control falls short compared to most others in his division. He doesn't fare well off his back, either, so use the clinch sparingly and try to get things done in the realm of stand up fighting, where Marius truly shines.

Fighting against: Marius Zaromskis—Tie up with Zaromskis to slow him down and exploit his lack of clinch control. Mash him against the fence and hurl elbows at his chin, hoping to rock the kickboxer. Slam him to the mat when he's forced to block, then begin to work "The Whitemare" over with some heavy ground and pound. Focus on controlling the clinch position against Marius to keep him off balance as you wear him down.

GROUND STRATEGIES

Zaromskis has good grappling defense, but his lack of submission ability means he only wants to be raining down blows from the top position. Don't roll against tap-out artists; use Marius's great skill at returning to his feet to pop up after each takedown. Employ Zaromskis's ground and pound against unskilled grapplers if you like, but try to remain on the feet, where "The Whitemare" can do the most damage.

Fighting against: Marius Zaromskis—Planting Marius on his back is a good way to rough him up. He

has good submission defense, but he won't threaten you from the bottom. Stuff Zaromskis on his back and work him over with steady ground and pound, targeting his vulnerable chin to score the KO victory from dominant position.

MATT LINDLAND
"THE LAW"

MATT LINDLAND
Born: Oregon City, Oregon

> FIGHT RECORD <

22—7—0 (WIN—LOSS—DRAW)

WINS	LOSSES
8 (T)KOs (36.36%)	3 (T)KOs (42.86%)
7 Submissions (31.82%)	3 Submissions (42.86%)
6 Decisions (27.27%)	1 Decisions (14.29%)
1 Other (4.55%)	

Specialty: Wrestling

Weight Classes: Light Heavy-weight, Middleweight

OPPONENT	RESULT	METHOD	DATE	ROUND	TIME
Kevin Casey	Win	TKO (Punches)	5/21/10	3	3:41
Ronaldo Souza	Loss	Submission (Arm-Triangle Choke)	12/19/09	1	4:18
Vitor Belfort	Loss	KO (Punches)	1/24/09	1	0:37
Fabio Nascimento	Win	Decision (Unanimous)	7/19/08	3	5:00
Fedor Emelianenko	Loss	Submission (Armbar)	4/14/07	1	2:58
Carlos Newton	Win	Submission (Guillotine Choke)	2/2/07	2	1:43
Jeremy Horn	Win	TKO (Punches)	9/9/06	2	0:21
Quinton Jackson	Loss	Decision (Split)	7/22/06	3	5:00
Mike Van Arsdale	Win	Submission (Guillotine Choke)	4/29/06	1	3:38
Fabio Leopoldo	Win	Submission (Rear Naked Choke)	3/3/06	3	3:25
Antonio Schembri	Win	TKO (Punches)	12/3/05	3	3:33
Joe Doerksen	Win	Decision (Unanimous)	8/20/05	3	5:00
Travis Lutter	Win	Submission (Guillotine Choke)	4/16/05	2	3:32
Landon Showalter	Win	Submission (Armbar)	1/8/05	1	2:43
Mark Weir	Win	TKO (Doctor Stoppage)	11/27/04	1	5:00
David Terrell	Loss	KO (Punches)	8/21/04	1	0:24
Tony Fryklund	Win	Decision (Unanimous)	5/7/04	3	5:00
Falaniko Vitale	Win	TKO (Punches)	11/21/03	3	4:23
Falaniko Vitale	Loss	TKO (Slam)	6/6/03	1	1:56
Phil Baroni	Win	Decision (Unanimous)	2/28/03	3	5:00
Ivan Salaverry	Win	Decision (Unanimous)	9/27/02	3	5:00
Murilo Bustamante	Loss	Submission (Guillotine Choke)	5/10/02	3	1:33
Pat Miletich	Win	TKO (Punches)	3/22/02	1	3:09
Phil Baroni	Win	Decision (Majority)	11/2/01	3	5:00
Ricardo Almeida	Win	DQ	5/4/01	3	4:21
Yoji Anjo	Win	TKO (Punches)	12/16/00	1	2:58
Travis Fulton	Win	Submission (Choke)	9/20/97	1	22:13
Mark Waters	Win	Submission (Punches)	9/20/97	1	2:20
Karo Davtyan	Win	TKO (Punches)	2/14/97	1	8:34

MATT LINDLAND

ATTRIBUTES

ATTRIBUTE	LIGHT HEAVYWEIGHT	MIDDLEWEIGHT
Stand Up	**77**	**77**
Foot Speed	73	73
Hand Speed	88	88
Kick Combo Speed	80	80
Kick Range	71	71
Movement Speed	78	78
Punch Combo Speed	88	88
Punch Range	72	72
Stand Up Left Foot Power	68	68
Stand Up Left Hand Power	77	77
Stand Up Right Foot Power	68	68
Stand Up Right Hand Power	77	77
Takedowns	88	88
Takedown Defense	81	81
Clinch	**86**	**86**
Clinch Combo	87	87
Clinch Control	92	92
Clinch Strike Speed	87	87
Clinch Striking Power	81	81
Ground	**83**	**83**
Grapple Defense	81	81
Ground Combo Speed	88	88
Ground Get Up	77	77
Ground Strike Speed	88	88
Ground Striking Power	81	81
Passing	88	88
Submission	**56**	**56**
Arm Submissions	66	66
Leg Submissions	33	33
Neck Submissions	71	71
Health	**80**	**80**
Blocking	73	73
Chin	78	78
Gut	78	78
Heart	87	87
Leg Health	84	84
Stamina Recovery	82	82

SPECIAL MOVES

NAME	TYPE	FROM
Americana	Submission (Arm)	(1) Full Mount Postured Up—Top; (2) Full Mount Tight—Top
Armbar	Submission (Arm)	(1) Full Guard—Bottom; (2) Full Guard Postured Up—Bottom; (3) Side Control—Top; (4) Back Mount Side Turtle—Top
Catch Punch	Parry	(1) Full Guard Postured Up—Bottom; (2) Full Guard Postured Up—Top; (3) Full Mount Postured Up—Top
Dashing Takedown	Takedown	Standing
Diving Punch	Strike	Standing vs. Open Guard
Guillotine Takedown	Submission (Neck)	Standing
Major Pass	Strike	Every Ground Position
Overhand Punch	Strike	Standing
Rear Naked Choke	Submission (Neck)	Back Mount—Top
Roundhouse Head Kick	Strike	Standing
Spinning Backfist	Strike	Standing
Superman Punch	Strike	Standing
Triangle Choke	Submission (Neck)	(1) Full Guard—Bottom; (2) Full Guard Postured Up—Bottom; (3) Full Mount Postured Up—Top; (4) Guard Stacked—Bottom

STAND UP STRATEGIES

Lindland is a seasoned veteran with balanced skills, but he falls short of average in many statistical categories. His best place to win a fight is the clinch, so use his hand speed to throw combos, back the opponent up, and bring the fight there.

Fighting against: Matt Lindland—"The Law" has poor defensive attributes, so fight him upright and look for the KO. Expect Lindland to close in and grapple, and prevent this from happening by striking carefully, keeping your distance and remaining ready to stuff his shots.

CLINCH STRATEGIES

Matt has great control in the clinch, making this an ideal place for him to fight. Back the opponent up on the feet so you may enter the clinch more easily, then focus on controlling the position as you score with strikes. Slam the opponent with a takedown once he is forced to block and start working Matt's ground and pound.

Fighting against: Matt Lindland—Avoid clinching up when fighting against Lindland—his clinch game is solid, and he's much easier to beat on the feet. If Matt ties you up, look to break free of his grip when he throws his somewhat sluggish strikes.

GROUND STRATEGIES

Matt has a number of submissions at his disposal, but his skill in forcing the tap is limited. Use his ground and pound to score points and inflict damage from top position instead. "The Law" has a pretty good shot, so use it on the feet to bring the fight to the mat when you're having trouble entering the clinch.

Fighting against: Matt Lindland—Matt's ground game is decent, but nothing spectacular. Don't fear rolling with him if you're using a skilled grappler, but try to score takedowns on the feet rather than from the clinch, where Matt has good control. Shoot in for a takedown and then work some ground and pound, ending the fight with a submission after wearing down "The Law."

MELVIN MANHOEF

"NO MERCY"

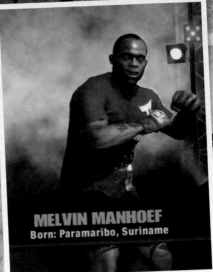

MELVIN MANHOEF
Born: Paramaribo, Suriname

Specialty: Muay Thai

Weight Classes: Light Heavyweight, Middleweight

> FIGHT RECORD <

24—8—1 (WIN—LOSS—DRAW)

WINS	LOSSES
23 (T)KOs (95.83%)	3 (T)KOs (37.5%)
1 Decision (4.17%)	5 Submissions (62.5%)

OPPONENT	RESULT	METHOD	DATE	ROUND	TIME
Tatsuya Mizuno	Loss	Submission (Kimura)	7/10/10	1	7:38
Robbie Lawler	Loss	KO (Punches)	1/30/10	1	3:33
Kazuo Misaki	Win	TKO (Punches)	12/31/09	1	1:49
Paulo Filho	Loss	Submission (Armbar)	7/20/09	1	2:36
Mark Hunt	Win	KO (Punches)	12/31/08	1	0:18
Gegard Mousasi	Loss	Submission (Triangle Choke)	9/23/08	1	1:28
Kazushi Sakuraba	Win	TKO (Punches)	6/15/08	1	1:30
Dae Won Kim	Win	TKO (Knees and Punches)	5/11/08	1	4:08
Yosuke Nishijima	Win	TKO (Punches)	12/31/07	1	1:49
Fabio Silva	Win	TKO (Punches)	9/17/07	1	1:00
Bernard Ackah	Win	KO (Punches)	7/16/07	1	2:13
Dong Sik Yoon	Loss	Submission (Armbar)	6/2/07	2	1:17
Kazuo Takahashi	Win	TKO (Punches)	3/12/07	1	2:36
Yoshihiro Akiyama	Loss	Submission (Armbar)	10/9/06	1	1:58
Shungo Oyama	Win	TKO (Strikes)	10/9/06	1	1:04
Crosley Gracie	Win	TKO (Punches)	8/5/06	1	9:12
Ian Freeman	Win	KO (Punches)	7/1/06	1	0:17
Shungo Oyama	Win	TKO (Cut)	3/15/06	1	2:51
Evangelista Santos	Win	KO (Punches)	2/4/06	2	3:51
Fabio Piamonte	Win	KO (Punches)	9/10/05	1	0:51
Paul Cahoon	Win	TKO	7/3/05	1	N/A
Bob Schrijber	Win	Decision (Unanimous)	6/12/05	2	5:00
Ladislav Zak	Win	TKO (Corner Stoppage)	4/30/05	1	0:37
Matthias Riccio	Win	TKO (Punches)	2/26/05	1	3:01
Rodney Glunder	Loss	KO (Punch)	5/20/04	2	4:43
Slavomir Molnar	Win	KO	4/8/04	1	N/A
Alexandr Garkushenko	Win	TKO (Punches)	4/6/03	1	6:57
Bob Schrijber	Loss	TKO (Punches)	3/16/03	1	4:01
Mika Ilmen	Win	KO (Punch)	9/29/02	1	0:28
Paul Cahoon	Win	TKO (Corner Stoppage)	6/2/02	2	2:07
Husein Cift	Win	KO	12/15/01	1	N/A
Rodney Glunder	Draw	Draw	6/20/99	2	5:00
Jordy Jonkers	Win	TKO (Palm Strike)	12/2/95	2	3:37

SPECIAL MOVES		
NAME	TYPE	FROM
Catch Kick	Parry	Standing
Diving Punch	Strike	Standing vs. Open Guard
Major Pass	Strike	Every Ground Position
Overhand Punch	Strike	Standing
Rear Naked Choke	Submission (Neck)	Back Mount—Top
Roundhouse Head Kick	Strike	Standing
Takedown Counter Strike	Strike	Standing
Teep Kick	Strike	Standing

MELVIN MANHOEF

ATTRIBUTES		
ATTRIBUTE	LHW	MW
Stand Up	**82**	**83**
Foot Speed	92	96
Hand Speed	92	96
Kick Combo Speed	92	96
Kick Range	75	75
Movement Speed	88	92
Punch Combo Speed	92	96
Punch Range	75	75
Stand Up Left Foot Power	85	85
Stand Up Left Hand Power	85	85
Stand Up Right Foot Power	85	85
Stand Up Right Hand Power	85	85
Takedowns	50	50
Takedown Defense	70	70
Clinch	**86**	**88**
Clinch Combo	92	96
Clinch Control	75	75
Clinch Strike Speed	92	96
Clinch Striking Power	85	85
Ground	**75**	**76**
Grapple Defense	70	70
Ground Combo Speed	90	94
Ground Get Up	70	70
Ground Strike Speed	92	94
Ground Striking Power	80	80
Passing	50	50
Submission	**33**	**33**
Arm Submissions	33	33
Leg Submissions	33	33
Neck Submissions	33	33
Health	**81**	**81**
Blocking	80	80
Chin	60	60
Gut	90	90
Heart	70	70
Leg Health	99	99
Stamina Recovery	90	90

STAND UP STRATEGIES

Melvin's greatest assets are his speed and power on the feet—he's a complete beast at Middleweight. Sling kicks and punches to rock opponents in a blink, but beware of takedowns—Manhoef is unskilled on the ground and can be easily controlled and tapped out in this position.

Fighting against: Melvin Manhoef—Melvin may be an offensive juggernaut, but his weak chin can be his downfall when trading blows with other heavy hitters. Try to rock Melvin in the stand up battle, looking to find his glass jaw. If things go poorly on the feet, shoot in and bring Manhoef to the floor—he has poor takedown defense and is a fish out of water when planted on his back.

CLINCH STRATEGIES

"No Mercy" retains his great power and speed in the clinch, but his lack of control can get him into trouble. Avoid the clinch, using it only to get out of dangerous positions, or to give Manhoef a chance to clear his head after he's been rocked by stiff a headshot.

Fighting against: Melvin Manhoef—Use the clinch against Manhoef to shut down his stand up game and gain control over the pace of the fight. Strike his chin to entice him to block, then quickly change levels and score a takedown to bring the feared striker out of his element.

GROUND STRATEGIES

The mat is the last place Melvin wants to be in a fight, so avoid the clinch when using him and be ready to stuff the opponent's takedown at all times. If Melvin is ever stuffed onto his back, work hard at denying the opponent's attempts to pass guard, and struggle to return to the feet as quickly as possible. Melvin can unleash some effective ground and pound, but his lack of passing ability and grappling defense make it difficult for him to maintain dominant posture.

Fighting against: Melvin Manhoef—Manhoef may have a weak chin, but there's no point in testing it on the feet—bring the feared striker to the ground and brutalize him with heavy strikes, targeting his chin for the knockout. Submissions are also very effective against Melvin, so no matter what your fighter's strengths are, keep the fight on the floor to neutralize Manhoef's devastating stand up.

MIZUTO HIROTA
Born: Isahaya, Japan

Specialty: Boxing
Weight Class: Lightweight

MIZUTO HIROTA

> FIGHT RECORD <

12—4—1 (WIN—LOSS—DRAW)

WINS	LOSSES
8 (T)KOs (66.67%)	1 Submission (25%)
4 Decisions (33.33%)	3 Decisions (75%)

OPPONENT	RESULT	METHOD	DATE	ROUND	TIME
Shinya Aoki	Loss	Technical Submission (Hammerlock)	12/31/09	1	1:17
Satoru Kitaoka	Win	TKO (Knees)	8/2/09	4	2:50
Mitsuhiro Ishida	Win	TKO (Punches)	5/10/09	1	1:33
Katsuya Inoue	Draw	Draw	2/28/09	3	5:00
Kazunori Yokota	Loss	Decision (Unanimous)	11/1/08	3	5:00
Ryan Schultz	Win	KO (Superman Punch)	8/24/08	2	4:25
Tomonari Kanomata	Win	TKO (Punches)	4/5/08	1	1:00
Johnny Frachey	Win	TKO (Punches)	2/11/08	2	0:08
Do Gi Sin	Win	KO (Punches)	12/1/07	1	0:16
Ganjo Tentsuku	Loss	Decision (Unanimous)	8/5/07	3	5:00
Takashi Nakakura	Loss	Decision (Unanimous)	2/17/07	3	5:00
Jin Kazeta	Win	Decision (Unanimous)	5/12/06	3	5:00
Danilo Cherman	Win	Decision (Unanimous)	2/17/06	3	5:00
Kabuto Kokage	Win	Decision (Unanimous)	12/17/05	2	5:00
Yoshihiro Koyama	Win	Decision (Unanimous)	9/23/05	2	5:00
Komei Okada	Win	TKO (Punches)	6/3/05	1	4:56
Masaaki Yamamori	Win	TKO (Punches)	2/6/05	2	1:27

SPECIAL MOVES		
NAME	TYPE	FROM
Catch Kick	Parry	Standing
Diving Punch	Strike	Standing vs. Open Guard
Flying Knee	Strike	Standing
Major Pass	Strike	Every Ground Position
Overhand Punch	Strike	Standing
Rear Naked Choke	Submission (Neck)	Back Mount—Top
Roundhouse Head Kick	Strike	Standing
Superman Punch	Strike	Standing
Teep Kick	Strike	Standing

MIZUTO HIROTA

ATTRIBUTES	
ATTRIBUTE	LW
Stand Up	**78**
Foot Speed	98
Hand Speed	96
Kick Combo Speed	96
Kick Range	70
Movement Speed	98
Punch Combo Speed	97
Punch Range	70
Stand Up Left Foot Power	60
Stand Up Left Hand Power	60
Stand Up Right Foot Power	60
Stand Up Right Hand Power	60
Takedowns	80
Takedown Defense	80
Clinch	**87**
Clinch Combo	99
Clinch Control	90
Clinch Strike Speed	99
Clinch Striking Power	60
Ground	**82**
Grapple Defense	75
Ground Combo Speed	99
Ground Get Up	80
Ground Strike Speed	99
Ground Striking Power	60
Passing	80
Submission	**44**
Arm Submissions	50
Leg Submissions	33
Neck Submissions	50
Health	**96**
Blocking	90
Chin	99
Gut	99
Heart	99
Leg Health	90
Stamina Recovery	99

STAND UP STRATEGIES

Mizuto is an accomplished boxer with excellent speed on the feet and respectable striking power. Use his footwork to keep the opponent guessing as you slip in to score damage with flying knees and superman punches. Hirota has good defensive attributes, so feel confident exchanging with other Lightweight strikers. Beware of takedowns by skilled grapplers, however—Hirota is often outmatched on the ground.

Fighting against: Mizuto Hirota—Don't trade strikes with this boxer—his speed, power, and defense are his greatest strengths. Get Mizuto to exchange, then drive in with a takedown to put him on his back and out of his depth.

CLINCH STRATEGIES

Hirota is overwhelming in the clinch, owning excellent control and capable of unleashing furious strikes. Use this position to control mobile opponents, working them over with elbows and knees. Avoid tying up with grapplers, however, as Mizuto finds himself in trouble when he's slammed to the mat.

Fighting against: Mizuto Hirota—The clinch can be used to slow Hirota down when fighting against him, but ensure your warrior has excellent control in this position before tying up. The ground is where you really want to be against Mizuto, so work for takedowns from the clinch and bring the fight there. Considering Mizuto's clinch prowess, it's better to shoot in for takedowns on the feet rather than entering the clinch game against him—Hirota doesn't have the "takedown counter strike" special, so all he can do is stuff your shots.

GROUND STRATEGIES

Your strategy on the ground with Hirota is simple: Get back to your feet. Mizuto has poor grappling and submission ability, so there's little sense in entering this dangerous realm of MMA.

Fighting against: Mizuto Hirota—Strive to take Hirota down in any fight against him, exploiting his poor grappling skill to punish him on the mat. Use takedowns instead of clinch slams to bring Hirota to the floor more safely, then work for submissions—Mizuto is durable and resilient against strikes.

MUHAMMED LAWAL
"KING MO"

MUHAMMED LAWAL
Born: Murfreesboro, Tennessee

Specialty: Wrestling

Weight Classes: Heavyweight, Light Heavyweight

> FIGHT RECORD <

7—1—0 (WIN—LOSS—DRAW)

WINS	LOSSES
5 (T)KOs (71.43%)	1 (T)KOs (100%)
2 Decisions (28.57%)	

OPPONENT	RESULT	METHOD	DATE	ROUND	TIME
Rafael Cavalcante	Loss	TKO (Punches and Elbows)	8/21/10	3	1:14
Gegard Mousasi	Win	Decision (Unanimous)	4/17/10	5	5:00
Mike Whitehead	Win	KO (Punches)	12/19/09	1	3:08
Mark Kerr	Win	TKO (Punches)	8/28/09	1	0:25
Ryo Kawamura	Win	Decision (Unanimous)	3/20/09	3	5:00
Yukiya Naito	Win	TKO (Punches)	1/4/09	1	3:54
Fabio Silva	Win	TKO (Punches)	11/1/08	3	0:41
Travis Wiuff	Win	TKO (Punches)	9/28/08	1	2:11

SPECIAL MOVES		
NAME	TYPE	FROM
Catch Punch	Parry	(1) Full Guard Postured Up—Bottom; (2) Full Guard Postured Up—Top; (3) Full Mount Postured Up—Top
Darce Choke	Submission (Neck)	Sprawl—Top
Dashing Takedown	Takedown	Standing
Diving Punch	Strike	Standing vs. Open Guard
Flying Knee	Strike	Standing
Guillotine Takedown	Submission (Neck)	Standing
Major Pass	Strike	Every Ground Position
Overhand Punch	Strike	Standing
Rear Naked Choke	Submission (Neck)	Back Mount—Top
Superman Punch	Strike	Standing
Takedown Fake	Strike	Standing

MUHAMMED LAWAL

ATTRIBUTES

ATTRIBUTE	HW	LHW
Stand Up	**79**	**81**
Foot Speed	74	80
Hand Speed	87	93
Kick Combo Speed	74	80
Kick Range	60	60
Movement Speed	84	88
Punch Combo Speed	87	93
Punch Range	88	88
Stand Up Left Foot Power	60	60
Stand Up Left Hand Power	93	93
Stand Up Right Foot Power	60	60
Stand Up Right Hand Power	93	93
Takedowns	90	90
Takedown Defense	80	80
Clinch	**90**	**93**
Clinch Combo	86	92
Clinch Control	97	97
Clinch Strike Speed	86	92
Clinch Striking Power	93	93
Ground	**92**	**94**
Grapple Defense	99	99
Ground Combo Speed	88	94
Ground Get Up	90	90
Ground Strike Speed	88	94
Ground Striking Power	95	95
Passing	95	95
Submission	**36**	**36**
Arm Submissions	33	33
Leg Submissions	33	33
Neck Submissions	44	44
Health	**94**	**94**
Blocking	90	90
Chin	99	99
Gut	99	99
Heart	99	99
Leg Health	91	91
Stamina Recovery	90	90

STAND UP STRATEGIES

"King Mo" Lawal has great speed and power in his hands and a durable chin, which allow him to mix things up on the feet. Bring the heat with Lawal, unleashing flying knees and superman punches to rock rivals from range and pressure them up close to achieve a clinch or takedown. Lawal is an outstanding grappler, so open up on the feet without fear of being taken down.

Fighting against: Muhammed Lawal—Lawal's good boxing and takedown ability make him a handful on the feet, but this is by far the best place to battle him. Expect him to wade in with punches in preparation for the takedown and circle away when he makes an advance. Try to engage Lawal on your terms, landing rangy leg kicks to slow "King Mo" down. Take away his speed to make him an easier target, but never throw more than a few strikes at a time or you'll most likely be grappled to the mat.

CLINCH STRATEGIES

Muhammed works the clinch to great effect, enjoying outstanding control that's only surpassed by legendary MMA warrior Randy Couture. Use Lawal's boxing to back the opponent up on the feet, then clinch up and smash rivals with fast-yet-heavy strikes. Control the position to wear out opponents before slamming them to the mat, where you can apply some of his ferocious ground and pound.

Fighting against: Muhammed Lawal—The clinch is a dangerous game to play against Lawal, so avoid tying up with him by keeping distance on the feet and being ready to stuff his clinch efforts. Don't allow "King Mo" to back you into a corner, and whenever he manages to tie you up, focus on minimizing damage and escaping.

GROUND STRATEGIES

One of the best ground fighters in MMA, "King Mo" uses his overwhelming grappling game to smother opponents on the mat, where he's free to unleash his brutal ground and pound. If Lawal is losing the stand up exchanges, shoot for a takedown and bring the fight to the floor, working into dominant position so "King Mo" may pour on the damage.

Fighting against: Muhammed Lawal—Lawal's submissions are nothing to fear, but his exceptional grappling and ground and pound makes him an overwhelming adversary on the mat.

Strive to remain upright throughout each fight against "King Mo," circling away from the cage, picking your strikes with care, and always being ready to stuff his powerful takedowns and clinch attempts. Avoid going for submissions on the bottom—Lawal is as tough to tap as they come, and failing a sub may land you in a very precarious position.

MURILO RUA
Born: Curitiba, Brazil

MURILO RUA
"NINJA"

> FIGHT RECORD <
20—10—1 (WIN—LOSS—DRAW)

WINS	LOSSES
9 (T)KOs (45%)	5 (T)KOs (50%)
9 Submissions (45%)	5 Decisions (50%)
2 Decisions (10%)	

Specialty: Muay Thai

Weight Classes: Light Heavy-weight, Middleweight

OPPONENT	RESULT	METHOD	DATE	ROUND	TIME
Jeremy May	Win	Submission (Guillotine Choke)	7/18/10	1	4:12
Arturo Arcemendes	Win	Submission (Arm Triangle Choke)	5/28/10	1	1:27
Jason Jones	Win	TKO (Punches)	12/12/09	2	3:20
Alex Stiebling	Win	TKO (Head Kick and Punches)	9/12/09	1	0:39
Riki Fukuda	Loss	Decision (Unanimous)	4/5/09	2	5:00
Benji Radach	Loss	TKO (Punches)	10/4/08	2	2:31
Tony Bonello	Win	TKO (Punches)	6/14/08	1	3:15
Xavier Foupa-Pokam	Win	Submission (Rear Naked Choke)	12/1/07	2	3:47
Robbie Lawler	Loss	KO (Punches)	9/15/07	3	2:04
Joey Villasenor	Win	TKO (Punches)	6/22/07	2	1:05
Alex Reid	Win	TKO (Cut on the Shin)	4/21/07	1	0:28
Mark Weir	Win	Submission (Arm Triangle Choke)	9/30/06	2	1:15
Denis Kang	Loss	KO (Punches)	6/4/06	1	0:15
Paulo Filho	Loss	Decision (Unanimous)	4/2/06	2	5:00
Murad Chunkaiev	Win	Submission (Heel Hook)	10/23/05	1	3:31
Quinton Jackson	Loss	Decision (Split)	2/20/05	3	5:00
Sergei Kharitonov	Loss	KO (Punches)	4/25/04	1	4:14
Alexander Otsuka	Win	Submission (Arm Triangle Choke)	2/1/04	1	1:25
Akira Shoji	Win	KO (Flying Knee)	12/31/03	1	2:24
Kevin Randleman	Loss	TKO (Cut)	12/23/02	3	0:20
Ricardo Arona	Loss	Decision (Unanimous)	11/24/02	3	5:00
Mario Sperry	Win	Decision (Unanimous)	4/28/02	3	5:00
Alex Andrade	Win	Decision (Unanimous)	12/23/01	3	5:00
Dan Henderson	Loss	Decision (Split)	11/3/01	3	5:00
Daijiro Matsui	Win	TKO (Soccer Kick and Stomps)	9/24/01	3	0:51
Rogerio Sagate	Win	Submission (Keylock)	6/9/01	1	3:54
Akihiro Gono	Draw	Draw	5/1/01	3	5:00
Leopoldo Serao	Win	TKO (Doctor Stoppage)	12/16/00	1	7:00
Luiz Claudio das Dores	Win	TKO (Retirement)	11/14/00	1	3:00
Israel Albuquerque	Win	Submission (Shoulder Injury)	8/12/00	1	1:36
Adriano Verdelli	Win	Submission (Triangle Choke)	5/27/00	1	3:08

MURILO RUA

ATTRIBUTES		
ATTRIBUTE	LHW	MW
Stand Up	**74**	**77**
Foot Speed	74	84
Hand Speed	77	87
Kick Combo Speed	77	87
Kick Range	74	74
Movement Speed	78	78
Punch Combo Speed	77	87
Punch Range	73	73
Stand Up Left Foot Power	71	71
Stand Up Left Hand Power	71	71
Stand Up Right Foot Power	71	71
Stand Up Right Hand Power	71	71
Takedowns	77	77
Takedown Defense	71	71
Clinch	**72**	**77**
Clinch Combo	74	84
Clinch Control	71	71
Clinch Strike Speed	74	84
Clinch Striking Power	70	70
Ground	**80**	**83**
Grapple Defense	99	99
Ground Combo Speed	77	87
Ground Get Up	73	73
Ground Strike Speed	77	87
Ground Striking Power	73	73
Passing	81	81
Submission	**79**	**79**
Arm Submissions	91	91
Leg Submissions	55	55
Neck Submissions	91	91
Health	**83**	**83**
Blocking	81	81
Chin	71	71
Gut	89	89
Heart	83	83
Leg Health	91	91
Stamina Recovery	88	88

SPECIAL MOVES		
NAME	TYPE	FROM
Americana	Submission (Arm)	(1) Full Mount Postured Up—Top; (2) Full Mount Tight—Top
Armbar	Submission (Arm)	(1) Full Guard—Bottom; (2) Full Guard Postured Up—Bottom; (3) Side Control—Top; (4) Back Mount Side Turtle—Top
Catch Kick	Parry	Standing
Catch Punch	Parry	(1) Full Guard Postured Up—Bottom; (2) Full Guard Postured Up—Top; (3) Full Mount Postured Up—Top
Dashing Takedown	Takedown	Standing
Diving Punch	Strike	Standing vs. Open Guard
Flying Knee	Strike	Standing
Head Arm Choke	Submission (Neck)	(1) Full Mount Tight—Top; (2) Side Control—Top
Heel Hook	Submission (Leg)	(1) Full Guard Postured Up—Top; (2) Guard Stacked—Top
Kimura	Submission (Arm)	Half Guard—Top
Major Pass	Strike	Every Ground Position
Overhand Punch	Strike	Standing
Rear Naked Choke	Submission (Neck)	Back Mount—Top
Roundhouse Head Kick	Strike	Standing
Takedown Counter Strike	Strike	Standing
Takedown Fake	Strike	Standing
Triangle Choke	Submission (Neck)	(1) Full Guard—Bottom; (2) Full Guard Postured Up—Bottom; (3) Full Mount Postured Up—Top; (4) Guard Stacked—Bottom

STAND UP STRATEGIES

"Ninja" Rua is a gifted submission artist, but his stand up game doesn't measure up to most other fighters in his weight classes. He's particularly vulnerable when he strikes at Light Heavyweight, so use his footwork and speed to set up takedowns. Mix in power strikes such as flying knees as well to avoid becoming predicable and potentially rock Rua's foes.

Fighting against: Murilo Rua—When striking against Murilo, strive to stuff his takedowns, thereby nullifying his ability to apply dangerous submissions. Pick "Ninja" apart with sharp kicks and punches from range, targeting his vulnerable chin and battering his body to wear him down.

CLINCH STRATEGIES

Rua's clinch game is weak compared to his peers, so avoid this position. Shoot in for takedowns on the feet instead of looking for clinch slams, and escape from the clinch if you're ever tied up—Rua has poor control here.

Fighting against: Murilo Rua—You can dominate Rua in the clinch if your fighter is skilled in this area, but dissecting "Ninja" with standing strikes is the safer option. Unless you're supremely confident in your fighter's ground defense and clinch control, don't do Rua the favor of closing in; keep your distance to give him little chance of scoring a takedown.

GROUND STRATEGIES

Rua's best chance of winning a fight is on the ground, so bring his opponents to the mat as fast as you can. His wrestling isn't great, but his grappling defense and submission ability are outstanding. Roll with opponents, looking

to lock in kimuras from half guard, or armbars and triangles from the bottom. Rua's leg submissions fail to impress, so stick with arm locks and chokes, and don't let your opponent back to his feet.

Fighting against: Murilo Rua—Don't go to the ground against Rua—he's almost impossible to submit and can tap you out in a heartbeat. Stay standing and beat "Ninja" to the punch with superior striking. Always be on guard to defend against his takedowns. Should Rua pin you down, focus on denying his submissions and getting back to your feet—his ground strikes aren't worthy of much concern.

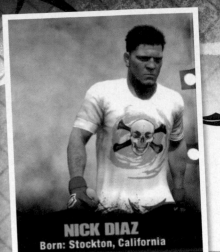

NICK DIAZ
Born: Stockton, California

Specialty: Jiu Jitsu

Weight Classes: Middleweight, Welterweight

NICK DIAZ

› FIGHT RECORD ‹

22—7—0 (WIN—LOSS—DRAW) (1 NC)

WINS	LOSSES
12 (T)KOs (54.55%)	2 (T)KOs (28.57%)
7 Submissions (31.82%)	5 Decisions (71.43%)
3 Decisions (13.64%)	

OPPONENT	RESULT	METHOD	DATE	ROUND	TIME
Hayato Sakurai	Win	Submission (Armbar)	5/29/10	1	3:54
Marius Zaromskis	Win	TKO (Punches)	1/30/10	1	4:38
Scott Smith	Win	Submission (Rear Naked Choke)	6/6/09	3	1:41
Frank Shamrock	Win	TKO (Punches)	4/11/09	2	3:57
Thomas Denny	Win	TKO (Punches)	7/26/08	2	0:30
Muhsin Corbbrey	Win	TKO (Punches)	6/14/08	3	3:59
Katsuya Inoue	Win	TKO (Corner Stoppage)	5/11/08	1	6:45
Karl James Noons	Loss	TKO (Doctor Stoppage)	11/10/07	1	5:00
Mike Aina	Win	Decision (Split)	9/15/07	3	5:00
Takanori Gomi	NC	No Decision—Overturned by NSAC	2/24/07	2	1:46
Gleison Tibau	Win	TKO (Punches)	11/18/06	2	2:27
Josh Neer	Win	Submission (Kimura)	8/26/06	3	1:42
Ray Steinbeiss	Win	Decision (Unanimous)	5/13/06	3	5:00
Sean Sherk	Loss	Decision (Unaminous)	4/15/06	3	5:00
Joe Riggs	Loss	Decision (Unaminous)	2/4/06	3	5:00
Diego Sanchez	Loss	Decision (Unanimous)	11/5/05	3	5:00
Koji Oishi	Win	KO (Punches)	6/4/05	1	1:24
Drew Fickett	Win	TKO (Punches)	2/5/05	1	4:40
Karo Parisyan	Loss	Decision (Split)	8/21/04	3	5:00
Robbie Lawler	Win	KO (Punches)	4/2/04	2	1:31
Jeremy Jackson	Win	Submission (Armbar)	9/26/03	3	2:04
Jeremy Jackson	Win	TKO (Punches)	7/19/03	1	4:17
Joe Hurley	Win	Submission (Kimura)	3/27/03	1	1:55
Kuniyoshi Hironaka	Loss	Decision (Split)	12/14/02	3	5:00
Harris Sarmiento	Win	TKO (Corner Stoppage)	10/24/02	2	1:47
Jeremy Jackson	Loss	TKO (Punches)	9/28/02	1	0:49
Adam Lynn	Win	Submission (Armbar)	9/28/02	1	2:51
Blaine Tyler	Win	TKO (Punches)	9/28/02	2	2:01
Chris Lytle	Win	Decision (Unanimous)	7/12/02	3	5:00
Mike Wick	Win	Submission (Triangle Choke)	8/31/01	1	3:43

NICK DIAZ

ATTRIBUTES

ATTRIBUTE	MW	WW
Stand Up	**82**	**82**
Foot Speed	77	87
Hand Speed	90	96
Kick Combo Speed	90	90
Kick Range	80	80
Movement Speed	88	91
Punch Combo Speed	90	96
Punch Range	90	90
Stand Up Left Foot Power	75	70
Stand Up Left Hand Power	77	72
Stand Up Right Foot Power	75	70
Stand Up Right Hand Power	77	72
Takedowns	80	80
Takedown Defense	80	80
Clinch	**88**	**88**
Clinch Combo	90	96
Clinch Control	88	88
Clinch Strike Speed	90	96
Clinch Striking Power	84	74
Ground	**82**	**84**
Grapple Defense	81	81
Ground Combo Speed	90	92
Ground Get Up	71	80
Ground Strike Speed	90	92
Ground Striking Power	80	74
Passing	85	85
Submission	**82**	**83**
Arm Submissions	88	88
Leg Submissions	66	66
Neck Submissions	93	95
Health	**85**	**89**
Blocking	95	95
Chin	71	71
Gut	66	90
Heart	99	99
Leg Health	90	90
Stamina Recovery	90	90

SPECIAL MOVES

NAME	TYPE	FROM
Americana	Submission (Arm)	(1) Full Mount Postured Up—Top; (2) Full Mount Tight—Top
Armbar	Submission (Arm)	(1) Full Guard—Bottom; (2) Full Guard Postured Up—Bottom; (3) Side Control—Top; (4) Back Mount Side Turtle—Top
Catch Kick	Parry	Standing
Catch Punch	Parry	(1) Full Guard Postured Up—Bottom; (2) Full Guard Postured Up—Top; (3) Full Mount Postured Up—Top
Dashing Takedown	Takedown	Standing
Diving Punch	Strike	Standing vs. Open Guard
Head Arm Choke	Submission (Neck)	(1) Full Mount Tight—Top; (2) Side Control—Top
Kimura	Submission (Arm)	Half Guard—Top
Major Pass	Strike	Every Ground Position
Overhand Punch	Strike	Standing
Rear Naked Choke	Submission (Neck)	Back Mount—Top
Roundhouse Head Kick	Strike	Standing
Takedown Counter Strike	Strike	Standing
Takedown Fake	Strike	Standing
Triangle Choke	Submission (Neck)	(1) Full Guard—Bottom; (2) Full Guard Postured Up—Bottom; (3) Full Mount Postured Up—Top; (4) Guard Stacked—Bottom

STAND UP STRATEGIES

Diaz is a well-rounded and dangerous fighter. He's one of the best strikers in the Welterweight division, though he gives up a lot of power when fighting at Middleweight. Nick's excellent punching range and speed are his greatest assets on the feet—use his long strikes to pick foes apart without exposing Nick's vulnerable chin to counters. If things aren't going your way in the stand up department, look to clinch or shoot for a takedown to employ Diaz's impressive grappling ability.

Fighting against: Nick Diaz—Outstriking a long-reaching and swift opponent like Diaz is tough, but finding his chin is a sure way toward victory. Target Nick's head with nearly every strike, attacking his legs when you want to mix things up. Nick has very few stand up specials, so you'll primarily see traditional strikes and takedowns. Always be prepared to stuff Nick's shots and clinch attempts as you look for the knockout.

CLINCH STRATEGIES

Nick's got a great clinch game—use it to keep his chin protected as you rough up opponents. Nick's strikes gain more weight in the clinch, especially during Middleweight bouts, so use this

position to your advantage when opponents try to slip past Nick's fists. Use the clinch to score heavy damage, bringing the fight to the mat with a huge slam the moment rivals begin to block.

Fighting against: Nick Diaz—Nick has more control in the clinch than in any other position, so break free of his grip whenever he attempts to tie up. If his reach is giving you trouble on the feet, initiate the clinch yourself to damage Diaz up close. Beware his clinch takedowns, however, and try to land knees and elbows to the head to rock Nick.

GROUND STRATEGIES

Nick's high submission skill makes him very dangerous on the floor, but he lacks the dominant control over the ground game that other fighters enjoy. It's therefore best to hit the mat on Diaz's terms, slamming the opponent from the clinch

or scoring with a standing takedown. The moment you hit the ground, look to apply one of Nick's lethal chokes or arm locks. Kimuras from half guard are your go-to subs, but Nick's a little better at choke holds—pass guard and use his head arm choke or triangle to end fights fast.

Fighting against: Nick Diaz—Rolling with a submission artist like Diaz is dangerous, but Nick's lack of grappling defense can be exploited by superior ground fighters. If you're getting picked apart by his long strikes, change levels with a takedown and see if you can finish Nick off with some ground and pound or a tight submission lock. Focus on controlling the action from the top and don't remain in Diaz's dangerous guard for long.

NICK THOMPSON
Born: Minneapolis, Minnesota

NICK THOMPSON
"THE GOAT"

> FIGHT RECORD <

38—13—1 (WIN—LOSS—DRAW)

WINS	LOSSES
10 (T)KOs (26.32%)	6 (T)KOs (46.15%)
22 Submissions (57.89%)	7 Submissions (53.85%)
6 Decisions (15.79%)	

Specialty: Muay Thai

Weight Classes: Middleweight, Welterweight

OPPONENT	RESULT	METHOD	DATE	ROUND	TIME
Taisuke Okuno	Loss	KO (Punch)	8/22/10	3	0:27
Dan Hornbuckle	Loss	TKO (Punches)	9/23/09	2	1:30
Tim Kennedy	Loss	Submission (Punches)	6/19/09	2	2:37
Paul Daley	Win	Decision (Unanimous)	2/20/09	3	5:00
Travis McCullough	Win	Submission (Punches)	1/17/09	1	2:38
Jake Shields	Loss	Submission (Guillotine Choke)	7/26/08	1	1:03
Michel Costa	Win	Submission (Kimura)	6/8/08	2	4:13
Fabricio Monteiro	Win	Decision (Unanimous)	3/5/08	3	5:00
John Troyer	Win	Submission (Rear Naked Choke)	2/1/08	1	3:46
Mark Weir	Win	TKO (Punches)	8/24/07	1	4:01
Eddie Alvarez	Win	TKO (Punches)	4/14/07	2	4:32
Dustin Denes	Win	TKO (Punches)	2/18/07	1	1:27
Ansar Chalangov	Win	Submission (Rear Naked Choke)	12/2/06	1	4:59
Joe Winterfeldt	Win	TKO (Referee Stoppage)	10/21/06	1	N/A
Davion Peterson	Win	Submission (Rear Naked Choke)	8/22/06	3	N/A
Steven Bratland	Win	Submission (Rear Naked Choke)	7/15/06	1	N/A
Yancy Cuellar	Win	TKO	7/15/06	1	N/A
Chris Wilson	Win	Submission (Kimura)	6/24/06	2	2:08
Karo Parisyan	Loss	Submission (Punches)	4/15/06	1	4:44
Alex Carter	Win	Submission (Triangle Choke)	2/1/06	N/A	N/A
Anthony White	Win	Submission (Strikes)	1/13/06	N/A	N/A
Keith Wisniewski	Win	Decision (Unanimous)	11/19/05	3	5:00
Josh Neer	Win	Submission (Rear Naked Choke)	10/15/05	2	2:19
Dereck Keasley	Win	Submission (Choke)	9/24/05	1	3:48
Victor Moreno	Win	Submission (Guillotine Choke)	9/24/05	2	N/A
Chris Conley	Win	Decision	9/24/05	2	5:00
Brian Fitzsimmons	Win	KO	7/9/05	N/A	N/A
Ed Herman	Loss	TKO (Injury)	6/17/05	1	N/A
Yushin Okami	Loss	Submission (Elbow Injury)	6/11/05	1	0:29
Marcel Ferreira	Win	TKO (Punches)	4/30/05	3	2:48
Joey Clark	Win	Submission (Armbar)	4/23/05	1	3:01
Nuri Shakir	Win	Submission (Triangle Choke)	4/2/05	2	3:07
Paul Purcell	Loss	KO (Punches)	3/5/05	2	N/A
Brian Green	Win	TKO (Punches)	2/19/05	N/A	N/A
Brian Gassaway	Win	Decision (Unanimous)	2/5/05	3	3:00
Jesse Chilton	Win	Submission (Rear Naked Choke)	1/8/05	3	N/A
Darren Hines	Win	Submission (Guillotine Choke)	12/3/04	1	0:19
Daryl Guthmiller	Draw	Draw	11/5/04	3	5:00
John Renken	Win	TKO (Punches)	9/24/04	1	N/A
Sean Huffman	Win	Submission (Choke)	9/24/04	2	N/A
Brian Ebersole	Loss	TKO (Punches)	9/24/04	1	N/A
Ricky Seleuce	Win	Submission (Twister)	8/21/04	1	N/A
Thiago Goncalves	Win	Submission (Punches)	6/12/04	2	2:39
Brian Moore	Win	Submission (Guillotine Choke)	6/4/04	1	0:28
Jeff Doyle	Win	TKO (Corner Stoppage)	5/15/04	2	N/A
Mike Quinlan	Loss	Submission (Rear Naked Choke)	5/1/04	2	0:16
Emyr Bussade	Win	Decision (Unanimous)	3/6/04	2	5:00
Kyle Helsper	Win	Submission (Rear Naked Choke)	1/10/04	2	2:16
Dan Hart	Loss	Submission (Guillotine Choke)	10/18/03	1	0:17
Dustin Denes	Loss	Submission (Triangle Choke)	9/5/03	1	1:45
Kyle Helsper	Win	Submission (Punches)	6/28/03	1	N/A
Dan Hart	Loss	KO (Punches)	3/22/03	1	N/A

NICK THOMPSON

ATTRIBUTES

ATTRIBUTE	MIDDLEWEIGHT	WELTERWEIGHT
Stand Up	**78**	**80**
Foot Speed	88	95
Hand Speed	88	95
Kick Combo Speed	88	95
Kick Range	78	78
Movement Speed	85	85
Punch Combo Speed	88	95
Punch Range	78	78
Stand Up Left Foot Power	71	71
Stand Up Left Hand Power	69	69
Stand Up Right Foot Power	71	71
Stand Up Right Hand Power	60	69
Takedowns	74	74
Takedown Defense	71	71
Clinch	**82**	**85**
Clinch Combo	88	95
Clinch Control	81	81
Clinch Strike Speed	88	95
Clinch Striking Power	72	72
Ground	**77**	**79**
Grapple Defense	64	64
Ground Combo Speed	88	95
Ground Get Up	73	73
Ground Strike Speed	88	95
Ground Striking Power	73	73
Passing	76	76
Submission	**89**	**89**
Arm Submissions	96	96
Leg Submissions	77	77
Neck Submissions	96	96
Health	**80**	**80**
Blocking	81	81
Chin	78	78
Gut	88	88
Heart	71	71
Leg Health	89	89
Stamina Recovery	74	74

SPECIAL MOVES

NAME	TYPE	FROM
Americana	Submission (Arm)	(1) Full Mount Postured Up—Top; (2) Full Mount Tight—Top
Armbar	Submission (Arm)	(1) Full Guard—Bottom; (2) Full Guard Postured Up—Bottom; (3) Side Control—Top; (4) Back Mount Side Turtle—Top
Darce Choke	Submission (Neck)	Sprawl—Top
Dashing Takedown	Takedown	Standing
Diving Punch	Strike	Standing vs. Open Guard
Gogoplata	Submission (Neck)	Rubber Guard—Bottom
Guillotine Takedown	Submission (Neck)	Standing
Kimura	Submission (Arm)	Half Guard—Top
Major Pass	Strike	Every Ground Position
Omoplata	Submission (Arm)	Rubber Guard—Bottom
Overhand Punch	Strike	Standing
Rear Naked Choke	Submission (Neck)	Back Mount—Top
Rubber Guard	Strike	Full Guard—Bottom
Takedown Counter Strike	Strike	Standing
Takedown Fake	Strike	Standing
Triangle Choke	Submission (Neck)	(1) Full Guard—Bottom; (2) Full Guard Postured Up—Bottom; (3) Full Mount Postured Up—Top; (4) Guard Stacked—Bottom

STAND UP STRATEGIES

Thompson is a submission fighter who comes up a bit short in the striking game. He's particularly weak in this department when fighting at Middleweight, so use his fast hands primarily to set up takedowns.

Fighting against: Nick Thompson—With weak strikes and a flimsy chin, Thompson can be dismantled on the feet by talented strikers. Tap-out artists with good grappling defense can overwhelm Thompson on the ground as well, so fight your fight when facing "The Goat."

CLINCH STRATEGIES

Thompson doesn't have the greatest control in the clinch, but his strikes gain power here, particularly when the position is used against Welterweight adversaries. Use Nick's clinch to slow down swift strikers, inflict damage, and bring the fight to the mat to work his submissions. Thompson must beware the opponent's takedowns in the clinch, however, as he isn't particularly good at ground defense.

Fighting against: Nick Thompson—Thompson can be worked over in the clinch, but it's best to avoid this position when fighting against him because it's one of his stronger areas. Batter him with strikes on the feet if you're looking for the KO, or shoot in and take him down to exploit his lack of grappling defense.

GROUND STRATEGIES

Nick's powerful submissions make him dangerous on the ground, but he suffers from a lack of grappling defense and passing ability. Fortunately, with an array of submissions and great skill in using them, "The Goat" has plenty of ways to end the fight on the mat. Score takedowns with Thompson on the feet or from the clinch, slapping on fast kimuras or armbars shortly after hitting the floor.

Fighting against: Nick Thompson—Respect Thompson's tap-out game, but exploit the gaping holes in his wrestling by denying his submission attempts and popping back to your feet each time he manages to take you down. Beware of Nick's kimuras from half guard and strive to prevent him from locking them in. If you're going to roll with Nick on the ground, make sure to pass his guard quickly and work methodically to maintain dominant top position. Wear him down with strikes and then turn his favorite finishers against him for the tap.

PAT MILETICH
Born: Bettendorf, Iowa

Specialty: Jiu Jitsu

Weight Classes: Middleweight, Welterweight

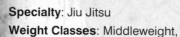

PAT MILETICH
"THE CROATIAN SENSATION"

> FIGHT RECORD <

29—7—2 (WIN—LOSS—DRAW)

WINS	LOSSES
5 (T)KOs (17.24%)	3 (T)KOs (42.86%)
18 Submissions (62.07%)	3 Submissions (42.86%)
6 Decisions (20.69%)	1 Decision (14.29%)

OPPONENT	RESULT	METHOD	DATE	ROUND	TIME
Thomas Denny	Win	KO (Punches)	12/11/08	2	0:50
Renzo Gracie	Loss	Submission (Guillotine Choke)	9/23/06	1	3:37
Matt Lindland	Loss	TKO (Punches)	3/22/02	1	3:09
Shonie Carter	Win	KO (Head Kick)	6/29/01	2	2:42
Carlos Newton	Loss	Submission (Bulldog Choke)	5/4/01	3	2:50
Kenichi Yamamoto	Win	Submission (Guillotine Choke)	12/16/00	2	1:58
Kiyoshi Tamura	Loss	Decision (Majority)	8/23/00	2	5:00
John Alessio	Win	Submission (Armbar)	6/9/00	2	1:43
Jose Landi-Jons	Loss	TKO (Corner Stoppage)	1/15/00	1	8:00
Shonie Carter	Win	Decision	8/21/99	1	20:00
Andre Pederneiras	Win	TKO (Cut)	7/16/99	2	2:20
Clayton Miller	Win	Submission (Triangle)	5/30/99	1	0:40
Jutaro Nakao	Loss	Technical Submission (Triangle Choke)	2/2/99	1	9:22
Jorge Patino	Win	Decision (Unanimous)	1/8/99	1	21:00
Mikey Burnett	Win	Decision	10/16/98	1	21:00
Dan Severn	Draw	Draw	8/22/98	1	20:00
Al Buck Jr.	Win	Submission (Choke)	6/27/98	2	2:49
Chris Brennan	Win	Submission (Choke)	3/13/98	1	9:02
Townsend Saunders	Win	Decision	3/13/98	1	15:00
Chris Brennan	Win	Decision	11/15/97	1	30:00:00
Chris Brennan	Draw	Draw	8/30/97	1	20:00
Chuck Kim	Win	Submission (Rear Naked Choke)	6/25/97	1	10:46
Matt Hume	Loss	TKO (Doc Stop from Broken Nose)	3/28/97	1	5:00
Chad Cox	Win	Submission	2/15/97	1	0.1
Paul Kimbro	Win	Submission (Armbar)	2/1/97	1	5:13
Jason Nicholsen	Win	Decision (Unanimous)	1/17/97	1	15:00
Earl Loucks	Win	Submission (Keylock)	11/23/96	1	7:00
Pat Assalone	Win	Submission (Armbar)	9/1/96	1	4:01
Matt Andersen	Win	Submission (Strikes)	7/26/96	N/A	N/A
Yasunori Matsumoto	Win	TKO (Doctor)	5/11/96	1	15:53
Andrey Dudko	Win	Submission (Rear Naked Choke)	2/10/96	1	2:49
Bob Gholson	Win	KO	2/10/96	1	2:20
Rick Graveson	Win	Submission (Rear Naked Choke)	2/10/96	1	0:46
Rick Graveson	Win	Submission (Rear Naked Choke)	1/20/96	1	1:53
Ed McLennan	Win	Submission (Armbar)	1/20/96	1	1:28
Kevin Marino	Win	Submission (Rear Naked Choke)	10/28/95	1	3:49
Angelo Rivera	Win	Submission (Rear Naked Choke)	10/28/95	1	1:40
Yasunori Matsumoto	Win	Submission (Rear Naked Choke)	10/28/95	1	7:40

PAT MILETICH

ATTRIBUTES

ATTRIBUTE	MW	WW
Stand Up	79	81
Foot Speed	85	85
Hand Speed	88	94
Kick Combo Speed	80	86
Kick Range	70	70
Movement Speed	88	88
Punch Combo Speed	88	94
Punch Range	85	85
Stand Up Left Foot Power	68	68
Stand Up Left Hand Power	68	68
Stand Up Right Foot Power	68	68
Stand Up Right Hand Power	68	68
Takedowns	92	92
Takedown Defense	88	88
Clinch	84	87
Clinch Combo	88	94
Clinch Control	91	91
Clinch Strike Speed	88	94
Clinch Striking Power	70	70
Ground	85	87
Grapple Defense	95	95
Ground Combo Speed	88	94
Ground Get Up	84	84
Ground Strike Speed	88	94
Ground Striking Power	73	73
Passing	86	86
Submission	77	77
Arm Submissions	91	91
Leg Submissions	44	44
Neck Submissions	97	97
Health	87	87
Blocking	90	90
Chin	82	82
Gut	92	92
Heart	81	81
Leg Health	88	88
Stamina Recovery	90	90

SPECIAL MOVES

NAME	TYPE	FROM
Americana	Submission (Arm)	(1) Full Mount Postured Up—Top; (2) Full Mount Tight—Top
Armbar	Submission (Arm)	(1) Full Guard—Bottom; (2) Full Guard Postured Up—Bottom; (3) Side Control—Top; (4) Back Mount Side Turtle—Top
Catch Kick	Parry	Standing
Catch Punch	Parry	(1) Full Guard Postured Up—Bottom; (2) Full Guard Postured Up—Top; (3) Full Mount Postured Up—Top
Darce Choke	Submission (Neck)	Sprawl—Top
Dashing Takedown	Takedown	Standing
Diving Punch	Strike	Standing vs. Open Guard
Guillotine Takedown	Submission (Neck)	Standing
Head Arm Choke	Submission (Neck)	(1) Full Mount Tight—Top; (2) Side Control—Top
Heel Hook	Submission (Leg)	(1) Full Guard Postured Up—Top; (2) Guard Stacked—Top
Kimura	Submission (Arm)	Half Guard—Top
Major Pass	Strike	Every Ground Position
Overhand Punch	Strike	Standing
Rear Naked Choke	Submission (Neck)	Back Mount—Top
Roundhouse Head Kick	Strike	Standing
Spinning Kick	Strike	Standing
Superman Punch	Strike	Standing
Takedown Counter Strike	Strike	Standing
Takedown Fake	Strike	Standing
Triangle Choke	Submission (Neck)	(1) Full Guard—Bottom; (2) Full Guard Postured Up—Bottom; (3) Full Mount Postured Up—Top; (4) Guard Stacked—Bottom

STAND UP STRATEGIES

An MMA icon, Pat Miletich is a very versatile fighter. His best positions are in the clinch and on the ground, however, so use his fast strikes to back the opponent up, aiming to close in and grapple. Be aggressive without fear of the takedown; Miletich is an exceptional grappler and can threaten with submissions off his back. If the opponent is winning the stand up battle, shoot in for a takedown and work Pat's strong submission game.

Fighting against: Pat Miletich—Miletich has solid stand up, but as he's much better in the clinch and on the ground, on the feet is the best place to fight him. Swing for Pat's chin, which isn't the strongest you'll find, and always be on guard against his powerful takedowns.

CLINCH STRATEGIES

Pat gains striking power in the clinch, and his control ranks among the highest in both of his weight classes. Use the clinch to score damage, manage the opponent, and protect Pat's chin. Bring the

opponent to the ground as he begins to block and start looking to force the tap.

Fighting against: Pat Miletich—Entering the clinch against Miletich is unwise, so avoid this position. Clinching with Miletich only puts you closer to his powerful grappling game, so keep your distance, strike with care, and avoid letting him corner you against the cage.

GROUND STRATEGIES

Use Pat's stand up and clinch game as a means of bringing the fight to the ground, where his submission skills can end the fight in short order. Pat has excellent grappling defense, so feel confident rolling with

anyone and go for broke with his subs. Try for kimuras immediately after you complete a takedown, or slip into side control and apply an even nastier head arm choke. Use triangles from Pat's back to end a fight unexpectedly as well.

Fighting against: Pat Miletich—Miletich is a handful on the ground, so it's best not to even go here against him. Defend against his powerful arm and neck submissions when he plants you on your back, aiming to stand up as soon as possible. Taking Pat down really isn't wise, so defend against his takedowns as you attempt to stagger him on the feet.

RANDY COUTURE
"THE NATURAL"

RANDY COUTURE
Born: Corvallis, Oregon

Specialty: Wrestling

Weight Classes: Heavyweight, Light Heavyweight

> FIGHT RECORD <

19—10—0 (WIN—LOSS—DRAW)

WINS	LOSSES
7 (T)KOs (36.84%)	5 (T)KOs (50%)
4 Submissions (21.05%)	4 Submissions (40%)
8 Decisions (42.11%)	1 Decision (10%)

OPPONENT	RESULT	METHOD	DATE	ROUND	TIME
James Toney	Win	Submission (Arm Triangle Choke)	8/28/10	1	3:19
Mark Coleman	Win	Submission (Rear Naked Choke)	2/6/10	2	1:09
Brandon Vera	Win	Decision (Unanimous)	11/14/09	3	5:00
Antonio Rodrigo Nogueira	Loss	Decision (Unanimous)	8/29/09	3	5:00
Brock Lesnar	Loss	TKO (Punches)	11/15/08	2	3:07
Gabriel Gonzaga	Win	TKO (Punches)	8/25/07	3	1:37
Tim Sylvia	Win	Decision (Unanimous)	3/3/07	5	5:00
Chuck Liddell	Loss	KO (Punch)	2/4/06	2	1:28
Mike Van Arsdale	Win	Submission (Anaconda Choke)	8/20/05	3	0:52
Chuck Liddell	Loss	KO (Punches)	4/16/05	1	2:06
Vitor Belfort	Win	TKO (Doctor Stoppage)	8/21/04	3	5:00
Vitor Belfort	Loss	TKO (Cut)	1/31/04	1	0:49
Tito Ortiz	Win	Decision (Unanimous)	9/26/03	5	5:00
Chuck Liddell	Win	TKO (Punches)	6/6/03	3	2:39
Ricco Rodriguez	Loss	Submission (Elbow)	9/27/02	5	3:04
Josh Barnett	Loss	TKO (Punches)	3/22/02	2	4:35
Pedro Rizzo	Win	TKO (Punches)	11/2/01	3	1:38
Pedro Rizzo	Win	Decision (Unanimous)	5/4/01	5	5:00
Valentijn Overeem	Loss	Submission (Guillotine Choke)	2/24/01	1	0:56
Tsuyoshi Kosaka	Win	Decision (Unanimous)	2/24/01	2	5:00
Kevin Randleman	Win	TKO (Strikes)	11/17/00	3	4:13
Ryushi Yanagisawa	Win	Decision (Majority)	10/9/00	2	5:00
Jeremy Horn	Win	Decision (Unanimous)	10/9/00	3	5:00
Mikhail Illoukhine	Loss	Submission (Kimura)	3/20/99	1	7:43
Enson Inoue	Loss	Submission (Armbar)	10/25/98	1	1:39
Maurice Smith	Win	Decision	12/21/97	1	21:00
Vitor Belfort	Win	TKO (Punches)	10/17/97	1	8:16
Steven Graham	Win	TKO (Punches)	5/30/97	1	3:13
Tony Halme	Win	Submission (Rear Naked Choke)	5/30/97	1	0:56

SPECIAL MOVES		
NAME	TYPE	FROM
Catch Punch	Parry	(1) Full Guard Postured Up—Bottom; (2) Full Guard Postured Up—Top; (3) Full Mount Postured Up—Top
Darce Choke	Submission (Neck)	Sprawl—Top
Dashing Takedown	Takedown	Standing
Diving Punch	Strike	Standing vs. Open Guard
Guillotine Takedown	Submission (Neck)	Standing
Head Arm Choke	Submission (Neck)	(1) Full Mount Tight—Top; (2) Side Control—Top
Major Pass	Strike	Every Ground Position
Overhand Punch	Strike	Standing
Rear Naked Choke	Submission (Neck)	Back Mount—Top
Takedown Fake	Strike	Standing

RANDY COUTURE

ATTRIBUTES		
ATTRIBUTE	HW	LHW
Stand Up	**78**	**79**
Foot Speed	80	80
Hand Speed	81	85
Kick Combo Speed	66	73
Kick Range	60	60
Movement Speed	80	80
Punch Combo Speed	80	85
Punch Range	80	80
Stand Up Left Foot Power	70	70
Stand Up Left Hand Power	78	78
Stand Up Right Foot Power	70	70
Stand Up Right Hand Power	83	83
Takedowns	96	95
Takedown Defense	95	95
Clinch	**91**	**91**
Clinch Combo	88	88
Clinch Control	99	99
Clinch Strike Speed	88	88
Clinch Striking Power	90	90
Ground	**88**	**89**
Grapple Defense	99	99
Ground Combo Speed	85	88
Ground Get Up	90	90
Ground Strike Speed	85	85
Ground Striking Power	92	92
Passing	82	82
Submission	**51**	**51**
Arm Submissions	40	40
Leg Submissions	33	33
Neck Submissions	82	82
Health	**84**	**84**
Blocking	81	81
Chin	72	72
Gut	90	90
Heart	96	96
Leg Health	72	72
Stamina Recovery	96	96

STAND UP STRATEGIES

Legendary MMA warrior Randy "The Natural" Couture is one of the best grapplers in existence, but his weak chin and vulnerable legs put him at risk while fighting on the feet. Fortunately, Couture has a terrific shot—use it to bring the action to the floor without delay.

Fighting against: Randy Couture—You've got to stay standing to have any chance of beating Couture. His grappling and clinch game are overwhelming, so stay light on your feet and be ready to stuff Randy's takedowns and clinch attempts. Keep him at a distance and pick away at his legs with long kicks. Counter his advances with fast jabs and straights, pouring on the offense when you at last manage to rock the MMA legend.

CLINCH STRATEGIES

The clinch is a perfect place for Couture, who has more dominant control in this position than any other fighter. Randy also gains a huge boost to his striking power in the clinch, allowing him to wear down and even KO opponents in short order. Score takedowns from the clinch when the opponent begins to block, passing to mount and dropping some bombs.

Fighting against: Randy Couture—Avoid clinching with Couture at all costs—the famed grappler has incredible control and can inflict great damage from this position. You're in trouble if Couture clinches up with you, so do your utmost not to end up in this position by striving to keep him at bay with footwork and counters.

GROUND STRATEGIES

Randy's a handful on the ground, with decent neck submissions and brutal ground and pound. His ground strikes are even more powerful than his clinch blows, so use Randy's ground and pound to batter opponents into unconsciousness. Head arm chokes are available from side control, but only attempt these against unskilled grapplers with poor submission defense. Randy's ability to pass guard isn't spectacular, so expect to work in order to achieve mount.

Fighting against: Randy Couture—Couture's phenomenal grappling defense makes him a challenge to roll with. He's nearly impossible to submit, so think twice before shooting in for takedowns unless you're simply looking to work some ground and pound from the top. The mat may be a better place to battle Couture than the clinch, but not when you're on bottom—deny his attempts at passing guard and get back to your feet as soon as possible. If you manage to plant Randy on his back, work patiently from the top and strive to keep him beneath you.

RENATO SOBRAL
"BABALU"

RENATO SOBRAL
Born: Rio de Janeiro, Brazil

Specialty: Wrestling

Weight Classes: Light Heavy-weight

> FIGHT RECORD <

36—8—0 (WIN—LOSS—DRAW)

WINS	LOSSES
5 (T)KOs (13.89%)	4 (T)KOs (50%)
18 Submissions (50%)	1 Submission (12.5%)
13 Decisions (36.11%)	3 Decisions (37.5%)

OPPONENT	RESULT	METHOD	DATE	ROUND	TIME
Robbie Lawler	Win	Decision (Unanimous)	6/16/10	3	5:00
Gegard Mousasi	Loss	KO (Punches)	8/15/09	1	1:00
Rameau Thierry Sokoudjou	Win	Submission (Brabo Choke)	1/24/09	2	2:36
Bobby Southworth	Win	TKO (Doctor Stoppage)	11/21/08	1	5:00
Mike Whitehead	Win	Decision (Unanimous)	7/19/08	3	5:00
Rodney Glunder	Win	Submission (Arm Triangle Choke)	12/9/07	3	N/A
David Heath	Win	Submission (Anaconda Choke)	8/25/07	2	3:30
Jason Lambert	Loss	KO (Punch)	3/3/07	2	3:26
Chuck Liddell	Loss	TKO (Punches)	8/26/06	1	1:35
Mike Van Arsdale	Win	Submission (Rear Naked Choke)	2/4/06	1	2:21
Chael Sonnen	Win	Submission (Triangle Choke)	10/7/05	2	1:20
Travis Wiuff	Win	Submission (Armbar)	4/16/05	2	0:24
Pierre Guillet	Win	Submission (Punches)	2/26/05	1	1:57
Cyrille Diabate	Win	Submission (Guillotine Choke)	11/27/04	1	3:38
Jose Landi-Jons	Win	Decision (Unanimous)	10/23/04	3	5:00
Jeremy Horn	Win	Decision (Unanimous)	9/6/03	3	5:00
Mauricio Rua	Win	Submission (Guillotine Choke)	9/6/03	3	3:07
Trevor Prangley	Win	Decision (Unanimous)	9/6/03	3	5:00
Marcelo Azevedo	Win	Decision (Unanimous)	7/31/03	3	5:00
Chuck Liddell	Loss	KO (Head Kick)	11/22/02	1	2:55
Elvis Sinosic	Win	Decision (Unanimous)	7/13/02	3	5:00
Kevin Randleman	Loss	Decision (Unanimous)	1/11/02	3	5:00
Fedor Emelianenko	Loss	Decision (Unanimous)	8/11/01	5	5:00
Tsuyoshi Kosaka	Win	Decision (Majority)	6/15/01	2	5:00
Kiyoshi Tamura	Win	Decision (Majority)	2/24/01	2	5:00
Maurice Smith	Win	Decision (Unanimous)	11/17/00	3	5:00
Valentijn Overeem	Loss	Submission (Toe Hold)	10/9/00	1	2:19
Tariel Bitsadze	Win	Submission (Armbar)	10/9/00	1	2:58
Hiromitsu Kanehara	Win	Decision (Unanimous)	6/15/00	2	5:00
Jacob Zobnin	Win	Submission (Rear Naked Choke)	5/20/00	1	3:20
Travis Fulton	Win	Submission (Armbar)	4/20/00	1	4:49
Dan Henderson	Loss	Decision (Majority)	2/26/00	2	5:00
Kiyoshi Tamura	Win	Decision (Majority)	2/26/00	2	5:00
Mikhail Illoukhine	Win	Submission (Armbar)	2/26/00	3	0:40
Brad Kohler	Win	KO (Soccer Kick)	1/15/00	2	0:50
Lee Hasdell	Win	Decision (Unanimous)	10/28/99	2	5:00
Zaza Tkeshelashvili	Win	Submission (Kimura)	10/28/99	2	1:11
Dario Amorim	Win	Submission (Punches)	7/24/99	1	2:14
Pedro Otavio	Win	Submission (Punches)	7/24/99	1	4:34
Augusto Menezes Santos	Win	Submission (Keylock)	7/24/99	1	0:56
Fernando Cerchiari	Win	KO (Punches)	1/20/99	1	4:41
Marco Vinicios	Win	TKO (Retirement)	9/27/97	2	4:58
Manoel Vicente	Win	TKO (Punches and Stomp)	9/27/97	1	6:27
Claudio Palma	Win	Submission (Leg Kicks)	9/27/97	1	2:08

RENATO SOBRAL

ATTRIBUTES

ATTRIBUTE	LH
Stand Up	**78**
Foot Speed	84
Hand Speed	87
Kick Combo Speed	87
Kick Range	78
Movement Speed	80
Punch Combo Speed	87
Punch Range	71
Stand Up Left Foot Power	73
Stand Up Left Hand Power	70
Stand Up Right Foot Power	70
Stand Up Right Hand Power	70
Takedowns	74
Takedown Defense	83
Clinch	**80**
Clinch Combo	88
Clinch Control	71
Clinch Strike Speed	88
Clinch Striking Power	76
Ground	**83**
Grapple Defense	95
Ground Combo Speed	87
Ground Get Up	76
Ground Strike Speed	87
Ground Striking Power	76
Passing	77
Submission	**81**
Arm Submissions	93
Leg Submissions	55
Neck Submissions	96
Health	**82**
Blocking	80
Chin	74
Gut	90
Heart	83
Leg Health	89
Stamina Recovery	81

SPECIAL MOVES

NAME	TYPE	FROM
Americana	Submission (Arm)	(1) Full Mount Postured Up—Top; (2) Full Mount Tight—Top
Armbar	Submission (Arm)	(1) Full Guard—Bottom; (2) Full Guard Postured Up—Bottom; (3) Side Control—Top; (4) Back Mount Side Turtle—Top
Catch Kick	Parry	Standing
Catch Punch	Parry	(1) Full Guard Postured Up—Bottom; (2) Full Guard Postured Up—Top; (3) Full Mount Postured Up—Top
Darce Choke	Submission (Neck)	Sprawl—Top
Dashing Takedown	Takedown	Standing
Diving Punch	Strike	Standing vs. Open Guard
Guillotine Takedown	Submission (Neck)	Standing
Head Arm Choke	Submission (Neck)	(1) Full Mount Tight—Top; (2) Side Control—Top
Kimura	Submission (Arm)	Half Guard—Top
Major Pass	Strike	Every Ground Position
Open Guard Takedown	Strike	Open Guard vs. Standing
Rear Naked Choke	Submission (Neck)	Back Mount—Top
Roundhouse Head Kick	Strike	Standing
Submission Chaining	Submission (varies)	After a failed Armbar, Omoplata, Rear Naked Choke, or Triangle
Takedown Fake	Strike	Standing
Teep Kick	Strike	Standing
Triangle Choke	Submission (Neck)	(1) Full Guard—Bottom; (2) Full Guard Postured Up—Bottom; (3) Full Mount Postured Up—Top; (4) Guard Stacked—Bottom

STAND UP STRATEGIES

"Babalu" Sobral is a submission wizard with below-average skill in most other areas of the fight game. This includes the stand up department, where Sobral suffers from a distinct lack of power. Considering he also owns a weak chin, Sobral's stand up is best used to bring the fight to the mat. Unfortunately, "Babalu" doesn't have a great shot, so you'll need to be patient on the feet, using his quick strikes to create openings to shoot in.

Fighting against: Renato Sobral—Stay upright when battling Sobral—his submission game is nasty. Be prepared to stuff his takedowns at any moment as you pick him apart on the feet. Aim for his chin and try to turn his lights out, but be patient and don't give him the chance to work on the floor.

CLINCH STRATEGIES

The clinch is a slightly better place for Sobral than the feet; his strikes gain weight here and his chin is better protected. Sobral has poor control in this position, however, so don't let him rest here for long. Use the clinch to bring the fight to the floor, where submission opportunities abound.

Fighting against: Renato Sobral—Renato's closer to a takedown when you tie up with him, but his sorry control allows clinch specialists to do a number on him in this position. Beating "Babalu" on the feet is always the best plan, but controlling him in a clinch and working him over with strikes can bring the fight to a sudden and dramatic end.

GROUND STRATEGIES

"Babalu" is at his best on the ground, with expert arm and neck submissions, and exceptional grappling defense. Kimuras are his best subs—they're available right after a takedown, so you don't need to worry about passing the opponent's guard (an aspect of the grappling game in which Sobral doesn't shine). Head arm chokes from side control and triangles from guard are also excellent submission options. Be quick to employ Renato's "submission chaining" ability following failed sub attempts to roll the opponent into another submission—and avoid have "Babalu" end up on his back.

Fighting against: Renato Sobral—Sobral is good at applying submissions from various angles and has excellent defense against such moves himself, so rolling with him isn't wise. His poor passing ability makes him somewhat easy to hold down if you score a takedown, however, and ground and pound can be used quite effectively against Renato if your fighter's good at it. Don't even consider hitting the mat with "Babalu" without a ton of grappling defense, however—Sobral's submissions are incredibly dangerous, and with the ability to string them together, he can end your night in a blink.

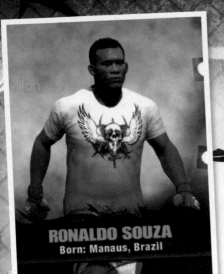

RONALDO SOUZA

"JACARE"

> FIGHT RECORD <

13—2—0 (WIN—LOSS—DRAW) (1 NC)

WINS	LOSSES
10 Submissions (76.92%)	2 (T)KOs (100%)
3 Decisions (23.08%)	

RONALDO SOUZA
Born: Manaus, Brazil

Specialty: Jiu Jitsu

Weight Class: Middleweight

OPPONENT	RESULT	METHOD	DATE	ROUND	TIME
Tim Kennedy	Win	Decision (Unanimous)	8/21/10	5	5:00
Joey Villasenor	Win	Decision (Unanimous)	5/15/10	3	5:00
Matt Lindland	Win	Submission (Arm-Triangle Choke)	12/19/09	1	4:18
Jason Miller	NC	NC (Cut from an Illegal Kick)	5/26/09	1	2:33
Gegard Mousasi	Loss	KO (Upkick)	9/23/08	1	2:15
Zelg Galesic	Win	Submission (Armbar)	9/23/08	1	1:27
Jason Miller	Win	Decision (Unanimous)	6/15/08	2	5:00
Ian Murphy	Win	Submission (Rear Naked Choke)	4/29/08	1	3:38
Wendell Santos	Win	Submission (Punches)	10/13/07	1	1:40
Jose Gomes de Ribamar	Win	Submission (Armbar)	9/29/07	1	3:28
Bill Vucick	Win	Submission (Punches)	5/19/07	1	1:59
Haim Gozali	Win	Submission (Rear Naked Choke)	12/17/06	1	1:33
Alexey Prokofiev	Win	Submission (Triangle Choke)	9/27/06	1	2:30
Alexander Shlemenko	Win	Submission (Arm Triangle Choke)	4/29/06	1	2:10
Victor Babkir	Win	Submission (Punches)	5/15/04	1	0:56
Jorge Patino	Loss	KO (Punch)	9/13/03	1	3:13

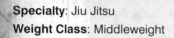

SPECIAL MOVES		
NAME	**TYPE**	**FROM**
Americana	Submission (Arm)	(1) Full Mount Postured Up—Top; (2) Full Mount Tight—Top
Armbar	Submission (Arm)	(1) Full Guard—Bottom; (2) Full Guard Postured Up—Bottom; (3) Side Control—Top; (4) Back Mount Side Turtle—Top
Catch Punch	Parry	(1) Full Guard Postured Up—Bottom; (2) Full Guard Postured Up—Top; (3) Full Mount Postured Up—Top
Darce Choke	Submission (Neck)	Sprawl—Top
Dashing Takedown	Takedown	Standing
Diving Punch	Strike	Standing vs. Open Guard
Guillotine Takedown	Submission (Neck)	Standing
Head Arm Choke	Submission (Neck)	(1) Full Mount Tight—Top; (2) Side Control—Top
Heel Hook	Submission (Leg)	(1) Full Guard Postured Up—Top; (2) Guard Stacked—Top
Inverted Kneebar	Submission (Leg)	Guard Stacked—Bottom
Kimura	Submission (Arm)	Half Guard—Top
Kneebar	Submission (Leg)	Full Guard—Top
Major Pass	Strike	Every Ground Position
Open Guard Takedown	Strike	Open Guard vs. Standing
Rear Naked Choke	Submission (Neck)	Back Mount—Top
Roundhouse Head Kick	Strike	Standing
Spinning Kick	Strike	Standing
Submission Chaining	Submission (varies)	After a failed Armbar, Omoplata, Rear Naked Choke, or Triangle
Takedown Fake	Strike	Standing
Teep Kick	Strike	Standing
Triangle Choke	Submission (Neck)	(1) Full Guard—Bottom; (2) Full Guard Postured Up—Bottom; (3) Full Mount Postured Up—Top; (4) Guard Stacked—Bottom

RONALDO SOUZA

ATTRIBUTES

ATTRIBUTE	MIDDLEWEIGHT
Stand Up	**79**
Foot Speed	90
Hand Speed	88
Kick Combo Speed	85
Kick Range	70
Movement Speed	84
Punch Combo Speed	88
Punch Range	70
Stand Up Left Foot Power	70
Stand Up Left Hand Power	72
Stand Up Right Foot Power	70
Stand Up Right Hand Power	72
Takedowns	90
Takedown Defense	90
Clinch	**86**
Clinch Combo	90
Clinch Control	90
Clinch Strike Speed	90
Clinch Striking Power	75
Ground	**89**
Grapple Defense	99
Ground Combo Speed	88
Ground Get Up	90
Ground Strike Speed	88
Ground Striking Power	75
Passing	99
Submission	**99**
Arm Submissions	99
Leg Submissions	99
Neck Submissions	99
Health	**87**
Blocking	80
Chin	80
Gut	99
Heart	85
Leg Health	99
Stamina Recovery	80

STAND UP STRATEGIES

The Middleweight division's most dominant submission grappler, "Jacare" Souza suffers from a lack of power and reach on the feet, making the stand up his weakest area. Be aggressive with Ronaldo's combos as you look for the takedown.

Fighting against: Ronaldo Souza—When facing a submission master like "Jacare," keeping the fight upright is paramount. Fear his explosive takedowns and be ready to sprawl at a moment's notice. Souza's chin is somewhat suspect, so sling sharp strikes at his head to eventually rock him.

CLINCH STRATEGIES

Souza is a force in the clinch, enjoying excellent striking speed and control. His strikes gain a bit of power here as well, but they remain comparatively weak, so primarily use the position to protect Ronaldo's chin and set up takedowns.

Fighting against: Ronaldo Souza—Steer clear of the clinch battle when facing "Jacare." Strike with caution so you can stuff his attempts to tie you up. Keep the fight standing and look to rock Jacare with precision headshots.

GROUND STRATEGIES

Ronaldo's masterful grappling and submission ability make him the most fearsome Middleweight ground fighter. He knows almost every submission and can apply them with tremendous force. Use Souza's excellent shot to bring the fight to the ground, then use his superior control and "submission chaining" ability to ensure the opponent doesn't get back up.

Fighting against: Ronaldo Souza—Ronaldo's a scary individual when rolling on the ground, so avoid going to the mat. If you find yourself flat on your back, focus on denying his submission attempts and be ready to counter his "submission chaining" ability each time you manage to slip free of a hold. Souza's stamina and ground and pound are slightly below average, so tire him out from the bottom by countering his moves.

SATORU KITAOKA

SATORU KITAOKA
Born: Nara, Japan

Specialty: Jiu Jitsu
Weight Class: Lightweight

> FIGHT RECORD <

26—10—9 (WIN—LOSS—DRAW)

WINS	LOSSES
14 Submissions (53.85%)	3 (T)KOs (30%)
12 Decisions (46.15%)	7 Decisions (70%)

OPPONENT	RESULT	METHOD	DATE	ROUND	TIME
Jorge Rodrigues	Win	Decision (Unanimous)	6/5/10	3	5:00
Jorge Masvidal	Loss	KO (Punches)	11/7/09	2	3:23
Mizuto Hirota	Loss	TKO (Knees)	8/2/09	4	2:50
Yukio Sakaguchi	Win	Submission (Achilles Lock)	6/7/09	1	1:26
Takanori Gomi	Win	Submission (Achilles Lock)	1/4/09	1	1:41
Kazunori Yokota	Win	Decision (Unanimous)	11/1/08	3	5:00
Eiji Mitsuoka	Win	Submission (Heel Hook)	11/1/08	1	1:16
Clay French	Win	Submission (Achilles Lock)	8/24/08	1	0:31
Ian James Schaffa	Win	Submission (Guillotine Choke)	5/18/08	1	0:50
Katsuya Inoue	Loss	Decision (Split)	1/30/08	3	5:00
Jason Palacios	Win	Decision (Split)	9/5/07	3	5:00
Fabricio Monteiro	Win	Submission (Arm Triangle Choke)	4/13/07	2	2:37
Gustavo Picone	Win	Decision (Unanimous)	2/28/07	3	5:00
Ju Pyo Hong	Win	Submission (Achilles Lock)	10/25/06	1	0:24
Paul Daley	Win	Submission (Guillotine Choke)	8/27/06	1	2:54
Daizo Ishige	Loss	Decision (Unanimous)	5/2/06	3	5:00
Tatsunori Tanaka	Win	Submission (Guillotine Choke)	3/19/06	2	2:53
Katsuya Inoue	Draw	Draw	1/26/06	3	5:00
Carlos Condit	Win	Submission (Heel Hook)	10/2/05	1	3:57
Thomas Schulte	Win	Submission (Heel Hook)	7/10/05	1	1:11
Hidehiko Hasegawa	Win	Decision (Split)	3/6/05	3	5:00
Katsuya Inoue	Loss	Decision (Unanimous)	11/7/04	3	5:00
Heath Sims	Draw	Draw	9/24/04	3	5:00
Kurt Pellegrino	Win	Submission (Guillotine Choke)	7/25/04	2	0:34
Takaichi Hirayama	Win	Submission (Guillotine Choke)	5/28/04	2	4:05
Eiji Ishikawa	Loss	Decision (Unanimous)	3/29/04	3	5:00
Tadahiro Hosaka	Draw	Draw	2/15/04	2	5:00
Naoki Seki	Win	Decision (Unanimous)	10/31/03	3	5:00
Yuji Hoshino	Draw	Draw	6/22/03	3	5:00
Takuya Wada	Draw	Draw	4/12/03	2	5:00
Hiroki Nagaoka	Win	Decision (Unanimous)	1/26/03	2	5:00
Taro Minato	Win	Decision (Majority)	10/29/02	2	5:00
Hidetaka Monma	Loss	KO (Knee)	7/28/02	1	0:05
Kenji Arai	Win	Submission (Toe Hold)	7/28/02	3	2:08
Hiroyuki Nozawa	Win	Decision (Unanimous)	7/28/02	2	5:00
Kenji Arai	Win	Decision (Majority)	5/11/02	2	5:00
Koji Oishi	Loss	Decision (Majority)	3/25/02	2	5:00
Hiroki Nagaoka	Draw	Draw	12/1/01	2	5:00
Yohei Ota	Win	Decision (39-38)	10/8/01	2	5:00
Junya Miyakawa	Draw	Draw	8/25/01	2	5:00
Kenichi Serizawa	Draw	Draw	8/15/01	2	3:00
Yuji Hoshino	Loss	Decision (Unanimous)	6/26/01	2	5:00
Kosei Kubota	Draw	Draw	3/31/01	2	5:00
Kazuhito Kikuchi	Win	Decision (Unanimous)	12/9/00	1	10:00
Yoshinori Kawasaki	Loss	Decision (Majority)	10/31/00	1	10:00

SATORU KITAOKA

ATTRIBUTES	
ATTRIBUTE	LIGHTWEIGHT
Stand Up	**74**
Foot Speed	98
Hand Speed	97
Kick Combo Speed	97
Kick Range	70
Movement Speed	99
Punch Combo Speed	98
Punch Range	55
Stand Up Left Foot Power	55
Stand Up Left Hand Power	55
Stand Up Right Foot Power	55
Stand Up Right Hand Power	55
Takedowns	66
Takedown Defense	66
Clinch	**77**
Clinch Combo	95
Clinch Control	71
Clinch Strike Speed	95
Clinch Striking Power	49
Ground	**81**
Grapple Defense	99
Ground Combo Speed	97
Ground Get Up	70
Ground Strike Speed	97
Ground Striking Power	49
Passing	77
Submission	**88**
Arm Submissions	88
Leg Submissions	88
Neck Submissions	88
Health	**88**
Blocking	80
Chin	80
Gut	91
Heart	82
Leg Health	99
Stamina Recovery	99

SPECIAL MOVES		
NAME	TYPE	FROM
Catch Kick	Parry	Standing
Catch Punch	Parry	(1) Full Guard Postured Up—Bottom; (2) Full Guard Postured Up—Top; (3) Full Mount Postured Up—Top
Darce Choke	Submission (Neck)	Sprawl—Top
Dashing Takedown	Takedown	Standing
Diving Punch	Strike	Standing vs. Open Guard
Guillotine Takedown	Submission (Neck)	Standing
Head Arm Choke	Submission (Neck)	(1) Full Mount Tight—Top; (2) Side Control—Top
Heel Hook	Submission (Leg)	(1) Full Guard Postured Up—Top; (2) Guard Stacked—Top
Inverted Kneebar	Submission (Leg)	Guard Stacked—Bottom
Jump Guard Takedown	Takedown	Muay Thai Clinch—Offensive
Kneebar	Submission (Leg)	Full Guard—Top
Major Pass	Strike	Every Ground Position
Rear Naked Choke	Submission (Neck)	Back Mount—Top
Roundhouse Head Kick	Strike	Standing

STAND UP STRATEGIES

Satoru is a decent striker, but the ground is where he wants to fight. His takedown ability is poor, unfortunately, so you'll need to work to bring the action to the floor. Be aggressive, slinging fast combos to set up opportunities to shoot.

Fighting against: Satoru Kitaoka—When fighting against Kitaoka, be careful with your striking and always be ready to stuff his unimpressive takedowns. Target his susceptible chin, hoping to rock him with a lucky shot. He has no special strikes to speak of, which makes his attacks slightly easier to predict and counter.

CLINCH STRATEGIES

Satoru suffers from sorry clinch control, so this isn't an ideal spot for him. Use it to bring the fight to the mat, performing his "jump guard takedown" ability from the offensive Muay Thai clinch to drag his opponent down when you're having difficulty scoring traditional takedowns.

Fighting against: Satoru Kitaoka—The clinch can be worked effectively against Kitaoka, but avoid sacrificing position here or giving up the takedown. Use superior control to keep Satoru in a defensive posture as you sneak in strikes, focusing on cracking his vulnerable chin.

GROUND STRATEGIES

Satoru's ground game is his greatest strength—he boasts excellent grappling defense, along with powerful leg and neck submissions. Kitaoka has no armbars or triangles, but his impressive array of

leg locks make him dangerous while lingering in his opponent's guard. In fact, this is the ideal place to be—fire punches at the opponent while postured up or stacked up in their guard, opening the foe up for heel hooks and kneebars. Satoru's outstanding grappling defense means he has little reason to fear begin submitted from these positions.

Fighting against: Satoru Kitaoka—The ground is the worst place to fight Kitaoka, but if you're using a skilled grappler, consider taking him to the ground and holding him there, exploiting his poor ability to get back to his feet as you score points with tactful ground and pound. Don't let Satoru remain in your guard—he has too many submissions from here. Sweep him or get back to your feet as soon as possible.

SCOTT SMITH
Born: Reno, Nevada

SCOTT SMITH
"HANDS OF STEEL"

▶ FIGHT RECORD ◀

17—7—0 (WIN—LOSS—DRAW) (1 NC)

WINS	LOSSES
14 (T)KOs (82.35%)	3 (T)KOs (42.86%)
3 Submissions (17.65%)	3 Submissions (42.86%)
	1 Decisions (14.29%)

Specialty: Muay Thai

Weight Classes: Light Heavyweight, Middleweight

OPPONENT	RESULT	METHOD	DATE	ROUND	TIME
Cung Le	Loss	KO (Kick to the Body)	6/26/10	2	1:46
Cung Le	Win	KO (Punches)	12/19/09	3	3:25
Nick Diaz	Loss	Submission (Rear Naked Choke)	6/6/09	3	1:41
Benji Radach	Win	KO (Punch)	4/11/09	3	3:24
Terry Martin	Win	KO (Punch)	11/21/08	1	0:24
Robbie Lawler	Loss	TKO (Kicks and Punches)	7/26/08	2	2:35
Robbie Lawler	NC	No Contest (Thumb in the Eye)	5/31/08	3	3:26
Kyle Noke	Win	KO (Punch)	2/16/08	2	0:07
Jeff Morris	Win	TKO	12/22/07	1	0:22
Ed Herman	Loss	Submission (Rear Naked Choke)	6/16/07	2	2:25
Troy Miller	Win	TKO (Doctor Stoppage)	3/22/07	1	1:06
Patrick Cote	Loss	Decision (Unanimous)	2/3/07	3	5:00
Pete Sell	Win	KO (Punch)	11/11/06	2	3:25
David Terrell	Loss	Submission (Rear Naked Choke)	4/15/06	1	3:08
Justin Levens	Win	KO (Punches)	1/13/06	1	1:58
Tait Fletcher	Win	TKO (Punches)	10/14/05	1	3:55
Tim McKenzie	Win	TKO (Punches)	10/14/05	1	2:25
John Seilhan	Win	TKO (Punches)	8/19/04	1	1:29
Isidro Gonzalez	Win	Submission (Rear Naked Choke)	4/17/04	1	4:07
James Irvin	Loss	KO	2/12/04	1	2:21
Jaime Jara	Win	Submission (Rear Naked Choke)	11/13/03	1	3:01
Jaime Jara	Win	KO	6/1/03	1	N/A
Levi Thornbrue	Win	TKO	4/14/02	1	2:20
Tim Kennedy	Win	TKO (Cut)	8/31/01	1	2:53
Ted Stamatelos	Win	Submission (Rear Naked Choke)	6/15/01	1	1:38

SPECIAL MOVES		
NAME	TYPE	FROM
Diving Punch	Strike	Standing vs. Open Guard
Guillotine Takedown	Submission (Neck)	Standing
Major Pass	Strike	Every Ground Position
Overhand Punch	Strike	Standing
Rear Naked Choke	Submission (Neck)	Back Mount—Top
Roundhouse Head Kick	Strike	Standing
Superman Punch	Strike	Standing
Takedown Counter Strike	Strike	Standing
Teep Kick	Strike	Standing

Scott   20/23
SMITH
Specialty   Muay Thai
Record   17-7

STAND UP	CLINCH	GROUND	SUBMISSION	HEALTH
82	83	78	47	82

SCOTT SMITH

ATTRIBUTES		
ATTRIBUTE	LHW	MW
Stand Up	**81**	**82**
Foot Speed	77	86
Hand Speed	84	94
Kick Combo Speed	77	84
Kick Range	80	80
Movement Speed	81	81
Punch Combo Speed	86	96
Punch Range	80	80
Stand Up Left Foot Power	81	77
Stand Up Left Hand Power	90	85
Stand Up Right Foot Power	81	77
Stand Up Right Hand Power	90	85
Takedowns	66	66
Takedown Defense	80	80
Clinch	**78**	**83**
Clinch Combo	82	91
Clinch Control	66	66
Clinch Strike Speed	82	91
Clinch Striking Power	84	84
Ground	**75**	**78**
Grapple Defense	81	81
Ground Combo Speed	82	92
Ground Get Up	71	71
Ground Strike Speed	82	92
Ground Striking Power	80	80
Passing	55	55
Submission	**47**	**47**
Arm Submissions	44	44
Leg Submissions	33	33
Neck Submissions	66	66
Health	**82**	**82**
Blocking	95	95
Chin	71	71
Gut	60	60
Heart	99	99
Leg Health	90	90
Stamina Recovery	77	77

STAND UP STRATEGIES

Smith is a fast puncher with knockout power, but his weak chin and vulnerable body must be taken into account when striking. Scott has excellent blocking ability—be sure to use it when trading with other powerful strikers. Be tactful with Scott's offense, throwing fast hands and leaving few openings for the opponent to grapple or counter your attacks.

Fighting against: Scott Smith—Trading punches with Smith is risky, so use movement to pick him apart with surgical strikes from range. Batter his soft body with kicks and punches, sapping away his unimpressive stamina.

CLINCH STRATEGIES

Smith has poor control in the clinch, so avoid this position when facing strong grapplers. The clinch only puts Scott closer to being taken down, and his vulnerable body is easier to batter while his hands are tied up. Remain on the feet, using Scott's strong blocking to buy time to recover when he's rocked instead of clinching.

Fighting against: Scott Smith—Use the clinch against Smith to neutralize his explosive striking. Attack Scott's body on the feet to get him backing up, then lock horns and stuff him into the cage. Focus on landing body shots in the clinch and dropping Scott with punishing knees to the ribs.

GROUND STRATEGIES

Scott has decent ground and pound, but his lack of mat defense makes the floor a dangerous place for him. Scott also has trouble getting off his back and lacks submission skill, so keep off the mat and go for the knockout on the feet instead, striking with care to avoid being taken down.

Fighting against: Scott Smith—Soften up Scott's body with calculated strikes to get him blocking, then stuff him onto the mat. Smith struggles at returning to his feet, so control him easily on the ground, slipping in body shots as you pass guard on your way to a KO or submission victory.

SHINYA AOKI

"TOBIKAN JUDAN"

SHINYA AOKI
Born: Shizuoka City, Japan

Specialty: Jiu Jitsu

Weight Classes: Welterweight, Lightweight

> FIGHT RECORD <

24—5—0 (WIN—LOSS—DRAW) (1 NC)

WINS	LOSSES
1 (T)KO (4.17%)	3 (T)KOs (60%)
15 Submissions (62.5%)	2 Decisions (40%)
6 Decisions (25%)	
2 Other (8.33%)	

OPPONENT	RESULT	METHOD	DATE	ROUND	TIME
Tatsuya Kawajiri	Win	Submission (Achilles Lock)	7/10/10	1	1:53
Gilbert Melendez	Loss	Decision (Unanimous)	4/17/10	5	5:00
Mizuto Hirota	Win	Technical Submission (Hammerlock)	12/31/09	1	1:17
Joachim Hansen	Win	Submission (Armbar)	10/6/09	2	4:56
Vitor Ribeiro	Win	Decision (Unanimous)	7/20/09	2	5:00
Hayato Sakurai	Loss	TKO (Knees and Punches)	4/5/09	1	0:27
David Gardner	Win	Submission (Rear Naked Choke)	3/8/09	1	5:58
Eddie Alvarez	Win	Submission (Heel Hook)	12/31/08	1	1:32
Todd Moore	Win	Submission (Neck Crank)	9/23/08	1	1:10
Joachim Hansen	Loss	TKO (Punches)	7/21/08	1	4:19
Caol Uno	Win	Decision (Unanimous)	7/21/08	2	5:00
Katsuhiko Nagata	Win	Submission (Gogoplata)	6/15/08	1	5:12
Gesias Cavalcante	Win	Decision (Unanimous)	4/29/08	2	5:00
Gesias Cavalcante	NC	NC (Aoki Injured by Illegal Elbows)	3/15/08	1	3:46
Bu Kyung Jung	Win	Decision (Unanimous)	12/31/07	2	5:00
Brian Lo-A-Njoe	Win	Submission (Armbar)	4/8/07	1	1:33
Akira Kikuchi	Win	Decision (Split)	2/17/07	3	5:00
Joachim Hansen	Win	Submission (Gogoplata)	12/31/06	1	2:24
Clay French	Win	Submission (Flying Triangle Choke)	11/5/06	1	3:57
George Sotiropoulos	Win	DQ (Groin Strike)	10/14/06	2	0:05
Jason Black	Win	Submission (Triangle Choke)	8/26/06	1	1:58
Akira Kikuchi	Win	Decision (Unanimous)	2/17/06	3	5:00
Kuniyoshi Hironaka	Win	TKO (Cut)	11/6/05	1	2:10
Hayato Sakurai	Loss	Decision (Unanimous)	8/20/05	3	5:00
Shigetoshi Iwase	Win	DQ (Low Blow)	7/30/05	1	0:35
Keith Wisniewski	Win	Submission (Standing Armlock)	1/29/05	1	2:22
Jutaro Nakao	Loss	KO (Punch)	10/30/04	1	4:29
Seichi Ikemoto	Win	Submission (Armbar)	7/3/04	2	0:52
Yasutoshi Ryu	Win	Submission (Armbar)	11/24/03	1	0:51
Dai Okimura	Win	Submission (Armbar)	11/24/03	1	3:14

STAND UP STRATEGIES

Shinya Aoki is one of the best submission fighters in MMA, but his stand up game is pretty awful—his reach is short and his strikes are among the weakest you'll find. Shinya wants to be on the ground, but his poor takedown ability can make bringing the fight here a challenge. Be brazen with Aoki's stand up, using his great speed to pressure the opponent until you manage to close in and grapple.

Fighting against: Shinya Aoki—Avoiding the ground game is paramount when facing off against Aoki, so be ready to sprawl against his unimpressive takedowns at all times. Tag Aoki's chin with fast, sharp strikes, looking to rock him as damage to his head piles up.

SHINYA AOKI

ATTRIBUTES

ATTRIBUTE	WW	LW
Stand Up	**73**	**74**
Foot Speed	95	99
Hand Speed	95	95
Kick Combo Speed	95	95
Kick Range	55	55
Movement Speed	99	99
Punch Combo Speed	95	95
Punch Range	55	55
Stand Up Left Foot Power	55	55
Stand Up Left Hand Power	55	55
Stand Up Right Foot Power	55	55
Stand Up Right Hand Power	55	55
Takedowns	71	71
Takedown Defense	81	81
Clinch	**80**	**80**
Clinch Combo	95	95
Clinch Control	80	80
Clinch Strike Speed	95	95
Clinch Striking Power	50	50
Ground	**86**	**86**
Grapple Defense	99	99
Ground Combo Speed	95	95
Ground Get Up	81	81
Ground Strike Speed	95	95
Ground Striking Power	55	55
Passing	95	95
Submission	**95**	**95**
Arm Submissions	99	99
Leg Submissions	88	88
Neck Submissions	99	99
Health	**86**	**88**
Blocking	90	90
Chin	80	81
Gut	90	90
Heart	71	71
Leg Health	90	99
Stamina Recovery	99	99

SPECIAL MOVES

NAME	TYPE	FROM
Americana	Submission (Arm)	(1) Full Mount Postured Up—Top; (2) Full Mount Tight—Top
Armbar	Submission (Arm)	(1) Full Guard—Bottom; (2) Full Guard Postured Up—Bottom; (3) Side Control—Top; (4) Back Mount Side Turtle—Top
Catch Kick	Parry	Standing
Catch Punch	Parry	(1) Full Guard Postured Up—Bottom; (2) Full Guard Postured Up—Top; (3) Full Mount Postured Up—Top
Climbing Armbar	Submission (Arm)	Muay Thai Clinch—Offensive
Darce Choke	Submission (Neck)	Sprawl—Top
Dashing Takedown	Takedown	Standing
Diving Punch	Strike	Standing vs. Open Guard
Gogoplata	Submission (Neck)	Rubber Guard—Bottom
Guillotine Takedown	Submission (Neck)	Standing
Head Arm Choke	Submission (Neck)	(1) Full Mount Tight—Top; (2) Side Control—Top
Heel Hook	Submission (Leg)	(1) Full Guard Postured Up—Top; (2) Guard Stacked—Top
Inverted Kneebar	Submission (Leg)	Guard Stacked—Bottom
Jump Guard Takedown	Takedown	Muay Thai Clinch—Offensive
Kimura	Submission (Arm)	Half Guard—Top
Kneebar	Submission (Leg)	Full Guard—Top
Major Pass	Strike	Every Ground Position
Omoplata	Submission (Arm)	Rubber Guard—Bottom
Open Guard Takedown	Strike	Open Guard vs. Standing
Rear Naked Choke	Submission (Neck)	Back Mount—Top
Roundhouse Head Kick	Strike	Standing
Rubber Guard	Strike	Full Guard—Bottom
Submission Chaining	Submission (varies)	After a failed Armbar, Omoplata, Rear Naked Choke, or Triangle
Takedown Fake	Strike	Standing
Teep Kick	Strike	Standing
Triangle Choke	Submission (Neck)	(1) Full Guard—Bottom; (2) Full Guard Postured Up—Bottom; (3) Full Mount Postured Up—Top; (4) Guard Stacked—Bottom

CLINCH STRATEGIES

Shinya has decent control in the clinch, but his strikes are even weaker here, so the position is best used to score takedowns when your standing shots are being countered. Use Aoki's Muay Thai clinch to perform the rare "climbing armbar" special, dragging opponents to the ground and immediately rolling them into dangerous armbar submissions.

Fighting against: Shinya Aoki—Aoki's "climbing armbar" special means he's able to tap you out from the clinch—an extremely high-level move. Beware this ability and strive to keep clear of his clutch. If Shinya manages to lock up with you, focus on denying his submissions and takedowns to tire him—you don't need to fear his feeble strikes.

GROUND STRATEGIES

Fighting on the ground is a blast when using Aoki. The submission whiz has mastery over every hold in the game and is able to tap his rivals from any position, including their own guard. His exceptional passing ability and grappling defense means he can work into or out of any position he chooses. Should the opponent manage to escape a joint lock or stranglehold, use Shinya's "submission chaining" skill to instantly roll your foe into another death lock. It's only a matter of time before the fight is brought to an end once Aoki gets his man on the mat.

Fighting against: Shinya Aoki—Don't even think of rolling with "Tobikan Judan" on the ground—stay as far away from his grasp as you can and be ever vigilant to stuff his takedowns and clinch attempts. If Aoki manages to drag you down, focus on denying his submissions and guard passes—his strikes aren't powerful enough to concern you unless he throws them in volume. Frustrate Aoki by denying his offensive grappling game until he's forced to open up with ground and pound, then sneak out and return to your feet.

TATSUYA KAWAJIRI
Born: Inashiki, Japan

TATSUYA KAWAJIRI
"CRUSHER"

> **FIGHT RECORD** <
26—6—2 (WIN—LOSS—DRAW)

WINS	LOSSES
11 (T)KOs (42.31%)	1 (T)KO (16.67%)
6 Submissions (23.08%)	3 Submissions (50%)
8 Decisions (30.77%)	2 Decisions (33.33%)
1 Other (3.85%)	

Specialty: Wrestling

Weight Classes: Welterweight, Lightweight

OPPONENT	RESULT	METHOD	DATE	ROUND	TIME
Shinya Aoki	Loss	Submission (Achilles Lock)	7/10/10	1	1:53
Kazunori Yokota	Win	Decision (Unanimous)	12/31/09	3	5:00
Melchor Manibusan	Win	TKO (Punches)	10/6/09	1	3:48
Gesias Cavalcante	Win	Decision (Unanimous)	5/26/09	2	5:00
Ross Ebanez	Win	Submission (Rear Naked Choke)	3/8/09	1	4:03
Eddie Alvarez	Loss	TKO (Punches)	7/21/08	1	7:35
Luiz Firmino	Win	Decision (Unanimous)	5/11/08	2	5:00
Kultar Gill	Win	Decision (Unanimous)	3/15/08	2	5:00
Luiz Azeredo	Win	Decision (Unanimous)	12/31/07	2	5:00
Gilbert Melendez	Loss	Decision (Unanimous)	12/31/06	2	5:00
Per Eklund	Win	TKO (Punches)	10/14/06	1	4:10
Chris Brennan	Win	TKO (Knee and Punches)	8/26/06	1	0:29
Charles Bennett	Win	Submission (Kneebar)	6/4/06	1	2:30
Joachim Hansen	Win	DQ (Kick to Groin)	2/17/06	1	0:08
Takanori Gomi	Loss	Submission (Rear Naked Choke)	9/25/05	1	7:42
Luiz Firmino	Win	Decision (Unaminous)	7/17/05	2	5:00
In Seok Kim	Win	TKO (Corner Stoppage)	5/22/05	1	3:28
Jani Lax	Win	TKO (Punches)	4/23/05	1	4:42
Vitor Ribeiro	Win	TKO (Punches)	12/14/04	2	3:11
Mindaugas Laurinaitis	Win	TKO (Punches)	9/26/04	2	2:00
Caol Uno	Draw	Draw	3/22/04	3	5:00
Ryan Bow	Win	TKO (Punches)	12/14/03	1	4:21
Yves Edwards	Win	Decision (Unanimous)	8/10/03	3	5:00
Takumi Nakayama	Win	TKO (Punches)	5/30/03	1	3:44
Vitor Ribeiro	Loss	Decision (Unanimous)	12/14/02	3	5:00
Ken Omatsu	Win	Submission (Armbar)	10/27/02	1	4:40
Tsutomu Shiiki	Win	Submission (Rear Naked Choke)	7/19/02	1	4:42
Daisuke Sugie	Win	TKO (Punches)	5/28/02	2	4:19
Takeshi Yamazaki	Win	Decision (Unanimous)	4/21/02	2	5:00
Masaya Takita	Win	TKO (Swollen Eye)	3/13/02	2	1:22
Kazumichi Takada	Win	Technical Submission (Triangle Armbar)	9/27/01	1	3:03
Yohei Suzuki	Win	Submission (Rear Naked Choke)	5/22/01	1	2:42
Yohei Suzuki	Draw	Draw	4/8/01	2	5:00
Takumi Nakayama	Loss	Submission (Rear Naked Choke)	4/12/00	1	2:44

TATSUYA KAWAJIRI

ATTRIBUTES

ATTRIBUTE	WELTERWEIGHT	LIGHTWEIGHT
Stand Up	**78**	**76**
Foot Speed	96	96
Hand Speed	97	97
Kick Combo Speed	97	97
Kick Range	70	70
Movement Speed	96	96
Punch Combo Speed	99	99
Punch Range	70	70
Stand Up Left Foot Power	60	54
Stand Up Left Hand Power	60	54
Stand Up Right Foot Power	60	54
Stand Up Right Hand Power	60	54
Takedowns	71	71
Takedown Defense	81	81
Clinch	**81**	**80**
Clinch Combo	95	95
Clinch Control	77	77
Clinch Strike Speed	95	95
Clinch Striking Power	60	54
Ground	**82**	**81**
Grapple Defense	83	83
Ground Combo Speed	97	97
Ground Get Up	81	81
Ground Strike Speed	97	97
Ground Striking Power	60	54
Passing	77	77
Submission	**58**	**58**
Arm Submissions	66	66
Leg Submissions	44	44
Neck Submissions	66	66
Health	**88**	**88**
Blocking	81	81
Chin	90	90
Gut	90	90
Heart	81	81
Leg Health	90	90
Stamina Recovery	99	99

SPECIAL MOVES

NAME	TYPE	FROM
Armbar	Submission (Arm)	(1) Full Guard—Bottom; (2) Full Guard Postured Up—Bottom; (3) Side Control—Top; (4) Back Mount Side Turtle—Top
Catch Punch	Parry	(1) Full Guard Postured Up—Bottom; (2) Full Guard Postured Up—Top; (3) Full Mount Postured Up—Top
Dashing Takedown	Takedown	Standing
Diving Punch	Strike	Standing vs. Open Guard
Head Arm Choke	Submission (Neck)	(1) Full Mount Tight—Top; (2) Side Control—Top
Heel Hook	Submission (Leg)	(1) Full Guard Postured Up—Top; (2) Guard Stacked—Top
Inverted Kneebar	Submission (Leg)	Guard Stacked—Bottom
Kneebar	Submission (Leg)	Full Guard—Top
Major Pass	Strike	Every Ground Position
Overhand Punch	Strike	Standing
Rear Naked Choke	Submission (Neck)	Back Mount—Top
Roundhouse Head Kick	Strike	Standing
Takedown Counter Strike	Strike	Standing
Takedown Fake	Strike	Standing
Teep Kick	Strike	Standing

STAND UP STRATEGIES

Kawajiri is an average Lightweight fighter who finds himself largely outclassed at Welterweight. His stand up is the weakest aspect of his game—use his speed to score fast strikes on your way into the clinch or takedown. Kawajiri has good defensive attributes, so don't worry about mixing things up with other strikers if you think you can exploit a weakness on the feet.

Fighting against: Tatsuya Kawajiri—Keep "Crusher" standing up when fighting him, preventing him from working his clinch game and ground and pound. Stuff his lackluster shots and strike back with your favorite combos. Kawajiri is equally strong in all areas of defense, so pick him apart however you like. Don't worry about Tatsuya's takedowns; they aren't great, and he isn't the most dominant fighter you could have on top of you.

CLINCH STRATEGIES

The clinch is a good place for Kawajiri, but his control could be better here, so only use the position when you're the instigator—defend and break free when your opponent ties you up. Maintain control in the clinch by striking with care, doing a bit of damage as you set up the takedown slam.

Fighting against: Tatsuya Kawajiri—If striking's your game, keep away from the clinch and pick Kawajiri apart on the feet—there's no need to take the fight here. However, if your warrior is a gifted grappler, use the clinch against Tatsuya to work him over and bring him to the mat on your terms.

GROUND STRATEGIES

Bring the fight to the mat when using Kawajiri, but don't feel overly confident down here—there are far better wrestlers than "Crusher" around. Focus on controlling the action from the top, using rapid strikes to set up passing opportunities. Tatsuya has a variety of submissions, but his skill in finishing them is poor—avoid risking submissions, especially leg locks, because failing one can land Kawajiri on his back. Simply strive to score points on the ground by controlling the action and grinding down opponents with strikes.

Fighting against: Tatsuya Kawajiri—Tatsuya's ground game is solid, but not overwhelming. If you're using a gifted grappler, put "Crusher" on his back and then work patiently, wearing him out with strikes as you move for the submission finish. When underneath Kawajiri, focus on countering his passes and returning to your feet instead of worrying over his weak ground strikes.

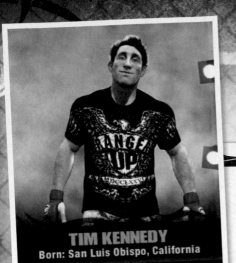

TIM KENNEDY

Born: San Luis Obispo, California

Specialty: Generalist

Weight Classes: Middleweight

> FIGHT RECORD <

12—3—0 (WIN—LOSS—DRAW)

WINS	LOSSES
5 (T)KOs (41.67%)	1 (T)KO (33.33%)
6 Submissions (50%)	2 Decisions (66.67%)
1 Decision (8.33%)	

OPPONENT	RESULT	METHOD	DATE	ROUND	TIME
Ronaldo Souza	Loss	Decision (Unanimous)	8/21/10	5	5:00
Trevor Prangley	Win	Submission (Rear Naked Choke)	6/16/10	1	3:35
Zak Cummings	Win	Submission (North-South Choke)	9/25/09	2	2:43
Nick Thompson	Win	Submission (Punches)	6/19/09	2	2:37
Elias Rivera	Win	KO (Punches)	12/29/07	1	2:00
Jason Miller	Loss	Decision (Unanimous)	12/15/07	3	5:00
Ryan McGivern	Win	Submission (Guillotine Choke)	5/19/07	2	1:25
Dante Rivera	Win	Submission (Punches)	2/23/07	2	2:29
Hector Urbina	Win	KO	9/23/06	1	N/A
Cruz Chacon	Win	TKO (Punches)	2/23/03	2	1:21
Jason Miller	Win	Decision (Unanimous)	2/23/03	3	5:00
Ryan Narte	Win	TKO (Punches)	2/23/03	1	1:22
Mack Brewer	Win	TKO (Punches)	10/18/02	1	1:03
Jody Burke	Win	Submission (Forearm Choke)	11/9/01	1	0:44
Scott Smith	Loss	TKO (Cut)	8/31/01	1	2:53

SPECIAL MOVES		
NAME	**TYPE**	**FROM**
Catch Punch	Parry	(1) Full Guard Postured Up—Bottom; (2) Full Guard Postured Up—Top; (3) Full Mount Postured Up—Top
Darce Choke	Submission (Neck)	Sprawl—Top
Dashing Takedown	Takedown	Standing
Diving Punch	Strike	Standing vs. Open Guard
Guillotine Takedown	Submission (Neck)	Standing
Head Arm Choke	Submission (Neck)	(1) Full Mount Tight—Top; (2) Side Control—Top
Major Pass	Strike	Every Ground Position
Overhand Punch	Strike	Standing
Rear Naked Choke	Submission (Neck)	Back Mount—Top
Roundhouse Head Kick	Strike	Standing
Superman Punch	Strike	Standing
Takedown Fake	Strike	Standing

TIM KENNEDY

ATTRIBUTES	
ATTRIBUTE	MIDDLEWEIGHT
Stand Up	**83**
Foot Speed	88
Hand Speed	90
Kick Combo Speed	88
Kick Range	78
Movement Speed	85
Punch Combo Speed	90
Punch Range	78
Stand Up Left Foot Power	76
Stand Up Left Hand Power	83
Stand Up Right Foot Power	80
Stand Up Right Hand Power	83
Takedowns	88
Takedown Defense	81
Clinch	**82**
Clinch Combo	88
Clinch Control	74
Clinch Strike Speed	88
Clinch Striking Power	78
Ground	**86**
Grapple Defense	95
Ground Combo Speed	88
Ground Get Up	76
Ground Strike Speed	88
Ground Striking Power	85
Passing	84
Submission	**63**
Arm Submissions	66
Leg Submissions	33
Neck Submissions	90
Health	**88**
Blocking	80
Chin	91
Gut	92
Heart	99
Leg Health	90
Stamina Recovery	81

STAND UP STRATEGIES

A well-rounded fighter, Kennedy can end a fight in any position. On the feet, he has good speed and excellent power for a Middleweight—punish the opponent with stiff punches and kicks. Tim also has good takedown ability and can work some brutal ground and pound from the top, allowing you to take the fight wherever you like.

Fighting against: Tim Kennedy—Kennedy's striking power and takedown ability must be respected, so attack with caution on the feet. Use speed and footwork to back him up while remaining ready to stuff his shots. Look to clinch up with Kennedy—he's most vulnerable there.

CLINCH STRATEGIES

The clinch is Tim's weakest area, so it's best to steer clear of this chaotic position. Get things done on the feet or ground instead, blocking the opponent's clinch strikes and breaking away from his grasp whenever he ties you up.

Fighting against: Tim Kennedy—Take the sting out of Kennedy's strikes by clinching up with him to deliver knees and elbows of your own. Focus on controlling the position, respecting Tim's takedown ability by being patient with your strikes. Keep Kennedy tied up to inflict damage, slamming him to the ground when he's forced to block.

GROUND STRATEGIES

Strike with opponents to get them focused on the stand up battle, then quickly change levels and use Tim's strong takedown ability to bring the fight to the mat. Tim has excellent grappling defense, good passing ability, heavy ground and pound, and great choke holds—use these talents to control the opponent as you move to dominant position, landing brutal ground strikes or locking in a nasty choke.

Fighting against: Tim Kennedy—Being stuck beneath Kennedy is no picnic, but he's far less threatening when he's the one on the bottom. When Tim's on top of you, prevent him from passing beyond half guard to limit his offensive options and get back up to your feet. If you manage to slam Kennedy to the mat, work to control him as you land strikes to score points. Tim has great grappling defense, but can have trouble getting off his back. Deny his attempts to sweep you while grinding away with point-scoring strikes.

TIM SYLVIA
"THE MAINE-IAC"

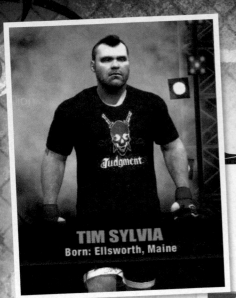

TIM SYLVIA
Born: Ellsworth, Maine

Specialty: Kickboxing

Weight Class: Heavyweight

> FIGHT RECORD <
27—6—0 (WIN—LOSS—DRAW)

WINS	LOSSES
18 (T)KOs (66.67%)	1 (T)KOs (16.67%)
3 Submissions (11.11%)	4 Submissions (66.67%)
6 Decisions (22.22%)	1 Decisions (16.67%)

OPPONENT	RESULT	METHOD	DATE	ROUND	TIME
Paul Buentello	Win	KO (Punch)	8/14/10	2	4:57
Mariusz Pudzianowski	Win	Submission (Punches)	5/21/10	2	1:43
Jason Riley	Win	TKO (Punches)	9/18/09	1	2:32
Ray Mercer	Loss	KO (Punch)	6/13/09	1	0:09
Fedor Emelianenko	Loss	Submission (Rear Nakcd Choke)	7/19/08	1	0:36
Antonio Rodrigo Nogueira	Loss	Submission (Guillotine Choke)	2/2/08	3	1:28
Brandon Vera	Win	Decision (Unanimous)	10/20/07	3	5:00
Randy Couture	Loss	Decision (Unanimous)	3/3/07	5	5:00
Jeff Monson	Win	Decision (Unanimous)	11/18/06	5	5:00
Andrei Arlovski	Win	Decision (Unanimous)	7/8/06	5	5:00
Andrei Arlovski	Win	TKO (Punches)	4/15/06	1	2:43
Assuerio Silva	Win	Decision (Unaminous)	1/16/06	3	5:00
Tra Telligman	Win	KO (Head Kick)	8/20/05	1	4:59
Mike Block	Win	TKO (Punches)	5/21/05	1	1:26
Andrei Arlovski	Loss	Submission (Achilles Lock)	2/5/05	1	0:47
Wes Sims	Win	TKO (Punches)	12/12/04	1	1:32
Frank Mir	Loss	Technical Submission (Armbar)	6/19/04	1	0:50
Gan McGee	Win	TKO (Punches)	9/26/03	1	1:54
Ricco Rodriguez	Win	TKO (Punches)	2/28/03	1	3:09
Wesley Correira	Win	TKO (Corner Stoppage)	9/27/02	2	1:43
Jeff Gerlick	Win	TKO (Punches)	7/27/02	1	3:17
Mike Whitehead	Win	TKO (Knee and Punches)	4/27/02	1	2:38
Jason Lambert	Win	TKO (Doctor Stoppage)	4/27/02	2	4:13
Boyd Ballard	Win	KO (Knee)	4/27/02	1	3:21
Mike Whitehead	Win	TKO (Punches)	4/26/02	1	3:46
Matt Fremmbling	Win	Decision (Unanimous)	3/16/02	2	5:00
Gino De La Cruz	Win	TKO	3/16/02	1	0:43
Ernest Henderson	Win	TKO (Fell out of the Ring)	3/16/02	1	0:29
Greg Wikan	Win	Submission (Choke)	11/17/01	3	2:20
Ben Rothwell	Win	Decision	8/24/01	3	5:00
Greg Wikan	Win	TKO (Towel)	6/2/01	1	5:00
Gabe Beauperthy	Win	Submission (Choke)	4/7/01	2	4:16
Randy Durant	Win	TKO	1/19/01	1	2:05

SPECIAL MOVES
NAME	TYPE	FROM
Diving Punch	Strike	Standing vs. Open Guard
Guillotine Takedown	Submission (Neck)	Standing
Major Pass	Strike	Every Ground Position
Overhand Punch	Strike	Standing
Rear Naked Choke	Submission (Neck)	Back Mount—Top
Roundhouse Head Kick	Strike	Standing
Superman Punch	Strike	Standing
Takedown Counter Strike	Strike	Standing
Teep Kick	Strike	Standing

TIM SYLVIA

ATTRIBUTES	
ATTRIBUTE	HEAVYWEIGHT
Stand Up	**81**
Foot Speed	70
Hand Speed	83
Kick Combo Speed	70
Kick Range	94
Movement Speed	76
Punch Combo Speed	80
Punch Range	99
Stand Up Left Foot Power	88
Stand Up Left Hand Power	91
Stand Up Right Foot Power	88
Stand Up Right Hand Power	87
Takedowns	60
Takedown Defense	73
Clinch	**76**
Clinch Combo	80
Clinch Control	60
Clinch Strike Speed	80
Clinch Striking Power	84
Ground	**71**
Grapple Defense	71
Ground Combo Speed	81
Ground Get Up	70
Ground Strike Speed	81
Ground Striking Power	86
Passing	41
Submission	**48**
Arm Submissions	42
Leg Submissions	33
Neck Submissions	71
Health	**74**
Blocking	80
Chin	81
Gut	97
Heart	66
Leg Health	54
Stamina Recovery	70

STAND UP STRATEGIES

Sylvia's long reach and powerful strikes make him very dangerous on the feet. His clinch game and grappling are weak, however, so strive to keep the fight standing when using Tim. Land long jabs and leg kicks to damage opponents from the outside, remaining constantly guarded against their attempts to clinch with you or slam you to the mat. Sylvia's long legs are highly vulnerable to kicks—look to counter the opponent's leg attacks with fast hooks and straights to potentially rock them.

Fighting against: Tim Sylvia—Striking with a powerful and rangy kickboxer like Sylvia isn't wise, but his shaky legs present a tantalizing target. Batter Tim's stalks with crisp leg kicks, but beware his ability to counter with stiff straights that can rock you. Use leg kicks to give Tim something to think about on the feet, then switch tactics and go for the clinch or a takedown.

CLINCH STRATEGIES

Sylvia's clinch control is abysmal, and being so close to his opponents negates the great reach advantage he often enjoys. Don't bother clinching up with Tim's opponents; use his long strikes to wear down rivals from range on the feet instead.

Fighting against: Tim Sylvia—When you tire of being knocked around by Sylvia's long reach, use movement to slip in and lock up with him. Stuff Tim into the fence and batter him with elbows and knees to the head, controlling the position for as long as possible. The moment he begins to block, plant him on his back with a demoralizing slam.

GROUND STRATEGIES

"The Maine-iac" is one of the worst ground fighters in the Heavyweight division, outdone only by Bob Sapp. He has almost no chance of passing guard, and his sorry ground defense leaves him open to sweeps and submissions. Use Sylvia's excellent reach and striking ability to keep the opponent at bay, making it difficult for him to shoot in with takedowns.

Fighting against: Tim Sylvia—Sylvia likely won't try for takedowns, so you'll be the one instigating the ground game. Use movement and leg kicks on the feet

to put him off balance, creating opportunities to dash in and grapple him to the mat. Tim has little ability to defend himself on his back and even less chance of mounting any offense. Pin Tim down and work him over with strikes as you move to secure the submission victory.

TYRON WOODLEY

"T-WOOD"

TYRON WOODLEY
Born: St Louis, Missouri

Specialty: Wrestling

Weight Class: Welterweight

> FIGHT RECORD <

7—0—0 (WIN—LOSS—DRAW)

WINS
6 Submissions (85.71%)
1 Decision (14.29%)

OPPONENT	RESULT	METHOD	DATE	ROUND	TIME
Nathan Coy	Win	Decision (Split)	5/21/10	3	5:00
Rudy Bears	Win	Submission (Arm Triangle Choke)	11/20/09	1	2:52
Zach Light	Win	Submission (Armbar)	9/25/09	2	3:38
Sal Woods	Win	Submission (Brabo Choke)	6/6/09	1	4:20
Jeff Carstens	Win	Submission (Rear Naked Choke)	4/30/09	1	0:48
Steve Schneider	Win	Submission (Punches)	2/7/09	1	1:09
Alex Carter	Win	Submission (Rear Naked Choke)	2/3/06	1	1:58

SPECIAL MOVES		
NAME	TYPE	FROM
Armbar	Submission (Arm)	(1) Full Guard—Bottom; (2) Full Guard Postured Up—Bottom; (3) Side Control—Top; (4) Back Mount Side Turtle—Top
Catch Kick	Parry	Standing
Catch Punch	Parry	(1) Full Guard Postured Up—Bottom; (2) Full Guard Postured Up—Top; (3) Full Mount Postured Up—Top
Darce Choke	Submission (Neck)	Sprawl—Top
Dashing Takedown	Takedown	Standing
Diving Punch	Strike	Standing vs. Open Guard
Guillotine Takedown	Submission (Neck)	Standing
Head Arm Choke	Submission (Neck)	(1) Full Mount Tight—Top; (2) Side Control—Top
Major Pass	Strike	Every Ground Position
Overhand Punch	Strike	Standing
Rear Naked Choke	Submission (Neck)	Back Mount—Top
Roundhouse Head Kick	Strike	Standing
Superman Punch	Strike	Standing
Takedown Fake	Strike	Standing
Teep Kick	Strike	Standing

TYRON WOODLEY

ATTRIBUTES	
ATTRIBUTE	WELTERWEIGHT
Stand Up	**81**
Foot Speed	90
Hand Speed	95
Kick Combo Speed	90
Kick Range	70
Movement Speed	95
Punch Combo Speed	95
Punch Range	70
Stand Up Left Foot Power	65
Stand Up Left Hand Power	70
Stand Up Right Foot Power	65
Stand Up Right Hand Power	70
Takedowns	90
Takedown Defense	90
Clinch	**87**
Clinch Combo	95
Clinch Control	90
Clinch Strike Speed	95
Clinch Striking Power	70
Ground	**89**
Grapple Defense	90
Ground Combo Speed	95
Ground Get Up	90
Ground Strike Speed	95
Ground Striking Power	75
Passing	90
Submission	**61**
Arm Submissions	75
Leg Submissions	33
Neck Submissions	75
Health	**96**
Blocking	90
Chin	95
Gut	99
Heart	99
Leg Health	99
Stamina Recovery	99

STAND UP STRATEGIES

"T-Wood" is a good Welterweight striker with excellent takedowns—use his striking ability to set up his shots. Woodley has great defense, so don't be afraid to mix things up on the feet. Be aggressive with fast punches, creating openings to shoot in and bring the fight to the floor.

Fighting against: Tyron Woodley—Woodley's weakest area is the stand up game, but you must respect his takedown ability when you fight him here. Pick your shots, remaining light on your feet and ready to deny his attempts at grappling. Woodley's a rugged and durable fighter, so expect to work hard before you break him down.

CLINCH STRATEGIES

Tyron can use the clinch very effectively, shutting down his opponents' offense and placing them in danger of a powerful slam. Employ Woodley's clinch against knockout strikers to dominate them with Tyron's excellent control in this position. Unleash a barrage of strikes the moment you clinch up, planting your opponent on his back the instant he is forced to block.

Fighting against: Tyron Woodley—Steer clear of the clinch game when battling "T-Wood"— the wrestler has too much control in this area. When Tyron ties you up, focus on denying his takedowns as you struggle to break away.

GROUND STRATEGIES

Woodley is at his best when he's on top of his grounded opponent, bashing him with heavy leather. Tyron's the best wrestler in the Welterweight division, so his control is dominant—but he lacks submission skill. Use Woodley's exceptional grappling ability to maintain top position, cracking the opponent with heavy shots to get him blocking before passing his guard. Work your way to mount, then rain down fists and elbows until the fight comes to a dramatic end.

Fighting against: Tyron Woodley—Unless your fighter has extremely poor ground defense, Woodley's submissions aren't worthy of concern. His excellent ground control is another matter— it's tough getting up when Woodley has got you pinned down. Strive to stuff Woodley's takedowns so the fight never comes here, and whenever you're brought to the mat, do your best to prevent Tyron from passing your guard as you look for a chance to scramble back up.

VITOR RIBEIRO

"SHAOLIN"

VITOR RIBEIRO
Born: Rio de Janeiro, Brazil

Specialty: Jiu Jitsu

Weight Class: Lightweight

> **FIGHT RECORD** <

20—4—0 (WIN—LOSS—DRAW)

WINS	LOSSES
2 (T)KOs (10%)	2 (T)KOs (50%)
11 Submissions (55%)	2 Decisions (50%)
6 Decisions (30%)	
1 Other (5%)	

OPPONENT	RESULT	METHOD	DATE	ROUND	TIME
Lyle Beerbohm	Loss	Decision (Split)	5/15/10	3	5:00
Shinya Aoki	Loss	Decision (Unanimous)	7/20/09	2	5:00
Katsuhiko Nagata	Win	TKO (Doctor Stoppage)	4/5/09	1	7:58
Gesias Cavalcante	Loss	TKO (Punches)	9/17/07	1	0:35
Kazuyuki Miyata	Win	Submission (Arm Triangle Choke)	7/16/07	2	1:54
Ryuki Ueyama	Win	Submission (Triangle Armbar)	3/12/07	1	1:48
Daisuke Nakamura	Win	Technical Submission (Straight Armbar)	12/9/06	1	3:55
Abdul Mohamed	Win	Submission (Kimura)	9/30/06	1	4:27
Chris Brennan	Win	Verbal Submission (Swollen Eye)	3/3/06	2	3:25
Eiji Mitsuoka	Win	Decision (Unanimous)	2/4/06	3	5:00
Jean Silva	Win	Submission (Arm Triangle Choke)	9/10/05	2	4:18
Gerald Strebendt	Win	Submission (Guillotine Choke)	7/2/05	1	1:13
Tetsuji Kato	Win	Submission (Arm Triangle Choke)	5/7/05	3	2:32
Tatsuya Kawajiri	Loss	TKO (Punches)	12/14/04	2	3:11
Mitsuhiro Ishida	Win	Decision (Unanimous)	7/9/04	3	5:00
Joachim Hansen	Win	Submission (Arm Triangle Choke)	12/14/03	2	2:37
Ivan Menjivar	Win	Decision (Unanimous)	7/19/03	3	5:00
Ryan Bow	Win	Decision (Unanimous)	5/4/03	3	5:00
Tatsuya Kawajiri	Win	Decision (Unanimous)	12/14/02	3	5:00
Eddie Yagin	Win	Technical Submission (Arm-Triangle Choke)	11/23/02	2	2:23
Hiroshi Tsuruya	Win	Decision (Unanimous)	9/16/02	3	5:00
Joe Hurley	Win	Technical Submission (Arm Triangle Choke)	7/5/02	2	1:19
Takumi Nakayama	Win	Submission (Arm Triangle Choke)	5/25/02	1	0:51
Charlie Kohler	Win	TKO (Cut)	11/3/01	1	3:50

VITOR RIBEIRO

ATTRIBUTES

ATTRIBUTE	LIGHTWEIGHT
Stand Up	**76**
Foot Speed	98
Hand Speed	98
Kick Combo Speed	70
Kick Range	98
Movement Speed	98
Punch Combo Speed	70
Punch Range	52
Stand Up Left Foot Power	52
Stand Up Left Hand Power	52
Stand Up Right Foot Power	52
Stand Up Right Hand Power	52
Takedowns	81
Takedown Defense	80
Clinch	**81**
Clinch Combo	98
Clinch Control	77
Clinch Strike Speed	98
Clinch Striking Power	52
Ground	**87**
Grapple Defense	99
Ground Combo Speed	98
Ground Get Up	84
Ground Strike Speed	98
Ground Striking Power	52
Passing	94
Submission	**84**
Arm Submissions	93
Leg Submissions	66
Neck Submissions	95
Health	**86**
Blocking	82
Chin	86
Gut	95
Heart	81
Leg Health	73
Stamina Recovery	99

SPECIAL MOVES

NAME	TYPE	FROM
Americana	Submission (Arm)	(1) Full Mount Postured Up—Top; (2) Full Mount Tight—Top
Armbar	Submission (Arm)	(1) Full Guard—Bottom; (2) Full Guard Postured Up—Bottom; (3) Side Control—Top; (4) Back Mount Side Turtle—Top
Catch Kick	Parry	Standing
Catch Punch	Parry	(1) Full Guard Postured Up—Bottom; (2) Full Guard Postured Up—Top; (3) Full Mount Postured Up—Top
Dashing Takedown	Takedown	Standing
Diving Punch	Strike	Standing vs. Open Guard
Head Arm Choke	Submission (Neck)	(1) Full Mount Tight—Top; (2) Side Control—Top
Inverted Kneebar	Submission (Leg)	Guard Stacked—Bottom
Kimura	Submission (Arm)	Half Guard—Top
Kneebar	Submission (Leg)	Full Guard—Top
Major Pass	Strike	Every Ground Position
Overhand Punch	Strike	Standing
Rear Naked Choke	Submission (Neck)	Back Mount—Top
Submission Chaining	Submission (varies)	After a failed Armbar, Omoplata, Rear Naked Choke, or Triangle
Takedown Counter Strike	Strike	Standing
Takedown Fake	Strike	Standing
Triangle Choke	Submission (Neck)	(1) Full Guard—Bottom; (2) Full Guard Postured Up—Bottom; (3) Full Mount Postured Up—Top; (4) Guard Stacked—Bottom

STAND UP STRATEGIES

Vitor has blazing speed on the feet, but his striking power is among the weakest in the Lightweight division. His defensive attributes also fail to impress, so don't trade blows on the feet for long. Be aggressive with Vitor, seeking to score a takedown that puts you in position to lock in one his arm-wrenching kimuras.

Fighting against: Vitor Ribeiro—Keep striking when fighting against Ribeiro, stuffing his shots to keep the fight on the feet. Vitor's lack of power makes him less than threatening in the stand up—keep your distance and kick his vulnerable legs out from under him.

CLINCH STRATEGIES

Though Vitor lacks clinch control, he can use the position to help him bring opponents to the mat, where his submission game can overwhelm. Use the clinch to score slams when opponents are countering your stand up shots with knees.

Fighting against: Vitor Ribeiro—Clinching up with Vitor isn't wise—it puts him closer to a takedown, which places you in danger of being quickly submitted. Stay away from the clinch game and keep Ribeiro at bay with rangy leg kicks that will eventually add up to slow him down.

GROUND STRATEGIES

Ribeiro is one of the strongest submission wrestlers in the Lightweight division, so use his speed on the feet to bring the fight to the ground, where he can force the tap with a lightning-fast kimura from half guard, along with plenty of other devious holds. If the opponent foolishly puts you on your back, look for triangles, armbars, and inverted kneebars from the bottom. Keep the action on the ground once you get here and use Vitor's "submission chaining" special to keep his holds rolling.

Fighting against: Vitor Ribeiro—Ribeiro is one of the scariest guys you could roll with in the Lightweight division, so you can never feel comfortable fighting him here. Keep Vitor on his feet and pick him apart with crisp jabs and leg kicks from range, wearing him down to take away from his ability to bring you to the mat. Play defense if Vitor ever gets you down, striving to deny his submissions and looking for any opportunity to get back up again.

VLADIMIR MATYUSHENKO
"THE JANITOR"

VLADIMIR MATYUSHENKO
Born: Retchisa, Belarus

Specialty: Wrestling

Weight Class: Light Heavyweight

> **FIGHT RECORD** <

24—5—0 (WIN—LOSS—DRAW)

WINS	LOSSES
7 (T)KOs (29.17%)	3 (T)KOs (60%)
7 Submissions (29.17%)	2 Decisions (40%)
10 Decisions (41.67%)	

OPPONENT	RESULT	METHOD	DATE	ROUND	TIME
Jon Jones	Loss	TKO (Elbows)	8/1/10	1	1:52
Eliot Marshall	Win	Decision (Split)	3/21/10	3	5:00
Igor Pokrajac	Win	Decision (Unanimous)	9/19/09	3	5:00
Jason Lambert	Win	Decision (Unanimous)	5/16/09	3	5:00
Antonio Rogerio Nogueira	Loss	KO (Knee)	1/24/09	2	4:26
Jamal Patterson	Win	TKO (Punches)	4/4/08	2	3:35
Alex Schoenauer	Win	Decision (Unanimous)	11/3/07	3	4:00
Tim Boetsch	Win	Decision (Unanimous)	8/2/07	3	4:00
Aaron Stark	Win	TKO (Punches)	6/1/07	1	2:49
Justin Levens	Win	TKO (Punches)	3/17/07	1	3:53
Dwayne Compton	Win	Submission (Armbar)	2/2/07	1	1:47
Anthony Ruiz	Win	Submission (Armbar)	6/3/06	1	2:03
Carlos Barreto	Win	TKO (Knee Injury)	5/21/05	1	0:26
Andrei Arlovski	Loss	KO (Punch)	9/26/03	1	1:59
Pedro Rizzo	Win	Decision (Unanimous)	2/28/03	3	5:00
Travis Wiuff	Win	Submission (Punches)	11/22/02	1	4:10
Antonio Rogerio Nogueira	Win	Decision (Unanimous)	8/8/02	3	5:00
Tito Ortiz	Loss	Decision (Unanimous)	9/28/01	5	5:00
Yuki Kondo	Win	Decision (Unanimous)	6/29/01	3	5:00
Tom Sauer	Win	TKO (Cut)	8/26/00	2	2:17
John Marsh	Win	Decision (Unanimous)	3/25/00	3	5:00
Vernon White	Loss	Decision (Split)	10/9/99	1	25:00:00
Travis Fulton	Win	Submission (Neck Crank)	4/2/99	1	15:33
Kenji Kawaguchi	Win	KO (Punches)	10/25/98	1	3:10
Joe Pardo	Win	Decision	9/4/98	3	N/A
Anthony Macias	Win	TKO (Doctor Stoppage)	5/30/98	1	0:16
Anthony Macias	Win	Submission (Punches)	9/5/97	1	2:59
Robert Lalonde	Win	Submission (Punches)	9/5/97	1	2:27
Vernon White	Win	Submission (Neck Crank)	9/5/97	1	5:44

Vladimir 9/19
MATYUSHENKO
Specialty Wrestling
Record 24-5

STAND UP CLINCH GROUND SUBMISSION HEALTH
79 82 80 71 79

Prima Official Game Guide

83 90 87

VLADIMIR MATYUSHENKO

ATTRIBUTES

ATTRIBUTE	LIGHT HEAVYWEIGHT
Stand Up	**79**
Foot Speed	75
Hand Speed	86
Kick Combo Speed	86
Kick Range	75
Movement Speed	80
Punch Combo Speed	86
Punch Range	75
Stand Up Left Foot Power	80
Stand Up Left Hand Power	80
Stand Up Right Foot Power	80
Stand Up Right Hand Power	80
Takedowns	75
Takedown Defense	75
Clinch	**82**
Clinch Combo	86
Clinch Control	78
Clinch Strike Speed	86
Clinch Striking Power	78
Ground	**80**
Grapple Defense	76
Ground Combo Speed	86
Ground Get Up	78
Ground Strike Speed	86
Ground Striking Power	82
Passing	75
Submission	**71**
Arm Submissions	70
Leg Submissions	70
Neck Submissions	75
Health	**79**
Blocking	80
Chin	80
Gut	80
Heart	80
Leg Health	81
Stamina Recovery	75

SPECIAL MOVES

NAME	TYPE	FROM
Armbar	Submission (Arm)	(1) Full Guard—Bottom; (2) Full Guard Postured Up—Bottom; (3) Side Control—Top; (4) Back Mount Side Turtle—Top
Catch Punch	Parry	(1) Full Guard Postured Up—Bottom; (2) Full Guard Postured Up—Top; (3) Full Mount Postured Up—Top
Darce Choke	Submission (Neck)	Sprawl—Top
Dashing Takedown	Takedown	Standing
Diving Punch	Strike	Standing vs. Open Guard
Flying Knee	Strike	Standing
Guillotine Takedown	Submission (Neck)	Standing
Head Arm Choke	Submission (Neck)	(1) Full Mount Tight—Top; (2) Side Control—Top
Major Pass	Strike	Every Ground Position
Overhand Punch	Strike	Standing
Rear Naked Choke	Submission (Neck)	Back Mount—Top
Spinning Backfist	Strike	Standing
Takedown Fake	Strike	Standing
Teep Kick	Strike	Standing

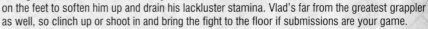

STAND UP STRATEGIES

Vladimir is a veteran Light Heavyweight who can get things done anywhere in a fight, but he doesn't particularly shine in any one area. Play to your opponents' weaknesses when using Matyushenko, taking the fight where they're least likely to overwhelm you with superior skill.

Fighting against: Vladimir Matyushenko—Matyushenko's a purely average striker—batter him with body blows on the feet to soften him up and drain his lackluster stamina. Vlad's far from the greatest grappler as well, so clinch up or shoot in and bring the fight to the floor if submissions are your game.

CLINCH STRATEGIES

Vladimir can get things going in the clinch, but his unimpressive control can allow superior grapplers to overwhelm him here. Use Matyushenko's clinch only if the opponent can be controlled; avoid tying up otherwise by keeping your distance and shooting for takedowns on the feet.

Fighting against: Vladimir Matyushenko—Many Light Heavyweight fighters can control Matyushenko in the clinch, so use the position against him if you feel like roughing him up on the inside. Be wary, though: the clinch places you in greater risk of Vladimir's takedowns, and "The Janitor" has some talent for ground fighting.

GROUND STRATEGIES

Matyushenko's ground game isn't spectacular, but his best position in a fight is on top of his opponent, hammering him with strikes. Unfortunately, Vlad's wrestling abilities are not great—strike tactfully on the mat, focusing on keeping your rival pinned down for as long as possible. Avoid going for submissions unless you're facing a very inexperienced grappler—Vlad isn't great at securing the tap, and failing a sub can land him on his back.

Fighting against: Vladimir Matyushenko—"The Janitor" has some skill at armbars and chokes, but most Light Heavyweight fighters have enough defense to easily avoid these submissions. Vladimir has trouble getting off his back, so feel free to roll with him if you're using a skilled grappler. Take your time on the ground and exploit Matyushenko's lack of defense here by sneaking him into a sub.

ROSTER ATTRIBUTES—LIGHTWEIGHT, CONT.

	EDDIE ALVAREZ	SHINYA AOKI	LYLE BEERBOHM	GESIAS CAVALCANTE	BILLY EVANGELISTA	KRON GRACIE	JOACHIM HANSEN	MIZUTO HIROTA	TATSUYA KAWAJIRI	SATORU KITAOKA	GILBERT MELENDEZ	VITOR RIBEIRO	HAYATO SAKURAI	JOSH THOMSON	AVERAGES
HEALTH	87	88	92	95	83	85	92	96	88	88	94	86	80	89	89
Blocking	56	90	88	90	71	55	90	90	81	80	90	82	71	90	80
Chin	94	81	97	92	77	95	70	99	90	80	92	86	78	90	87
Gut	91	90	91	96	90	95	99	99	90	91	96	95	82	90	93
Heart	98	71	98	99	97	95	99	99	81	82	99	81	78	85	90
Leg Health	90	99	87	99	83	75	99	90	90	99	88	73	77	80	88
Stamina Recovery	96	99	91	99	82	95	99	99	99	99	100	99	99	99	97

CREATE-A-FIGHTER ATTRIBUTES

Reference the following tables to quickly compare the minimum, maximum, and starting attribute scores for created fighters.

BOXING ATTRIBUTES

	HEAVYWEIGHT			LIGHT HEAVYWEIGHT			MIDDLEWEIGHT			WELTERWEIGHT			LIGHTWEIGHT		
	MIN	STARTING	MAX	MIN	STARTING	MAX	MIN	STARTING	MAX	MIN	STARTING	MAX	MIN	STARTING	MAX
STAND UP															
Foot Speed	59	59	81	62	62	84	65	65	86	68	68	89	70	70	89
Hand Speed	68	80	91	71	80	94	73	85	97	75	85	100	75	85	100
Kick Combo Speed	59	59	81	62	62	84	65	65	86	68	68	89	70	70	89
Kick Range	50	50	89	50	50	89	50	50	89	50	50	89	50	50	89
Movement Speed	63	79	84	66	80	88	69	80	92	75	85	100	75	85	100
Punch Combo Speed	68	80	91	71	80	94	73	85	97	75	85	100	75	85	100
Punch Range	75	85	100	75	85	100	75	85	100	75	85	100	75	85	100
Stand Up Left Foot Power	60	60	89	60	60	85	50	50	76	50	50	67	46	46	58
Stand Up Left Hand Power	60	80	95	60	75	90	50	68	81	50	59	71	46	52	62
Stand Up Right Foot Power	60	60	89	60	60	85	50	50	76	50	50	67	46	46	58
Stand Up Right Hand Power	60	80	95	60	75	90	50	68	81	50	59	71	46	52	62
Takedowns	33	33	89	33	33	89	33	33	89	33	33	89	33	33	89
Takedown Defense	33	73	95	33	77	95	33	72	95	33	73	95	33	76	95
CLINCH															
Clinch Combo	68	82	91	71	80	94	73	85	97	75	85	100	75	85	100
Clinch Control	33	80	95	33	80	95	33	80	95	33	78	95	33	80	95
Clinch Strike Speed	68	81	91	71	80	94	73	85	97	75	85	100	75	85	100
Clinch Striking Power	60	80	95	60	79	90	50	70	81	50	59	71	46	52	62
GROUND															
Grapple Defense	33	33	92	33	33	92	33	33	92	33	33	92	33	33	92
Ground Combo Speed	68	81	91	71	80	94	73	83	97	75	85	100	75	85	100
Ground Get Up	33	80	95	33	80	95	33	80	95	33	76	95	33	81	95
Ground Strike Speed	68	81	91	71	80	94	73	85	97	75	85	100	75	85	100
Ground Striking Power	60	80	95	60	80	90	50	70	81	50	59	71	46	51	62
Passing	33	33	89	33	33	89	33	33	89	33	33	89	33	33	89
SUBMISSION															
Arm Submissions	33	33	89	33	33	89	33	33	89	33	33	89	33	33	89
Leg Submissions	33	33	89	33	33	89	33	33	89	33	33	89	33	33	89
Neck Submissions	33	33	89	33	33	89	33	33	89	33	33	89	33	33	89
HEALTH															
Blocking	75	85	100	75	85	100	75	85	100	75	85	100	75	85	100
Chin	33	80	95	33	80	95	33	80	95	33	78	95	33	80	95
Gut	33	80	95	33	80	95	33	80	95	33	78	95	33	80	95
Heart	75	85	100	75	85	100	75	85	100	75	85	100	75	85	100
Leg Health	33	79	95	33	80	95	33	80	95	33	75	95	33	80	95
Stamina Recovery	75	85	100	75	85	100	75	85	100	75	85	100	75	85	100

APPENDIX

BRAWLER ATTRIBUTES

	HEAVYWEIGHT			LIGHT HEAVYWEIGHT			MIDDLEWEIGHT			WELTERWEIGHT			LIGHTWEIGHT		
	MIN	STARTING	MAX	MIN	STARTING	MAX	MIN	STARTING	MAX	MIN	STARTING	MAX	MIN	STARTING	MAX
STAND UP															
Foot Speed	59	59	81	62	62	84	65	65	86	68	68	89	70	70	89
Hand Speed	59	71	86	62	73	89	65	76	92	68	75	95	70	78	95
Kick Combo Speed	59	71	86	62	73	89	65	76	92	68	75	95	70	78	95
Kick Range	50	50	89	50	50	89	50	50	89	50	50	89	50	50	89
Movement Speed	59	59	75	62	62	78	65	65	82	68	68	89	70	70	89
Punch Combo Speed	59	71	86	62	73	89	65	76	92	68	75	95	70	78	95
Punch Range	75	85	100	75	85	100	75	85	100	75	84	100	75	84	100
Stand Up Left Foot Power	60	60	89	60	60	85	50	50	76	50	50	67	46	46	58
Stand Up Left Hand Power	75	85	100	71	81	95	64	72	85	56	64	75	46	55	65
Stand Up Right Foot Power	60	60	89	60	60	85	50	50	76	50	50	67	46	46	58
Stand Up Right Hand Power	75	85	100	71	81	95	64	72	85	56	64	75	46	55	65
Takedowns	33	78	95	33	79	95	33	78	95	33	78	95	33	78	95
Takedown Defense	33	73	95	33	75	95	33	75	95	33	76	95	33	75	95
CLINCH															
Clinch Combo	59	76	86	62	73	89	65	77	92	68	75	95	70	79	95
Clinch Control	75	85	100	75	85	100	75	85	100	75	85	100	75	85	100
Clinch Strike Speed	59	70	86	62	73	89	65	76	92	68	75	95	70	78	95
Clinch Striking Power	75	85	100	71	85	95	64	73	85	56	65	75	49	58	65
GROUND															
Grapple Defense	33	33	92	33	33	92	33	33	92	33	33	92	33	33	92
Ground Combo Speed	59	71	86	62	75	89	65	76	92	68	75	95	70	78	95
Ground Get Up	75	85	100	75	85	100	75	85	100	75	85	100	75	85	100
Ground Strike Speed	59	70	86	62	73	89	65	76	92	68	75	95	70	78	95
Ground Striking Power	75	85	100	71	85	95	64	73	85	56	66	75	49	55	65
Passing	33	33	89	33	33	89	33	33	89	33	33	89	33	33	89
SUBMISSION															
Arm Submissions	33	33	89	33	33	89	33	33	89	33	33	89	33	33	89
Leg Submissions	33	33	89	33	33	89	33	33	89	33	33	89	33	33	89
Neck Submissions	33	80	95	33	78	95	33	78	95	33	75	95	33	78	95
HEALTH															
Blocking	33	78	95	33	70	95	33	78	95	33	75	95	33	78	95
Chin	75	85	100	75	85	100	75	85	100	75	85	100	75	85	100
Gut	75	85	100	75	85	100	75	85	100	75	85	100	75	85	100
Heart	75	85	100	75	85	100	75	85	100	75	85	100	75	85	100
Leg Health	75	85	100	75	85	100	75	85	100	75	85	100	75	85	100
Stamina Recovery	33	65	89	33	65	89	33	65	89	33	65	89	33	65	89

GENERALIST ATTRIBUTES

	HEAVYWEIGHT			LIGHT HEAVYWEIGHT			MIDDLEWEIGHT			WELTERWEIGHT			LIGHTWEIGHT		
	MIN	STARTING	MAX	MIN	STARTING	MAX	MIN	STARTING	MAX	MIN	STARTING	MAX	MIN	STARTING	MAX
STAND UP															
Foot Speed	59	67	86	62	67	89	65	68	92	68	68	95	70	70	95
Hand Speed	59	67	86	62	67	89	65	68	92	68	68	95	70	70	95
Kick Combo Speed	59	67	86	62	67	89	65	68	92	68	68	95	70	70	95
Kick Range	50	67	95	50	67	95	50	68	95	50	66	95	50	65	95
Movement Speed	59	66	80	62	69	84	65	68	87	68	68	95	70	70	95
Punch Combo Speed	59	67	86	62	67	89	65	68	92	68	68	95	70	70	95
Punch Range	50	67	95	50	67	95	50	68	95	50	66	95	50	65	95
Stand Up Left Foot Power	60	60	89	60	60	95	50	50	76	50	50	67	46	46	58
Stand Up Left Hand Power	60	60	89	60	60	95	50	50	76	50	50	67	46	46	58
Stand Up Right Foot Power	60	60	89	60	60	95	50	50	76	50	50	67	46	46	58
Stand Up Right Hand Power	60	60	89	60	60	95	50	50	76	50	50	67	46	46	58
Takedowns	33	67	95	33	66	95	33	69	95	33	65	95	33	65	95
Takedown Defense	33	68	95	33	67	95	33	68	95	33	64	95	33	65	95

GENERALIST ATTRIBUTES, CONT.

	HEAVYWEIGHT			LIGHT HEAVYWEIGHT			MIDDLEWEIGHT			WELTERWEIGHT			LIGHTWEIGHT		
	MIN	STARTING	MAX	MIN	STARTING	MAX	MIN	STARTING	MAX	MIN	STARTING	MAX	MIN	STARTING	MAX
CLINCH															
Clinch Combo	59	65	86	62	67	89	65	68	92	68	68	95	70	71	95
Clinch Control	33	67	95	33	67	95	33	68	95	33	66	95	33	64	95
Clinch Strike Speed	59	67	86	62	67	89	65	68	92	68	68	95	70	70	95
Clinch Striking Power	60	60	89	60	60	85	50	50	76	50	50	67	46	46	58
GROUND															
Grapple Defense	33	67	95	33	67	95	33	68	95	33	66	95	33	65	95
Ground Combo Speed	59	67	86	62	66	89	65	68	92	68	68	95	70	70	95
Ground Get Up	33	67	95	33	66	95	33	68	95	33	63	95	33	65	95
Ground Strike Speed	59	67	86	62	66	89	65	68	92	68	68	95	70	70	95
Ground Striking Power	60	60	89	60	60	85	50	50	76	50	50	67	46	46	58
Passing	33	67	95	33	67	95	33	68	95	33	66	95	33	65	95
SUBMISSION															
Arm Submissions	33	67	95	33	66	95	33	68	95	33	65	95	33	65	95
Leg Submissions	33	67	95	33	66	95	33	68	95	33	65	95	33	65	95
Neck Submissions	33	67	95	33	66	95	33	68	95	33	65	95	33	65	95
HEALTH															
Blocking	33	67	95	33	67	95	33	68	95	33	66	95	33	64	95
Chin	33	67	95	33	66	95	33	68	95	33	65	95	33	65	95
Gut	33	66	95	33	66	95	33	68	95	33	65	95	33	65	95
Heart	33	75	95	33	75	95	33	75	95	33	75	95	33	75	95
Leg Health	33	67	95	33	67	95	33	68	95	33	66	95	33	65	95
Stamina Recovery	75	85	100	75	85	100	75	85	100	75	85	100	75	85	100

JIU JITSU ATTRIBUTES

	HEAVYWEIGHT			LIGHT HEAVYWEIGHT			MIDDLEWEIGHT			WELTERWEIGHT			LIGHTWEIGHT		
	MIN	STARTING	MAX	MIN	STARTING	MAX	MIN	STARTING	MAX	MIN	STARTING	MAX	MIN	STARTING	MAX
Stand Up															
Foot Speed	59	59	81	62	62	84	65	65	86	68	68	89	70	70	89
Hand Speed	59	59	81	62	62	84	65	65	86	68	68	89	70	70	89
Kick Combo Speed	59	59	81	62	62	84	65	65	86	68	68	89	70	70	89
Kick Range	50	50	89	50	50	89	50	50	89	50	50	89	50	50	89
Movement Speed	59	66	80	62	69	84	65	72	87	68	70	95	70	75	95
Punch Combo Speed	59	59	81	62	62	84	65	65	86	68	68	89	70	70	89
Punch Range	50	50	89	50	50	89	65	65	89	50	50	89	50	50	89
Stand Up Left Foot Power	60	60	89	60	60	85	50	50	76	50	50	67	46	46	58
Stand Up Left Hand Power	60	60	89	60	60	85	50	50	76	50	50	67	46	46	58
Stand Up Right Foot Power	60	60	89	60	60	85	50	50	76	50	50	67	46	46	58
Stand Up Right Hand Power	60	60	89	60	60	85	50	50	76	50	50	67	46	46	58
Takedowns	33	77	95	33	78	95	33	76	95	33	75	95	33	77	95
Takedown Defense	33	79	95	33	79	95	33	76	95	33	74	95	33	75	95
CLINCH															
Clinch Combo	59	70	86	62	66	89	65	70	92	68	68	95	70	71	95
Clinch Control	33	70	95	33	68	95	33	70	95	33	60	95	33	55	95
Clinch Strike Speed	59	70	86	62	68	89	65	70	92	68	68	95	70	70	95
Clinch Striking Power	60	70	95	60	68	90	50	60	81	50	50	71	46	46	62
GROUND															
Grapple Defense	75	85	100	75	85	100	75	85	100	75	85	100	75	85	100
Ground Combo Speed	59	70	86	62	68	89	65	70	92	68	68	95	70	70	95
Ground Get Up	33	70	95	33	68	95	33	78	95	33	74	95	33	60	95
Ground Strike Speed	59	70	86	62	68	89	65	70	92	68	68	95	70	70	95
Ground Striking Power	60	70	95	60	68	90	50	60	81	50	50	71	46	46	62
Passing	75	85	100	75	85	100	75	85	100	75	85	100	75	85	100
SUBMISSION															
Arm Submissions	75	85	100	75	85	100	75	85	100	75	85	100	75	85	100
Leg Submissions	75	85	100	75	85	100	75	85	100	75	85	100	75	85	100
Neck Submissions	75	85	100	75	85	100	75	85	100	75	85	100	75	85	100

APPENDIX

JIU JITSU ATTRIBUTES, CONT.

	HEAVYWEIGHT			LIGHT HEAVYWEIGHT			MIDDLEWEIGHT			WELTERWEIGHT			LIGHTWEIGHT		
	MIN	STARTING	MAX	MIN	STARTING	MAX	MIN	STARTING	MAX	MIN	STARTING	MAX	MIN	STARTING	MAX
HEALTH															
Blocking	33	70	95	33	68	95	33	70	95	33	65	95	33	61	95
Chin	33	33	89	33	33	89	33	33	89	33	33	89	33	33	89
Gut	33	33	89	33	33	89	33	33	89	33	33	89	33	33	89
Heart	33	78	95	33	75	95	33	75	95	33	75	95	33	75	95
Leg Health	33	72	95	33	68	95	33	75	95	33	60	95	33	65	95
Stamina Recovery	75	85	100	75	84	100	75	84	100	75	83	100	75	82	100

JUDO ATTRIBUTES

	HEAVYWEIGHT			LIGHT HEAVYWEIGHT			MIDDLEWEIGHT			WELTERWEIGHT			LIGHTWEIGHT		
	MIN	STARTING	MAX	MIN	STARTING	MAX	MIN	STARTING	MAX	MIN	STARTING	MAX	MIN	STARTING	MAX
STAND UP															
Foot Speed	59	59	81	62	62	84	65	65	86	68	68	89	70	70	89
Hand Speed	59	59	81	62	62	84	65	65	86	68	68	89	70	70	89
Kick Combo Speed	59	59	81	62	62	84	65	65	86	68	68	89	70	70	89
Kick Range	50	50	89	50	50	89	50	50	89	50	50	89	50	50	89
Movement Speed	59	66	80	62	69	84	65	74	87	68	75	95	70	77	95
Punch Combo Speed	59	59	81	62	62	84	65	65	86	68	68	89	70	70	89
Punch Range	50	50	89	50	50	89	50	50	89	50	50	89	50	50	89
Stand Up Left Foot Power	60	78	95	60	74	90	50	66	81	50	59	71	46	51	62
Stand Up Left Hand Power	60	78	95	60	74	90	50	66	81	50	59	71	46	51	62
Stand Up Right Foot Power	60	78	95	60	74	90	50	66	81	50	59	71	46	51	62
Stand Up Right Hand Power	60	78	95	60	74	90	50	66	81	50	59	71	46	51	62
Takedowns	75	84	100	75	85	100	75	82	100	75	83	100	75	85	100
Takedown Defense	75	85	100	75	83	100	75	80	100	75	84	100	75	83	100
CLINCH															
Clinch Combo	59	71	86	62	71	89	65	70	92	68	71	95	70	71	95
Clinch Control	75	85	100	75	85	100	75	85	100	75	85	100	75	85	100
Clinch Strike Speed	59	71	86	62	72	89	65	70	92	68	71	95	70	71	95
Clinch Striking Power	60	60	89	60	60	85	50	50	76	50	50	67	46	46	58
GROUND															
Grapple Defense	75	85	100	75	85	100	75	85	100	75	85	100	75	85	100
Ground Combo Speed	68	77	91	71	80	94	73	82	97	75	85	100	75	85	100
Ground Get Up	33	75	95	33	75	95	33	76	95	33	75	95	33	75	95
Ground Strike Speed	68	77	91	71	80	94	73	82	97	75	85	100	75	85	100
Ground Striking Power	75	85	100	71	81	95	66	72	86	56	60	75	46	55	65
Passing	75	85	100	75	85	100	75	85	100	75	85	100	75	85	100
SUBMISSION															
Arm Submissions	33	75	95	33	75	95	33	75	95	33	75	95	33	78	95
Leg Submissions	33	33	89	33	33	89	33	33	89	33	33	89	33	33	89
Neck Submissions	33	75	95	33	75	95	33	75	95	33	75	95	33	75	95
HEALTH															
Blocking	33	33	89	33	33	89	33	33	89	33	33	89	33	33	89
Chin	33	33	89	33	33	89	33	33	89	33	33	89	33	33	89
Gut	33	70	95	33	71	95	33	75	95	33	70	95	33	70	95
Heart	33	75	95	33	75	95	33	75	95	33	75	95	33	78	95
Leg Health	33	33	89	33	33	89	33	33	89	33	33	89	33	33	89
Stamina Recovery	33	71	95	33	71	95	33	71	95	33	69	95	33	71	95

www.primagames.com

KICKBOXING ATTRIBUTES

	HEAVYWEIGHT			LIGHT HEAVYWEIGHT			MIDDLEWEIGHT			WELTERWEIGHT			LIGHTWEIGHT		
	MIN	STARTING	MAX	MIN	STARTING	MAX	MIN	STARTING	MAX	MIN	STARTING	MAX	MIN	STARTING	MAX
STAND UP															
Foot Speed	68	77	91	71	80	94	73	82	97	75	85	100	75	85	100
Hand Speed	59	71	86	62	73	89	65	76	92	68	75	95	70	78	95
Kick Combo Speed	68	77	91	71	80	94	73	82	97	75	85	100	75	85	100
Kick Range	75	85	100	75	85	100	75	84	100	75	85	100	75	85	100
Movement Speed	59	66	80	62	69	84	65	72	87	68	75	95	70	78	95
Punch Combo Speed	59	70	86	62	73	89	65	76	92	68	75	95	70	78	95
Punch Range	50	75	95	50	77	95	50	78	95	50	75	95	50	78	95
Stand Up Left Foot Power	75	85	100	71	81	95	64	72	85	56	64	75	49	55	65
Stand Up Left Hand Power	60	78	95	60	74	90	50	66	81	50	59	71	46	51	62
Stand Up Right Foot Power	75	85	100	71	81	95	64	72	85	56	64	75	49	55	65
Stand Up Right Hand Power	60	78	95	60	74	90	50	64	81	50	59	71	46	51	62
Takedowns	33	33	89	33	33	89	33	33	89	33	33	89	33	33	89
Takedown Defense	75	83	100	75	84	100	75	85	100	75	83	100	75	84	100
CLINCH															
Clinch Combo	59	70	86	62	71	89	65	76	92	68	72	95	70	77	95
Clinch Control	33	33	89	33	33	89	33	33	89	33	33	89	33	33	89
Clinch Strike Speed	59	70	86	62	70	89	65	75	92	68	71	95	70	78	95
Clinch Striking Power	60	60	89	60	60	85	50	50	76	50	50	67	46	46	58
GROUND															
Grapple Defense	33	33	92	33	33	92	33	33	92	33	33	92	33	33	92
Ground Combo Speed	59	70	86	62	70	89	65	75	92	68	75	95	70	78	95
Ground Get Up	33	75	95	33	75	95	33	75	95	33	75	95	33	78	95
Ground Strike Speed	59	70	86	62	70	89	65	75	92	68	75	95	70	78	95
Ground Striking Power	60	75	95	60	70	90	50	66	81	50	59	71	46	51	62
Passing	33	33	89	33	33	89	33	33	89	33	33	89	33	33	89
SUBMISSION															
Arm Submissions	33	33	89	33	33	89	33	33	89	33	33	89	33	33	89
Leg Submissions	33	33	89	33	33	89	33	33	89	33	33	89	33	33	89
Neck Submissions	33	33	89	33	33	89	33	33	89	33	33	89	33	33	89
HEALTH															
Blocking	75	85	100	75	85	100	75	85	100	75	85	100	75	85	100
Chin	33	75	95	33	75	95	33	75	95	33	75	95	33	78	95
Gut	33	75	95	33	77	95	33	75	95	33	75	95	33	78	95
Heart	33	75	95	33	78	95	33	75	95	33	75	95	33	78	95
Leg Health	75	85	100	75	85	100	75	85	100	75	85	100	75	85	100
Stamina Recovery	75	85	100	75	85	100	75	84	100	75	85	100	75	85	100

MUAY THAI ATTRIBUTES

	HEAVYWEIGHT			LIGHT HEAVYWEIGHT			MIDDLEWEIGHT			WELTERWEIGHT			LIGHTWEIGHT		
	MIN	STARTING	MAX	MIN	STARTING	MAX	MIN	STARTING	MAX	MIN	STARTING	MAX	MIN	STARTING	MAX
STAND UP															
Foot Speed	68	76	91	71	80	94	73	82	97	75	85	100	75	85	100
Hand Speed	59	71	86	62	73	89	65	76	92	68	76	95	70	78	95
Kick Combo Speed	59	72	86	62	75	89	65	77	92	68	78	95	70	78	95
Kick Range	75	85	100	75	85	100	75	85	100	75	85	100	75	85	100
Movement Speed	59	69	80	62	71	84	65	75	87	68	78	95	70	78	95
Punch Combo Speed	59	59	81	62	62	84	65	65	86	68	68	89	70	70	89
Punch Range	50	78	95	50	78	95	50	78	95	50	78	95	50	78	95
Stand Up Left Foot Power	75	85	100	71	81	95	64	72	85	56	64	75	49	56	65
Stand Up Left Hand Power	60	60	89	60	60	85	50	50	76	50	50	67	46	46	58
Stand Up Right Foot Power	75	85	100	71	81	95	64	72	85	56	64	75	49	56	65
Stand Up Right Hand Power	60	60	89	60	60	85	50	50	76	50	50	67	46	46	58
Takedowns	33	33	89	33	33	89	33	33	89	33	33	89	33	33	89
Takedown Defense	33	75	95	33	73	95	33	75	95	33	76	95	33	75	95

APPENDIX

MUAY THAI ATTRIBUTES, CONT.

	HEAVYWEIGHT			LIGHT HEAVYWEIGHT			MIDDLEWEIGHT			WELTERWEIGHT			LIGHTWEIGHT		
	MIN	STARTING	MAX	MIN	STARTING	MAX	MIN	STARTING	MAX	MIN	STARTING	MAX	MIN	STARTING	MAX
CLINCH															
Clinch Combo	68	85	91	71	85	94	73	86	97	75	85	100	75	85	100
Clinch Control	75	85	100	75	85	100	75	85	100	75	85	100	75	85	100
Clinch Strike Speed	68	85	91	71	85	94	73	85	97	75	85	100	75	85	100
Clinch Striking Power	75	85	100	71	85	95	64	80	85	56	65	75	49	60	65
GROUND															
Grapple Defense	33	33	92	33	33	92	33	33	92	33	33	92	33	33	92
Ground Combo Speed	59	72	86	62	73	89	65	78	92	68	75	95	70	78	95
Ground Get Up	33	79	95	33	78	95	33	78	95	33	74	95	70	77	95
Ground Strike Speed	59	72	86	62	73	89	65	78	92	68	75	95	70	78	95
Ground Striking Power	60	78	95	60	74	90	50	66	81	50	59	71	46	51	62
Passing	33	33	89	33	33	89	33	33	89	33	33	89	33	33	89
SUBMISSION															
Arm Submissions	33	33	89	33	33	89	33	33	89	33	33	89	33	33	89
Leg Submissions	33	33	89	33	33	89	33	33	89	33	33	89	33	33	89
Neck Submissions	33	33	89	33	33	89	33	33	89	33	33	89	33	33	89
HEALTH															
Blocking	33	80	95	33	80	95	33	80	95	33	75	95	33	78	95
Chin	75	85	100	75	85	100	75	85	100	75	85	100	75	85	100
Gut	33	80	95	33	80	95	33	80	95	33	78	95	33	79	95
Heart	33	80	95	33	80	95	33	79	95	33	77	95	33	78	95
Leg Health	75	85	100	75	85	100	75	85	100	75	85	100	75	85	100
Stamina Recovery	33	79	95	33	78	95	33	78	95	33	78	95	33	79	95

SAMBO ATTRIBUTES

	HEAVYWEIGHT			LIGHT HEAVYWEIGHT			MIDDLEWEIGHT			WELTERWEIGHT			LIGHTWEIGHT		
	MIN	STARTING	MAX	MIN	STARTING	MAX	MIN	STARTING	MAX	MIN	STARTING	MAX	MIN	STARTING	MAX
STAND UP															
Foot Speed	59	59	81	62	62	84	65	65	86	68	68	89	70	70	89
Hand Speed	59	71	86	62	73	89	65	76	92	68	76	95	70	78	95
Kick Combo Speed	59	59	81	62	62	84	65	65	86	68	68	89	70	70	89
Kick Range	50	50	89	50	50	89	50	50	89	50	50	89	50	50	89
Movement Speed	59	66	80	62	69	84	65	72	87	68	75	95	70	78	95
Punch Combo Speed	59	71	86	62	73	89	65	76	92	68	78	95	70	78	95
Punch Range	50	78	95	50	78	95	50	79	95	50	79	95	50	78	95
Stand Up Left Foot Power	60	60	89	60	60	85	50	50	76	50	50	67	46	46	58
Stand Up Left Hand Power	60	78	95	60	74	90	50	66	81	50	59	71	46	51	62
Stand Up Right Foot Power	60	60	89	60	60	85	50	50	76	50	50	67	46	46	58
Stand Up Right Hand Power	60	78	95	60	74	90	50	66	81	50	59	71	46	51	62
Takedowns	75	85	100	75	85	100	75	85	100	75	83	100	75	86	100
Takedown Defense	75	84	100	75	85	100	75	85	100	75	83	100	75	85	100
CLINCH															
Clinch Combo	59	71	86	62	73	89	65	77	92	68	74	95	70	75	95
Clinch Control	75	85	100	75	85	100	75	85	100	75	85	100	75	85	100
Clinch Strike Speed	59	71	86	62	73	89	65	77	92	68	74	95	70	78	95
Clinch Striking Power	60	60	89	60	60	85	50	50	76	50	50	67	46	46	58
GROUND															
Grapple Defense	75	85	100	75	85	100	76	85	100	75	85	100	75	85	100
Ground Combo Speed	59	70	86	62	70	89	65	75	92	68	75	95	70	75	95
Ground Get Up	33	70	95	33	74	95	33	79	95	33	75	95	33	74	95
Ground Strike Speed	59	70	86	62	70	89	65	75	92	68	75	95	70	75	95
Ground Striking Power	60	75	95	60	70	90	50	66	81	50	59	71	46	51	62
Passing	75	85	100	75	85	100	75	85	100	75	85	100	75	85	100
SUBMISSION															
Arm Submissions	75	85	100	75	85	100	75	85	100	75	85	100	75	85	100
Leg Submissions	75	85	100	75	85	100	75	85	100	75	85	100	75	85	100
Neck Submissions	33	33	89	33	33	89	33	33	89	33	33	89	33	33	89

SAMBO ATTRIBUTES, CONT.

	HEAVYWEIGHT			LIGHT HEAVYWEIGHT			MIDDLEWEIGHT			WELTERWEIGHT			LIGHTWEIGHT		
	MIN	STARTING	MAX	MIN	STARTING	MAX	MIN	STARTING	MAX	MIN	STARTING	MAX	MIN	STARTING	MAX
HEALTH															
Blocking	33	33	89	33	33	89	33	33	89	33	33	89	33	33	89
Chin	33	33	89	33	33	89	33	33	89	33	33	89	33	33	89
Gut	33	78	95	33	75	95	33	75	95	33	70	95	33	75	95
Heart	33	78	95	33	75	95	33	75	95	33	75	95	33	75	95
Leg Health	33	33	89	33	33	89	33	33	89	33	33	89	33	33	89
Stamina Recovery	33	78	95	33	78	95	33	76	95	33	73	95	33	73	95

WRESTLING ATTRIBUTES

	HEAVYWEIGHT			LIGHT HEAVYWEIGHT			MIDDLEWEIGHT			WELTERWEIGHT			LIGHTWEIGHT		
	MIN	STARTING	MAX	MIN	STARTING	MAX	MIN	STARTING	MAX	MIN	STARTING	MAX	MIN	STARTING	MAX
STAND UP															
Foot Speed	59	59	81	62	62	84	65	65	86	68	68	89	70	70	89
Hand Speed	59	70	86	62	70	89	65	70	92	68	70	95	70	70	95
Kick Combo Speed	59	59	81	62	62	84	65	65	86	68	68	89	70	70	89
Kick Range	50	50	89	50	50	89	50	50	89	50	50	89	50	50	89
Movement Speed	59	66	80	62	69	84	65	70	87	68	75	95	70	72	95
Punch Combo Speed	59	70	86	62	70	89	65	70	92	68	70	95	70	70	95
Punch Range	50	69	95	50	70	95	50	70	95	50	70	95	50	71	95
Stand Up Left Foot Power	60	60	89	60	60	85	50	50	76	50	50	67	46	46	58
Stand Up Left Hand Power	60	70	95	60	70	90	50	65	81	50	59	71	46	51	62
Stand Up Right Foot Power	60	60	89	60	60	85	50	50	76	50	50	67	46	46	58
Stand Up Right Hand Power	60	70	95	60	70	90	50	65	81	50	59	71	46	51	62
Takedowns	75	85	100	75	84	100	75	85	100	75	83	100	75	85	100
Takedown Defense	75	85	100	75	85	100	75	85	100	75	85	100	75	85	100
CLINCH															
Clinch Combo	68	77	91	71	80	94	73	81	97	75	85	100	75	85	100
Clinch Control	75	85	100	75	85	100	75	85	100	75	85	100	75	85	100
Clinch Strike Speed	59	73	86	62	69	89	65	76	92	68	75	95	70	71	95
Clinch Striking Power	75	85	100	71	81	95	64	72	85	56	60	75	49	55	65
GROUND															
Grapple Defense	75	85	100	75	85	100	75	85	100	75	85	100	75	85	100
Ground Combo Speed	68	75	91	71	80	94	73	82	97	75	85	100	75	85	100
Ground Get Up	33	75	95	33	75	95	33	72	95	33	68	95	33	75	95
Ground Strike Speed	68	77	91	71	80	94	73	82	97	75	85	100	75	85	100
Ground Striking Power	75	85	100	71	81	95	64	72	85	56	60	75	49	55	65
Passing	75	85	100	75	85	100	75	85	100	75	85	100	75	85	100
SUBMISSION															
Arm Submissions	33	33	89	33	33	89	33	33	89	33	33	89	33	33	89
Leg Submissions	33	33	89	33	33	89	33	33	89	33	33	89	33	33	89
Neck Submissions	33	75	95	33	75	95	33	70	95	33	70	95	33	75	95
HEALTH															
Blocking	33	33	89	33	33	89	33	33	89	33	33	89	33	33	89
Chin	33	33	89	33	33	89	33	33	89	33	33	89	33	33	89
Gut	33	72	95	33	69	95	33	70	95	33	70	95	33	70	95
Heart	33	75	95	33	75	95	33	75	95	33	75	95	33	75	95
Leg Health	33	33	89	33	33	89	33	33	89	33	33	89	33	33	89
Stamina Recovery	75	85	100	75	83	100	75	85	100	75	81	100	75	82	100

APPENDIX

CAREER MODE EXERCISES

Use this informative table to help you quickly identify the ideal training sessions for your Career fighters.

TRAINING EXERCISES

EXERCISE	MAJOR BENEFITS	MINOR BENEFITS	ELITE MMA (BAS)	INTERNATIONAL JIU JITSU	MILETICH FIGHTING SYSTEMS	XTREME COUTURE	BUSHIDO CLUB	BALLISTIC BOXING	EIGHT VENOMS	INFERNO INTERNATIONAL GYM
STAND UP										
Blocking and Parry 1	Chin	Blocking, Gut, Leg Health	X		X	X		X	X	
Blocking and Parry 2	Gut, Blocking	Chin, Leg Health			X	X		X	X	
Blocking and Parry 3	Leg Health, Blocking	Chin, Gut			X			X	X	
Blocking and Parry 4	Blocking	Chin, Gut, Leg Health						X		
Boxing Combo 1	Punch Combo Speed	Punch Range, Stand Up Left Hand Power, Stand Up Right Hand Power, Hand Speed	X		X	X		X	X	
Boxing Combo 2	Hand Speed	Stand Up Left Hand Power, Stand Up Right Hand Power, Punch Combo Speed, Punch Range			X	X		X	X	
Boxing Combo 3	Stand Up Left Hand Power	Hand Speed, Punch Combo Speed, Stand Up Right Hand Power, Punch Range			X			X	X	
Boxing Combo 4	Stand Up Right Hand Power	Stand Up Left Hand Power, Hand Speed, Punch Combo Speed, Punch Range						X		
Movement and Range 1	None	Movement Speed, Stamina Recovery, Punch Range, Kick Range	X	X	X			X	X	
Movement and Range 2	Movement Speed, Kick Range	Punch Range, Stamina Recovery		X	X			X	X	
Movement and Range 3	Movement Speed, Punch Range	Kick Range, Stamina Recovery			X			X	X	
Movement and Range 4	Movement Speed	Punch Range, Kick Range, Stamina Recovery							X	
Kick Boxing Combo 1	Kick Combo Speed	Kick Range, Stand Up Left Foot Power, Stand Up Right Foot Power, Foot Speed	X		X		X		X	
Kick Boxing Combo 2	Foot Speed	Stand Up Left Foot Power, Stand Up Right Foot Power, Kick Combo Speed, Kick Range			X		X		X	
Kick Boxing Combo 3	Stand Up Left Foot Power	Food Speed, Kick Combo Speed, Stand Up Right Foot Power, Kick Range.			X				X	
Kick Boxing Combo 4	Stand Up Right Foot Power	Stand Up Left Foot Power, Foot Speed, Kick Range, Kick Combo Speed							X	
Takedown Defense 1	Ground Get Up	Takedown Defense, Stamina Recovery, Takedowns	X			X	X	X	X	
Takedown Defense 2	Ground Get Up, Takedown Defense	Takedowns, Stamina Recovery				X	X	X	X	
Takedown Defense 3	Takedown Defense	Ground Get Up, Stamina Recovery, Takedowns					X	X	X	
Takedown Defense 4	Takedown Defense	Ground Get Up, Stamina Recovery, Takedowns						X		
CLINCH										
Clinch Combo 1	Clinch Combo, Clinch Striking Power	Clinch Striking Power, Clinch Strike Speed, Stamina Recovery	X		X	X		X	X	
Clinch Combo 2	Clinch Strike Speed, Clinch Striking Power	Stamina Recovery, Clinch Combo			X	X		X	X	
Clinch Combo 3	Clinch Striking Power, Clinch Strike Speed, Clinch Combo	Stamina Recovery			X			X	X	
Clinch Combo 4	Clinch Striking Power	Clinch Strike Speed, Clinch Combo, Stamina Recovery							X	
Clinch Control 1	Clinch Control	Clinch Control, Stamina Recovery	X				X	X	X	
Clinch Control 2	Clinch Control	Stamina Recovery					X	X	X	
Clinch Control 3	Clinch Control	Stamina Recovery							X	
GROUND										
Grappling 1	Grapple Defense	Passing, Stamina Recovery	X	X			X	X		X
Grappling 2	Grapple Defense, Passing	Stamina Recovery		X			X	X		X
Grappling 3	Passing	Grapple Defense, Stamina Recovery					X			X
Grappling 4	Passing	Grapple Defense, Stamina Recovery								X
Ground Combos 1	Ground Combo Speed	Ground Striking Power, Ground Strike Speed, Stamina Recovery	X		X	X		X		X
Ground Combos 2	Ground Striking Speed, Ground Striking Power	Ground Combo Speed, Stamina Recovery			X	X		X		X
Ground Combos 3	Ground Striking Power, Ground Strike Speed	Ground Combo Speed, Stamina Recovery			X			X		X
Ground Combos 4	Ground Striking Power	Ground Strike Speed, Ground Combo Speed, Stamina Recovery						X		
Takedowns 1	None	Takedowns, Stamina Recovery, Takedown Defense		X			X			X
Takedowns 2	Takedowns	Stamina Recovery, Takedown Defense		X			X			X
Takedowns 3	Takedowns	Stamina Recovery, Takedown Defense		X			X			X
Takedowns 4	Takedowns	Stamina Recovery, Takedown Defense					X			
SUBMISSIONS										
Arm Submissions 1	None	Arm Submissions, Grapple Defense, Stamina Recovery	X	X				X		X
Arm Submissions 2	Arm Submissions	Grapple Defense, Stamina Recovery		X				X		X
Arm Submissions 3	Arm Submissions	Grapple Defense, Stamina Recovery		X						X
Choke Submissions 1	None	Neck Submissions, Grapple Defense, Stamina Recovery	X	X				X		X
Choke Submissions 2	Neck Submissions	Grapple Defense, Stamina Recovery		X				X		X
Choke Submissions 3	Neck Submissions	Grapple Defense, Stamina Recovery								X
Leg Submissions 1	Leg Submissions	Grapple Defense, Stamina Recovery	X	X				X		X
Leg Submissions 2	Leg Submissions	Grapple Defense, Stamina Recovery		X				X		X
Leg Submissions 3	Leg Submissions	Grapple Defense, Stamina Recovery								X
Submission Defense 1	None	Grapple Defense, Stamina Recovery, Arm Submissions, Leg Submissions, Neck Submissions	X	X				X		X
Submission Defense 2	Grapple Defense	Stamina Recovery, Arm Submissions, Leg Submissions, Neck Submissions		X				X		X
Submission Defense 3	Grapple Defense	Stamina Recovery, Arm Submissions, Leg Submissions, Neck Submissions		X				X		X
Submission Defense 4	Grapple Defense	Stamina Recovery, Arm Submissions, Leg Submissions, Neck Submissions								X

PRIMA Official Game Guide

Written by:

STEPHEN STRATTON

Prima Games
An Imprint of Random House, Inc.
3000 Lava Ridge Court, Suite 100
Roseville, CA 95661

Product Manager: Todd Manning
Design: In Color Design
Layout: In Color Design
Copyedit: Sara Wilson
Manufacturing: Stephanie Sanchez & Suzanne Goodwin

Important:

Stephen Stratton has authored over 40 guides in his seven years with Prima. His personal favorites include *Mass Effect*, *Command & Conquer 4: Tiberian Twilight*, *Command & Conquer: Red Alert 3*, *WWE Raw 2*, and the *WWE Smackdown* series.

Steve is a lifelong video gamer who attended the Rochester Institute of Technology in Rochester, NY. In addition to his Prima Games guides, he also held a staff position with Computec Media and managed the strategy section of their incite.com video game website.

We want to hear from you! E-mail comments and feedback to **sstratton@primagames.com**.

ISBN: 978-0-307-46987-8
Library of Congress Catalog Card Number: 2010938225

Printed in the United States of America
10 11 12 13 LL 10 9 8 7 6 5 4 3 2 1